Internationalisation and Enterprise Development in Ghana

Published by
Adonis & Abbey Publishers Ltd
P.O. Box 43418
London
SE11 4XZ
http://www.adonis-abbey.com

First Edition, March 2005

British Library Cataloguing-in-Publication Data
A catalogue record of this book is available from the British Library

ISBN 0-9545037-9-1 (Pb)
ISBN 0-9545037-8-3 (Hb)

Cover Design: Ifeanyi Adibe

Printed and bound in Great Britain by Lightning Source UK Ltd.

Internationalisation and Enterprise Development in Ghana

Edited by

John Kuada

Adonis & Abbey
Publishers Ltd

Other Books by Adonis & Abbey Publishers include:

Broken Dreams by Jideofor Adibe

The Making of the Africa-nation: Pan-Africanism and the African Renaissance edited by Mammo Muchie

Nigeria and the Politics of Unreason by Victor E. Dike

The Challenge of Authenticity: African Culture and Faith Commitment by Jacob Hevi

Table of Contents

Preface

Economists generally agree that countries that manage their export growth strategies effectively can reap the benefits of employment generation, resource creation, innovation and efficiency. Thus, internationalisation provides developing economies with a promising avenue for growth and poverty alleviation. Paradoxically, internationalisation is, by itself, resource-demanding. Exporting firms must acquire knowledge and critical resources to be able to react swiftly to customer needs in their target export markets and to match their competitors' marketing strategies. Building a vibrant export sector in developing countries such as Ghana therefore requires the design of policies and strategies that optimise the resource leveraging potentials of the country.

Offshore resource leveraging has been suggested by a number of economists as a viable approach to mitigating the resource deficiency problem in developing countries. This may take the form of inward foreign investments, especially the location of value-adding production facilities by foreign companies in the developing countries. It has been argued that the presence of foreign firms would introduce capital, advanced technology and managerial skills into the developing economies. Through their linkages with local firms, the foreign companies are able to pass on these skills to a large number of other firms and thereby contribute positively to overall competence upgrade in the economies. Economists refer to these impacts as positive externalities or spillovers. Developing country governments have therefore been encouraged to design incentive packages that can attract foreign direct investments in their countries, i.e. attracting foreign firms that are in search of immobile locational advantages such as cheap skilled labour.

Offshore resources may also be leveraged through non-equity collaborations with foreign firms located outside the developing economies. Such collaborations may also facilitate the transfer of technology and knowledge from the developed country firms to their developing country co-partners.

The merits and demerits of these policy instruments and the impact of internationalisation (or globalisation, if you like) on the developing economies continue to be fiercely debated in both the academic and popular literature. The papers presented in this volume reflect the complexity of the issues involved in the internationalisation processes of developing country firms. Do developing countries have realistic expectations of their export sectors? Are governments willing to commit the required resources to the development of enabling conditions for private sector growth in general and internationalisation in particular? If they do, are foreign firms willing to reward such efforts and policies by locating their businesses in these countries? Are top managers willing to develop appropriate organisational structures and management practices that would enhance the learning capacities of their firms? These are but a few of a long catalogue of issues requiring attention. The authors have done a laudable job covering most of these issues in the nine chapters of the book.

The book itself is a product of cross-border collaboration. Since 1995, the Centre for International Studies at Aalborg University and the School of Administration, University of Ghana, have been engaged in research collaborations under the Danish International Development Assistance's (Danida) research capacity enhancement programme. During this period the researchers have worked on various joint projects, focusing on many aspects of the internationalisation processes of Ghanaian firms. The outputs of these research projects have been consistently published and have contributed to the body of knowledge about business management in Ghana. The current volume adds further to the pool of knowledge produced through this collaboration.

It is a delight to be part of this research team. I would like to use the opportunity to extend my sincere thanks to Danida for providing us with the financial resources for the projects. We are also grateful to the heads of the two institutions, Professor Kofi

Nti, Director of the School of Administration, University of Ghana, and Professor Thomas Nielsen, Head of the Department of Business Studies, Aalborg University, for providing us with the institutional facilities that support the collaboration. The nearly ten years of collaboration have brought the researchers closer and have also taught us that collaborations succeed through mutual commitment and patience. My sincere thanks also go to Professor Olav Jull Sørensen who initiated this collaboration and has consistently provided it with intellectual and administrative support. Our colleagues in both Ghana and Denmark have also provided us with critical comments to earlier versions of the papers and have encouraged us to think through some of our ideas. To them I say thank you.

John Kuada
Associate Professor, International Management
Aalborg University
July, 2004

1

GENERAL INTRODUCTION

MANAGING THE INTERNATIONALISATION PROCESSES IN GHANA: THEORIES AND PRACTICES

John Kuada

Introduction

The past three decades have witnessed an intensive academic interest in the international activities of firms. Several strands of concern have stimulated studies in the field. One group of researchers have concerned themselves with downstream internationalisation (Kuada and Sørensen 1999), exploring issues such as export motives and methods (Cavusgil and Nevin 1981), export barriers (Rabino 1980, Cavusgil 1984), and the importance of government policies and support to new export firms (Czinkota and Ricks 1983, Seringhaus 1986).

Another group of scholars have concerned themselves with upstream internationalisation, focusing on the establishment of links with foreign suppliers (Welch and Luostarinen 1993). Despite the increasing volume of literature in the field, there has been a manifest lack of work on developing country-based firms. The limited geographical coverage of these studies is one of the weaknesses in the literature on international businesses in the light of the increasing involvement of developing country firms in global economic activities. The need to help address this weakness is one of the reasons why we chose to publish this volume.

The papers provide fresh insight into issues of profound concern to most African countries. The theoretical inspirations for the contributions are diverse and rich. They range from Porter's concern with competitiveness of nations and factors stimulating national competitiveness to Mintzberg's views on management. The breadth of the contributions therefore covers most of the concerns of theorists, policy makers and managers.

The present chapter is guided by two objectives. First, it provides an overview of the theoretical viewpoints that have guided international business discussions in the developing countries. Second, it introduces the papers, highlighting their contributions to the body of knowledge in the area.

Internationalisation and Business Development

The literature on development economics generally acknowledges that domestic demand plays a critical role in shaping national competitive advantages (Porter 1990, Fafchamps et al 2001). Where domestic demand for a particular product is high and buyers are sophisticated, local firms are pressured to innovate and to achieve more sophisticated competitive advantages.

Furthermore, serving large domestic markets allows local firms to reap economies of scale and learning. It also spurs them on to invest and upgrade their production technologies since they are relatively certain about recouping their investments relatively quickly. Conversely, when demand stagnates or is declining, firms would be reluctant to embrace new technologies. Building on this theoretical understanding, it can be argued that economic growth in African countries hinges mainly on the integration of their economies into the global economic structure. Three reasons support this observation. First, the domestic demand for nearly all goods and services in many African countries is very small. Second, due to the limited domestic demand for consumer goods, support industries that serve the producers of the consumer goods are virtually non-existent in most African countries.

African manufacturers of consumer goods must either produce their own inputs or import them from the industrialised countries. Third, Africa's colonial past has resulted in the creation of an infrastructure that links them commercially to Europe and hampers intra-African trade (Fafchamps et al 2001).

The above viewpoints have powerful theoretical, strategic and policy implications for Africa. To start with, African country-based firms must pursue upstream and downstream internationalisations concurrently (Kuada and Sørensen 1999, 2000).

Upstream internationalisation is required for input flows and acquisition of other essential resources (including technology, finance and knowledge). In addition, downstream internationalisation is required from the onset of the operations of most manufacturing firms to enable them meet the minimum volume of output required for optimal usage of their technologies. Downstream internationalisation processes of African firms cannot, however, proceed in a gradual, sequential manner as suggested by the mainstream internationalisation theories (Johanson and Vahlne 1977). The reason is that they cannot start their internationalisation process from the near-by markets partly due to limited demand in these markets and the infrastructural constraints alluded to above. Exporting to Europe and/or other developed countries is therefore a necessity even for newly established firms. Effective management of relationships with European firms in the short run provides the resources for domestic economic growth and inter-African trade. This point seems to make an economic sense but presents a politically unpleasant choice. For how long should Africa allow itself to be dependent on Europe after her political independence? The unpleasantness of this political choice has been vividly reflected in the enterprise development strategies that have been pursued in Ghana since independence. The collection of papers in this volume reveals some of the errors of the past and new policy directions for the future.

Some Ghanaian evidence and policies

The available data on Ghana provides illustrative evidence of limited domestic demand in African countries. They also provide justification for the arguments made above. The evidence shows that private and public consumption in Ghana has shown consistent decline during the past three decades because real GDP per capita has actually declined from 100 points in 1960 to 83 in 1994.

In response to this decline macro policies and incentive packages have been designed by successive Ghanaian governments to stimulate growth. Particular emphasis was placed on diversification within the export sector. The Rawlings government adopted the World Bank/IMF sponsored structural adjustment policies in 1984 aimed at controlling inflation, stimulating exports, and mobilizing both domestic and foreign resources through increases in the levels of savings and investment. Kastner's paper provides an overview of the government's export promotional policies and the results achieved so far.

Existing export promotional institutions such as the Ghana Export Promotion Council (GEPC) were revamped and new ones established. A three-year Export Development Plan (1988-1990) was initiated. This resulted in a modest export performance improvement; export earnings from the non-traditional export products increased from US$23.8 million in 1986 to US$62.34 million in 1990. A follow-up export development programme was implemented from 1991 to 1995, again with some modest success. By the end of 2000 export earnings from the non-traditional export sector had increased to US$400.65 million, an impressive rise when compared with the meagre figure of US$ 23.8 million in 1984. But this figure dwarfs in comparison with the $11 billion target set by the government for 2020.

According to Kastner's analysis, the contributions of horticultural products to the agricultural non-traditional export sector have been quite significant over the years. This sub-sector contributed US$28.1 million (or 37.7%) of the total of US$74.5 million revenue generated by the non-traditional agricultural exports in 2000. But the competitiveness of the sector has been constrained by the fragmentation and small sizes of the firms. Kastner argues that the fragmentation within the sector may be due to the low entry barriers that characterise the sector as a whole combined with the low level of trust among the local producers and exporters. Some degree of inter-firm linkages has, however, been registered within the sector, presumably due to the increasing degree of geographical clustering of the production activities. Linkages between export firms and suppliers, out-growers, channel members, local retailers and the local food processing industry are now emerging. These linkages present opportunity for the development of external resource leveraging capabilities, as well as other capabilities for crafting and sustaining competitive advantages.

The impact of the Ghanaian government's export support initiatives on export sector growth and inter-firm linkages is the theme taken up in Kuada's contribution. Export Processing Zones (EPZs) have become popular in developing economies because economists expect them to stimulate investment/capital inflows, technology transfer and employment generation (ILO 1998). The location of foreign firms in these zones would produce industrial clusters that would then stimulate the establishment of a wide range of local support industries. Linkages between the local and foreign firms would then create positive spillover effects that can set off a dynamic economic growth process (Cling and Letilly 2001). Kuada's paper reports the degree of linkages and upgrading within both Ghanaian and foreign firms located within the export processing zones and the impact it has on their operations.

The evidence suggests limited foreign capital inflow, weak linkages and limited stimulus of competence development within the local firms. The results are therefore consistent with views expressed in prior literature. Regarding the limited foreign capital inflow, a study conducted by Asiedu (2002) has shown that while FDI in European and Central Asian countries increased by about 5 times between 1980 and 1998, Sub-Saharan African (SSA) countries registered a modest increase of 1.6 times. Such factors as infrastructure development, political stability, and openness of the host country have had a modest impact on foreign investors' preparedness to place their investments in African countries. She therefore argues that there is an adverse regional effect on investors' perception of the attractiveness of SSA countries as investment targets. That is, being an African country is itself enough to be excluded from foreign investors' radar.

Previous studies have also shown that foreign operations established through joint ventures or mergers and acquisitions are more likely to source their inputs locally than wholly owned foreign companies. The reason is that, while joint venture firms can take advantages of the supplier relationships of their local partners, it takes the wholly owned firms a lot more effort and resources to develop linkages with local suppliers and this may deter them from doing so. Finally, the low level of trust within Ghanaian business as a whole has earlier been offered as a plausible explanation for the limited degree of interfirm relations. Thus, the general conclusion from Kuada's paper is that the establishment of export processing zone, cannot, by itself, produce any radical change in the export sector of Ghana, unless other structural and cultural changes take place at the same time.

Internal factors that influence enterprise growth have received attention in Ansah–Ofei's paper. He focuses on the organisational structure and management processes in the exporting firms. The underlying premises of the study is that changes in the strategies, functions and administrative structures of firms impact on their patterns of decision making and processes of managing resources.
The key findings from a sample of 36 exporting firms showed that their administrative structures tend to be related to their degree of internationalisation measured in terms of export's share of total sales. Firms exporting more than 75% of their

products are relatively large and highly structured. They have centralised decision-making systems and well established role positions. This contrasts with the structures of the smaller and medium-sized enterprises (SMEs). Many of the SMEs in the study do not have middle level managers and only a few of them had board of directors. But both the larger firms and the SMEs have created export departments through which their export activities are organised.

The study also shows that large firms in Ghana are more planning-oriented than the smaller firms. The larger firms showed considerable interest in monitoring and controlling all aspects of their operations. While the degree of formalisation of authority, planning and decision-making appears not to have any significant impact on export performance for the SMEs, the situation is different for the larger firms. For them, increase in the percentage of exports has stimulated organisational innovations that have resulted in improvements in their production, marketing, environment intelligence, research and development, and long-term planning activities.

Puplampu's contribution extends Ansah-Ofei's study by focusing attention on skills competencies and leadership and comparing the successful exporting firms with the less successful ones on these dimensions. The relationship between skills, structures and leadership is explained in the paper as follows:

> "Skills create (or enable) structures and once created, structures host skill deployment. ......It is the leadership of the organisation, which will craft a strategy and policy framework, which will enable employees to effect the goals and aspirations of the firm. It is the behaviour of leaders and their willingness to use appropriate structures, which will hold the organisation together through its learning cycles. Leadership is in essence a facilitator. "

The paper reports the results of an empirical investigation conducted on a sample of 12 Ghanaian SMEs drawn from the manufacturing sector all of them exporting to neighbouring West African countries with different degrees of operation in the West African regional market.

The results suggest a positive relationship between the degree of internationalisation (regional involvement) of firms and their levels of competence. Firms with higher levels of international involvement did not report skill deficiencies, while those with lower levels of international involvement reported severe skills deficiencies. Furthermore, ownership appeared to influence competence development. Firms with foreign ownership involvement have highly skilled workers, while those without foreign ownership are less competent. The general conclusion from the study is that the three variables: skills, leadership and structure do impact SMEs' internationalisation.

Together, Ansah-Ofei and Puplampu's studies provide empirical evidence in support of some of the theoretical viewpoints found in the internationalisation literature. For example, the relationship between firm size and the degree of internationalisation of firms has received attention in the extant literature. The general proposition is that the larger the firm the higher the propensity to export (Cavusgil and Nevin 1981). The underlying argument for this assumption is found in the economies of scale thesis. Granting that all firms aim at maximising the use of their productive resources, larger firms, it is argued, will tend to seek new markets for their products in order to minimise their unit cost of operation and therefore improve their competitive positions and growth opportunities.

Despite the volume of empirical research on the issue, no conclusive support has however been found for the proposition that firm size has positive influence on export activity (Katsikeas and Morgan 1994). It has been empirically demonstrated that although smaller firms have relatively limited resources, they can enter into export business by adopting less costly approaches of market involvement (Bonaccorsi 1992).

Bedman's work continues with the discussion of skills and competence development in Ghanaian firms. He draws extensively on theories of organisational learning and inter-firm relations to explore the extent to which international strategic alliances impact the transfer, generation as well as dissemination of knowledge within Ghanaian firms. The empirical part of this study is based on five cases of Danish-Ghanaian business collaborations. The results suggest that the Ghanaian firms benefited substantially from the collaborations. Not only were their technologies upgraded, they also acquired new and relevant knowledge that enhanced their operations. The employees were trained in both technical and managerial aspects of their work.

It must be noted that these collaborations were purposefully designed and monitored by the Danish International Development Assistance (Danida). The modalities of Danida assistance required detailed plans for training and documented post training impact. The question may be asked if firms would plan and execute such training programmes with the same degree of formalisation if this was not contractually required by a donor organisation.

There were evident weaknesses in the relationships of the 5 case companies. The degree of managerial capacity enhancement has been relatively low in some of the relationships and the resource contributions of Danish firms are limited to their participation in training and advising on technology transfer. As such some of the collaborations were starved of working capital, placing severe constraints on the operations of the Ghanaian firms. Bedman's recommendations include increased resource commitment from Danish firms and more rigorous financial discipline to improve performance.

Kragelund's paper is also on the Danida-sponsored collaborations between Danish and Ghanaian firms. His study, however, has a different focus and the empirical base is broader than Bedman's study. Kragelund argues that donor-sponsored inter-firm collaborations aim at attaining the twin objectives of enterprise growth and socio-economic development of the developing countries. The fulfilment of these objectives depends on a combination of both internal (firm-level) and external (contextual) factors. He argues further that any comprehensive evaluation of a programme of this type must take this set of objectives and factors into account.

He conducted a detailed study of 45 of the nearly 80 private sector collaborative projects that Danida has sponsored over the past ten years. His analysis of the empirical data shows that a small group of firms have registered performance improvements in such areas as increase in the number of employees, product quality and productivity improvements. Consistent with Bedman's findings, most Ghanaian firms in Kragelund's study have upgraded their technical capabilities through acquisition of improved machinery and training. Technical training of workers improved the operation and maintenance of the acquired machines and therefore resulted in the enhancement of production capabilities.

But these improvements did not immediately translate into higher turnover or profitability. Consequently, a few of the companies have experienced delays in their loan repayments, while others incurred losses. The reasons are many. The main ones include conflicts, tensions and low levels of trust between the partners. The sources of the problems could be traced to both Danish and Ghanaian firms. To address these weaknesses, Kragelund emphasises the importance of openness among partners and a greater attention to the development of administrative systems that can help build trust among the partners. He also saw the Ghanaian business system in general and the business culture in particular (e.g. employment of family members at top management positions without them possessing the requisite qualifications) as a major contributor to the relatively modest performance of the collaborative projects.

The issues of context received attention in the last two papers as well. Kuada and Thomsen draw attention to the contextual challenges involved in cross-border knowledge transfers, thereby returning to a theme earlier taken up in Bedman's paper. They argue that both knowledge-specific variables (i.e. tacitness and complexity) and partner-specific variables (i.e. prior experience, cultural distance, and organisational distance) have an impact on the processes of knowledge transfer. In their view, the owner-managers of

Ghanaian firms tend to perceive themselves as centres of knowledge. Ghanaian managers are likely to adopt authoritarian leadership styles and are therefore unwilling to solicit suggestions from their workers. Where suggestions are volunteered, they may endorse only those that appear to fit into their prior structures of understanding. Workers tend to be less innovative and respond to instructions from their superiors. As such their motivations to learn with a view to improving organisational performance are low, and this may negatively affect their capacity to absorb new knowledge.

The implications are clear. Partners need to gain a good understanding of the cultural context within which their co-partners operate in order to develop effective knowledge transfer strategies for them. A first step in the knowledge transfer process may be to help the owner-managers of Ghanaian firms change their leadership styles and allow workers to question existing practices within their companies. The real challenge lies in helping Ghanaian managers gain legitimacy for their authority without hampering the learning capacities of their companies. This involves changing the mode of using power without losing power.

Again, on the issue of context, Aboagye reports the results of his investigation of the impact of financial liberalisation on economic output in a number of sub-Saharan African countries, including Ghana, using a production function within the context of an endogenous growth model. His analysis reveals that the banking and stock market development variables do not have significant impact on output. He therefore argues that African countries must vigorously pursue policies that encourage more financial deepening in their economies and create economic environments in which economic agents realise positive real returns on their savings and equity investments. This will improve the impact of the financial sector on the growth of their economies.

Discussions

Taken together, these empirical investigations provide significant insights into the relevance of existing international business economics theories on enterprise development in African countries. The empirical evidence presented is illustrative of what obtains in many African countries. The issues covered are diverse and each paper provides not only an academic treatment of the specific issues of its focus but seeks to offer guidelines for policy and strategy formulation.

A recurrent theme in most of the papers is the importance of linkages and networks in relations to resource leveraging and internal capacity development of firms. Let us take a closer look at some of the pertinent issues addressed under this theme.

Several of the authors have reminded us that no business today is an island in the increasingly globalised world economy. Both upstream and downstream internationalisation processes require some form of inter-firm relationship; some are close, intensive in interaction and diversified in content while others are loose with intermittent interactions between partners. Inter-firm collaboration necessitates coordination and control of co-partners' activities to ensure that resources are allocated in the best desirable manner. What are the acceptable and most effective modalities of this coordination process?

Gereffi et al (2003) have identified five basic types of inter-firm relationships; markets, modular, relational, captive and hierarchy. Markets and hierarchies are opposite ends of the typology, representing the lowest and highest degrees of specification of rules of behaviour. In market type relationships partners are not dependent on each other since the costs of breaking out of the relationships and switching to other partners is low. The relationship may, however, persist over time in the form of repeat purchases if the vendor and buyer are satisfied with the conditions of purchase and if there are no significantly rewarding alternatives. The reverse conditions obtain in hierarchies. In between them are what Gereffi and his colleagues term the intermediate or "network" types of relationship.

Modular relationships apply when suppliers produce to customer specification based on some standardised components. The transaction specific investments required for such value-added activities are low, just as the degree of dependence of the partners is equally limited. Larger buyers are, however, likely to have stronger bargaining power in their relationship with smaller suppliers and govern the relationship with various instruments of power. Relational governance is applied where the degree of dependence is relatively balanced, i.e. partners are mutually vulnerable to changes in co-partners' transactional behaviour.

That is, governance is characterised by negotiation, consultations and joint actions. In captive relationships, however, one partner may be dependent on the other. For example, when suppliers are small, they are transactionally dependent on their buyers and stand in a weaker bargaining position vis-à-vis these buyers. The reasons are that they might have asset-specific investments and face significant switching costs, hence the label "captive" relationships.

Although the original intention of Gereffi and his colleagues is to develop a typology of supplier-customer relationship (with a focus on the role of lead firms in international value chains) the typology can be used to discuss upstream relationships as well. Ghanaian firms are the weaker partners in both upstream and downstream international business relations. They therefore end up in either market or captive relationships. Their export products are usually standardised (e.g. agricultural products or simple manufactures), and can be obtained from a large number of competitors on the global market.

Hierarchies are seldom used in these relationships. The literature shows that the reason for a company to build a joint venture is to overcome its own lack of knowledge or competence by partnering with an organisation that is recognised to have this expertise. Since the domestic market in Ghana is small, very few companies consider it strategically worthwhile to invest equity capital in the country for reasons of market access.

In conclusion these papers provide useful insights into the challenges confronting Ghana in the internationalisation process of her economy and enterprises. They also provide pointers for important themes that are worth exploring in future research. For example, it is important to discuss the merits and demerits of market driven (compared with policy-driven) inter-firm collaborations. It has been argued that collaborations are resource-demanding just as they facilitate resource creation. Firms must invest in their implementation capacities in order to absorb and effectively apply new knowledge and other intangible resources that may be produced through the collaboration.

Where there are enormous implementation constraints, the collaborations may not generate the expected benefits. The question that requires attention is under what local conditions would internationalisation result in the advantages that many scholars envisage.

References

Asiedu, Elizabeth, (2002): "On the Determinants of Foreign Direct Investment to Developing Countries: Is Africa Different?" World Development Vol. 30 No. 1 pp. 107-119

Bonaccorsi, Andrea (1992): "On the relationship between firm size and export intensity" *Journal of International Business* Vol. 23 No.4 pp.605- 635

Cavusgil, S. Tamer and John R. Nevin (1981): "Internal determinants of export marketing behaviour: an empirical investigation" *Journal of Marketing Research* Vol. XVIII

Cavusgil, S. Tamer (1984): "Organisational characteristics associated with export activity" *Journal of Management Studies* 21, 1

Cling, Jean-Pierre and Letilly, Gaëlle, (2001): "Export Processing Zones: A Threatened Instrument for Global Economy Insertion?" *Document de Travail* DT/2001/17 pp.1-50

Czinkota, Michael R. and D. A. Ricks (1983): "The use of a multi-measurement approach in the determination of company export priorities" *Journal of the Academy of Marketing Sciences* Vol. 11 No. 3 pp. 283 - 91

Fafchamps, Marcel (1996): "The enforcement of commercial contracts in Ghana" *World Development* Vol. 24 No. 3 pp 427-448

Fafchamps, Marcel, Teal, Francis, and Toye, John (2001): *Towards a Growth Strategy for Africa* (University of Oxford Centre for the Study of African Economies Working Paper REP/2001-06)

Gereffi, G. Humphrey, J., and Sturgeon, T. (2004): "The Governance of Global Value Chains" forthcoming in *Review of International Political Economy*

ILO (1998): 'Export Processing zones: Addressing the social and labour issues', available on the Internet [www.ilo.org].

Johanson, J. and J.-E. Vahlne (1977): "The Internationalisation Process of the Firm -- A Model of Knowledge Development and Increasing Foreign Market Commitments," *Journal of International Business Studies* 8 (1), 23-32.

Katsikeas, Constantine S. and Robert E. Morgan (1994): "Differences in Perceptions of Exporting Problems Based on Firm Size and Export Market Experience" *European Journal of Marketing* Vol, 28 No. 5

Kuada, John and Olav Jull Sørensen (1999b): "Upstream and Downstream Processes of Internationalisation : Some Ghanaian Evidence" *The Journal of Euromarketing* Vol 7 No. 4 pp: 7-41

Kuada, John and Olav Jull Sørensen (2000): *Internationalisation of Companies from Developing Countries:* (NY. The Haworth Press Inc.)

Porter, Michael E., (1990): *Competitive Advantage of Nations* (NY: Free Press)

Rabino, S. (1980): "An examination of barriers to exporting encountered by small manufacturing companies" *Management International Review* Vol. 1 pp: 67-73

Seringhaus, F.H. (1986): "The role of information assistance in small firms' export involvement" *International Small Business Journal* Vol. 5 No. 2 208-217

Welch, Lawrence S. and Luostarinen, Reijo (1993): "Inward-outward connections in internationalisation", *Journal of Internaitonal Marketing*, Vol. 1, no. 1, 44-56.

2

COMPETITIVENESS OF GHANA'S HORTICULTURAL EXPORT SECTOR

Adelaide Naa Amerley Kastner

Introduction

First, the chapter will show the importance of exports to Ghana's economic development. Second, it will establish the potential of horticultural products to contribute to export earnings from the agricultural sub-sector. Third, it will provide an overview of the *industry structure* in terms of parameters like the nature of products, number of products, number of exporters, firm sizes and industry density. Some of these parameters will help understand the nature of competition within the industry. Fourth, it will discuss the dynamics that shape the nature of competition at industry-level such as the threat of new entrants, and the bargaining power of suppliers/buyers. Fifth, the existing linkages within the industry will be highlighted, since linkages can positively impact on competitive advantages. Finally, the geographical clustering of the farms will be discussed to reveal the implications for competitiveness.

According to the European Management Forum (1984), "Competitiveness is the immediate and future ability of, and opportunities for entrepreneurs to design, produce and market goods world-wide whose price and non-price qualities form a more attractive package than those of foreign and domestic competitors" (Buckley, Pass and Prescott, 1988). It stands to reason, therefore, that *competitiveness* of Ghana's horticultural sector has to be *strategically* achieved and sustained through *present and future efforts* of both the government and the private sectors if the sector's earnings are to contribute effectively to economic development.

The Importance of Non-traditional Exports to Ghana's Economic Development

Since the introduction of the Economic Recovery Programme (ERP) in April 1983, Ghana has been intent on promoting economic development through exports, particularly non-traditional exports (NTE)[1]. Hitherto, the emphasis on exports had been on traditional products, namely cocoa, timber, gold, bauxite and other minerals. Non-traditional export promotion was thus intensified in order to diversify Ghana's export base. By the mid-eighties, this new direction saw the rejuvenation of the Ghana Export Promotion Council (GEPC), which was established in 1969 under the Legislation, NLC[2] Decree 396, with the mandate to develop and promote exports.

Against this background, and as part of Ghana Government's promotional activities, the GEPC embarked on a *Three-Year Export Development Plan* (1988-1990) in collaboration with the Ministry of Trade, MOTI (Amenuvor, 1993; Sey, 1997). By the end of the plan period, earnings from NTEs had increased from US$23.8 million corresponding to 3.2% of total export earnings in 1986 to US$62.34 million or 7.0% of total export earnings in 1990 (Akyea, 1993; Asenso-Okyere and Asante, 1997; Kastner, 1995, p.7). However, the improvement fell short of the target to raise NTEs from 2% to 15% of Ghana's total earnings. Therefore, as a follow-up, a *Medium-Term Non-Traditional Export Development Programme* was implemented from 1991 to 1995 (Akyea, 1993; Amenuvor, 1993; ISSER, 1994; Kastner, 1995; Asenso-Okyere and Asante, 1997). Mainly, the objectives of this programme were: (1) the diversification of the export base; (2) increasing the share of NTEs to traditional exports from 8% to the 15% target by the end of the plan period; and the diversification of producers and the doubling of the then 1,000 registered export producers (ISSER, 1994, p.116).

Through the collaborative efforts of GEPC and MOTI, export incentive schemes aimed at encouraging private sector export development have included the following:

Export Proceeds Retention Scheme
The scheme gave exporters complete access to their export earnings and the privilege of converting all (i.e. 100%) of such foreign currency earnings into cedis (i.e. Ghana's local currency) at competitive rates negotiated with the exporters' bankers.

Customs Duty Drawback
This allowed exporters to draw back (i.e. receive a refund) of up to 100% of duties paid on materials imported to produce goods for export.

Bonded Warehousing
A system that allowed manufacturers to seek customs licence to hold imported raw materials intended for manufacture for export in secured warehouses without payment of duty.

Corporate Tax Rebate
In this regard, Ghanaian firms engaged in manufacturing and exporting of agricultural products were allowed to claim between 40% and 75% of their tax liability as tax rebate.

Human Resource Development through GEPC's Export School Programmes

The GEPC has established the Export School to develop training programmes covering production, processing, marketing, packaging, procedures and documentation and all other aspects of the export trade. The training programmes include seminars and workshops using both Ghanaian and foreign resource persons.[3]

Market Identification and Development through Trade Fairs and Exhibitions

In this regard, GEPC assists exporters to locate foreign buyers for their products. Market information is usually obtained through Ghana's Foreign Missions.[4]

Other special promotional programmes were the Trade and Investment Programme (TIP) (1993-1997) and the Ghana Free Zone (GFZ) programme, which is long-term. The Trade and Investment Programme (TIP) was initiated with the support of the United States Agency for International Development (USAID) mission in Ghana. This five-year programme consisted of economic and technical assistance to address the constraints that limited private sector investment and production for export (Asenso-Okyere and Asante, 1997). Particularly, TIP influenced changes in official policies, reduced confusing rules and regulations that hindered exports and promoted simplification of export procedures. For instance, the programme engineered the abolition of the *export proceeds retention scheme,* which required exporters to deposit with banks 65% of their proceeds free of interest (Kuada and Sørensen, 2000).

The Ghana Free Zone (GFZ) programme is an integrated programme aimed at promoting the processing and manufacturing of goods through the establishment of Export Processing Zones (EPZs).[5] By the end of the *Medium-Term Non-Traditional Export Development Programme,* earnings from NTEs had increased to US$276.2 million, which represented 17.6% of total export earnings in 1996 (Asenso-Okyere and Asante, 1997). In the year 2000 earnings from NTE were US$400.65 million.[6]

The present NPP Government[7] has "repackaged" the economic development vision of Ghana, by declaring what is popularly known as the "Golden Age of Business" at a national economic dialogue in the year 2001. By the "Golden Age of Business", labour, the private sector, the civil society and the Government are to work as corporate Ghana with a shared common vision that will allow all to win. The concept adds that Ghanaians must use their limited time to reach consensus on the extent of the difficulties that confront them and agree on the solutions that will resolve the problems. The fundamental objective of this concept is to create a booming business sector to accelerate economic development for sustainable improved standard of living. The realisation of the "Golden Age of Business" is also largely dependent on export development, which requires sustainable competitive advantages. Towards this end the NPP Government has launched what is known as the President's Special Initiative on Garments/Textiles and Cassava Starch. The programme is to promote the competitive export of the named NTE products, particularly to the United States of America in response to opportunities presented by the African Growth Opportunity Act (AGOA).

However, it has been projected that for Ghana to move into a middle income status, total exports must contribute US$16.3 billion in foreign earnings with US$11.9 billion coming from NTEs, which represents 73% of total export earnings.[8] Ghana therefore has a great deal more to do to push NTEs to the desired level and even beyond. There is, therefore, the need to strategically identify and develop the competitiveness of production sectors that have high earnings potential. One of these is the horticultural sub-sector.

Potential of the Horticultural Sub-sector

Basically, Ghana's non-traditional agricultural export sub-sector is divided into four groups, namely: *horticultural products, fish and seafood products, game and wildlife and other (unclassified) agricultural products.* The contributions of horticultural products to the sub-sector have been quite significant over the years. In 1999 and 2000 horticultural products were the leading contributors. In 2000 total revenue from non-traditional agricultural exports was US$74.5 million with thirty-two *horticultural products* contributing approximately US$28.1 million (i.e. 37.7%), ten *fish and seafood products* approximately US$18.6 million (i.e. 25%), and three *game and wildlife* approximately US$0.305 million (i.e. 0.4%). An assortment of twenty-nine *unclassified agricultural products* such as cashew nuts, shea nuts, and sugar cane contributed the remaining 36.9%. These statistics indicate that horticultural products have great potential in terms of both variety and export earnings within the agricultural non-traditional export sub-sector. It is the recognition of this potential that has motivated the focus of this chapter on the horticultural non-traditional export sub-sector.

Against this background, the chapter will attempt to answer the composite question: *How do industry-related factors, namely industry structure, industry dynamics (e.g. the threat of new entrants), linkages and geographical clustering influence the competitiveness of the Ghanaian horticultural export sector?*

Overview: The Structure of the Horticultural Sub-sector

Although theoretically, horticultural products include *flowers, fruits and vegetables*, fruits and vegetables dominate Ghana's non-traditional horticultural exports. From GEPC records only one floral product was exported in both 1999 (two exporters) and 2000 (three exporters). The range of fruits includes *pineapple, papaya, orange, mangoes, banana, lime and watermelon*. The variety of vegetables is, among others, *aubergine/garden egg, bean, okra, cucumber, pepper and root vegetables like yam and cocoyam*. From 1996 to 2000, the number of horticultural products within Ghana's NTE sector increased from 26 to 32, while the number of exporters in those years were 1008 in 1996, 1053 in 1997, declining to 843 in 1999 and increasing to 1075 in 2000 (see Table 1).

Table 1: Non-Traditional Horticultural Exports, 1996-2000

Item	1996	1997	1998	1999	2000*
Number of Products	26	31	32	33	32
Number of Exporters	1,008	1,053	886	843	1,075
Value of Exports in US$ million	20.7	19.2	19.8	27.2	28.1

Source: Ghana Export Promotion Council/ISSER, 2001, p. 77
*Provisional Figures

In as much as there is a wide variety of horticultural products, the number of exporters is relatively large. Using available GEPC statistics on volume of exports, I classify the exporters into: large – US$1,000,000 and above; medium – US$999,000 – US$150,000; and small – US$149,000 and below. The classifications are by Ghanaian standards and may appear relatively small by international standards.

The non-traditional horticultural export sector is to a great extent fragmented[9] due to the existence of a relatively *large number of small firms*. Table 2 shows data extracted from GEPC statistics on the horticultural sector. The products in the table were selected based on the number of exporters being equal to, or above thirty (i.e. ≥30 exporters). It must be noted that within the horticultural industry, pineapple is the highest revenue earner, followed by yam. Banana comes third, with US$3,694,998.40 in 2000 (i.e. contribution of 4.97%). However, banana was not included in the table because the number of exporters is few (i.e. five in 2000). Thus considering banana's small number of exporters, and its third position in the industry, it appears to be an exception to the prevailing industry fragmentation phenomenon. Indeed in the banana product-sector, there is *only one large firm,* which exported bananas worth US$3,614,245.40 (i.e. 97.8% product-sector contribution in 2000).

The second banana exporter is relatively small, with total export of only US$80,150.00.

In contrast, pineapples contributed 15.95% to non-traditional agricultural exports, which translates into 42.2% (i.e. US$11,853,127.83 of US$28,082,158.87) of total earnings from the horticultural industry in 2000. However, *four* firms exported US$1,000,000 and above (i.e. large firms), *ten* exported between US$999,000 and US$150,000 (i.e. medium firms) and the remaining *forty-two* exported below US$149,000 (i.e. small firms). This implies 67% of pineapple exporters are small. Although the case of pineapples seems to project a *virtual concentration*, such a conclusion would be product-biased, without due cognisance of other product areas within the horticultural industry. Thus, adding large exporters from other product areas like banana would swell the number of large exporters in the industry. Secondly, an argument of concentration in terms of pineapples would be rational if the *four firms* generated at least 50% of total industry revenue. However, the earnings of the *four firms* total US$6,275,319.39, which represents only 22.35% (i.e. US$6,275,319.39 of US$28,082,158.87) of total horticultural exports.

The degree of fragmentation is even greater with respect to the aubergine/garden egg exporters. They number 126 and constitute the second largest number of exporters within the horticultural industry, which has a total number of 1,075 exporters. This represents 11.72% of the total number of exporters within the industry. Meanwhile, they contribute only 0.58% to non-traditional agricultural exports and 1.55% (i.e. US$434,126.57 of US$28,082,158.87) to horticultural export earnings. In addition to this, only the leading exporter could be classified as a medium-sized firm, with export earnings of US$181,734.22. The second highest exporter for the year under review recorded an export earning of US$51,593.46. Thus, excepting the leading exporter, the remaining 125 firms are small-sized.

Furthermore, the fragmentation argument may be supported by the assumption that the Ghanaian horticultural industry does not have any large *non*-exporting firms with dominant market share. The rationale behind the argument is that the horticultural industry in Ghana started as an export sub-sector in response to national export promotion in the 1970s, with cultivation of exotic varieties to satisfy international demand. This argument is further supported by previous research findings, which showed that Ghanaian exporters usually have bypassed the domestic market (Kuada and Sørensen, 2000; Kastner, 1995, 1996). As such, most *non-exporters* would mainly serve as *indirect exporters and suppliers* to the direct exporters, in the capacity of *out-growers*. This would render the non-export proportion within the industry insignificant. The insignificance of the local market, however, defeats Porter's (1990) theory, which requires a substantial and sophisticated local demand to propel innovation. The phenomenon could therefore impair the creation of competitive advantage(s) for the Ghanaian horticultural industry. To address the problem, Ghanaian exporters may have to depend on international market demand signals to motivate innovation. Alternatively, they may have to indulge in copying international competitors and technology transfer in their effort to compete internationally. Another factor that could possibly compound the problem is the inclination of Ghanaians to *imitate* rather than innovate (Sørensen, 2001).

It must, however, be noted that although the horticultural sector's paramount objective is the satisfaction of international demand, there is a flow of non-exportable but consumable output into the local market, as well as the processed food sector. As regards pineapple, for example, approximately 60% of the industry's output is exported as fresh fruit. Part of the remaining 40% is consumed locally and part of it is processed.

Another plausible reason for the fragmentation of the industry is the low level of *trust* within the industry participants. Sørensen (2001) explained that companies would tend to be small as the owner has to directly oversee all activities himself or herself. As demonstrated by Sørensen and Nyanteng (2000), because of distrust, a Ghanaian trader and his/her commodities are inseparable from the time of buying in the rural areas to the selling of the commodities in the urban markets. This tends to *increase transaction cost and prevent companies from growing or innovating.* Thus, to circumvent the problem of trust and engender growth would require employing family members and other people the entrepreneur can control, which is not always feasible because of the difficulties involved if family members have to be dismissed.

Table 2: Horticultural Export Products with 30 Exporters and above

Product	No. of Exporters	Value in US$	% Contribution to Agricultural NTE's
Yams	163	7,171,764.50	9.65
Aubergines/Garden eggs	126	434,126.57	0.58
Pepper/Chillies	94	1,255,206.97	1.69
Plantain	91	161,955.70	0.22
Cocoyam	73	54,395.69	0.07
Pineapples	62	11,853,127.83	15.93
Fresh Okra	59	44,626.11	0.06
Tinda	50	474,314.82	0.64
Mangoes	47	117,717.50	0.16
Beans	45	213.109.68	0.29
Onions/Shallots	45	15,150.46	0.02
Ginger	44	18,266.37	0.02
Marrow	35	130,088.88	0.18
Pawpaw	35	1,361,445.94	1.83
Totals	969	23,305,297.02	31.34
Horticultural Industry Totals	1,075	28,082,158.87	*37.79
Agricultural NTE Totals	1,520	**74,306,509.12	100.00
National NTE Totals	3,203	400,475,309.23	100.00

Source: Ghana Export Promotion Council (Provisional figures, 2000)

Notes: *Contribution of all horticultural products to agricultural NTE's (2000)

**This figure represents 18.55% of national NTE's, which was US$400,475,309.23 in 2000.

Drawing from the above discussions, consolidation of the industry might be necessary to generally reduce transaction cost, increase firm-level capitalisation, and improve firms' capabilities and competencies. These would promote innovation and creation of sustainable competitive advantages.

Industry Dynamics

Having provided an overview of the industry, to create a picture from parameters like the nature of products, number of products, number of exporters, firm sizes and industry density (i.e. fragmentation) the stage is now set for discussions on industry dynamics to provide deeper understanding of the competitiveness of the industry. Of the main, Porter's (1990) five forces driving industry competition will guide the discussions.

Theoretical Framework of Forces Driving Industry Competition

Industry dynamics are the forces that shape competition within the industry. In business literature, these forces are seen as environmental threats[10] that increase a firm's costs, decrease a firm's revenues, or in other ways reduce a firm's performance (Barney, 2002). Thus, environmental threats tend to increase competition within an industry and force firm performance to a normal level. Porter's (1990) framework of "five competitive forces" is a widely known model of environmental threats in the field of strategic management. The model attempts to assist managers in analysing environmental threats so that they can be more effective in developing strategies to neutralise them and generate competitive advantage(s). Specifically, these forces are grouped under the headings of: (1) threat of new entrants (2) bargaining power of suppliers (3) bargaining power of buyers (4) threat of substitute products or services, and (5) rivalry among existing firms. They are diagrammatically presented in Figure 1.

Figure 1: Forces Driving Industry Competition

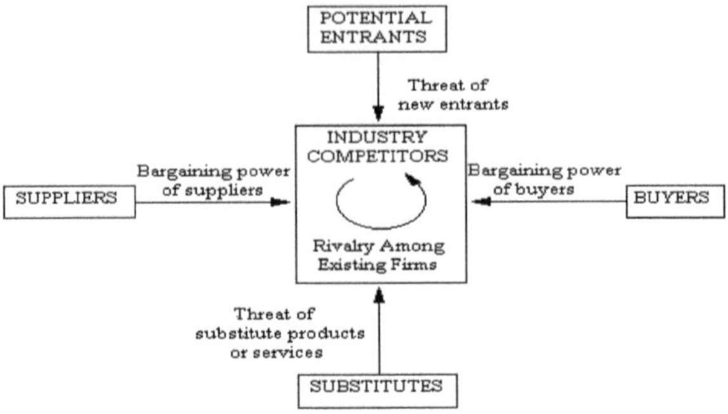

Source: Porter Michael (1990) *Competitive Strategy: Techniques for Analysing Industry and Competitors,* (New York: The Free Press), p.4.

The Threat of New Entrants: Porter espouses that new entrants bring new capacity and seek market share, which usually results in increased competition and consequently lower margins. New entrants are firms that have either recently begun operations in an industry or that threaten to begin operations in an industry soon. According to the structure-conduct-performance (S-C-P) model[11] new entrants are motivated to enter into an industry by the *above-normal economic profits* that some incumbent firms in that industry may be earning (Barney, 2002). The magnitude of threat depends on the barriers present and the expected reaction from existing competitors. If barriers to entry are high and newcomers can expect sharp retaliation from the entrenched competitors, obviously the newcomers will not pose a serious threat.

The Threat of Substitute Products or Services: Through research and development (R&D) competitors can generate close *substitute products* and thereby limit the price the firm could charge for the authentic product. The effect is reduced competitiveness.

The Bargaining Power of Suppliers and Buyers: Porter argues that powerful suppliers or buyers *bargain* away the profits for themselves, thereby eroding the profit and competitive base of the firm.

The Rivalry among the Existing Competitors: Finally, Porter asserts that fierce *competitive rivalry* erodes profits by dramatically increasing costs of competing. Such costs include those for advertising, sales expense (e.g. travels abroad) and R&D. In addition, competitors sometimes undercut the competition (i.e. offer products at lower prices) thereby passing on profits to customers.

Forces Driving Competition within Ghana's Horticultural Industry

The chapter will now proceed to examine how facts on the ground approximate the forces within the above model and how they influence competition in Ghana's horticultural industry.

Threat of New Entrants

Theory holds that new entrants bring new capacity and seek market share, which usually results in increased competition and consequently lower margins (Porter, 1990). Major barriers to entry into an industry are: (1) economies of scale, (2) product differentiation, (3) capital requirements, (4) cost advantages independent of size/scale, (5) access to distribution channels, and (6) government policy (Porter, 1998; Barney, 2002).

Findings showed that the Ghanaian horticultural export sector does not impose entry or exit barriers on potential entrants. The fragmented nature of the industry confirms this finding. Several reasons account for the absence of entry barriers. One, *national export promotion programmes,* usually implemented through GEPC, deter entry barriers. As stated earlier, the clarion call has been to export in order to diversify Ghana's export base, with the objective of using exports as an engine for economic growth. Thus, government policy has rather encouraged entry into the horticultural export sector through these schemes.

Two, *product differentiation* has been minimal, for the basic fact that most of the horticultural products are exported in their raw and fresh state. The observation was that at a very low level, differentiation has been attempted by some of the firms, mainly through packaging strategies. For instance, a firm has developed a simple *packaging* technology that keeps beans and other exported vegetables fresh through transit. The development of the packaging technology had been made possible because of the *unique innovative capabilities of the managing director*. The firm states that the packaging technology, which has been kept a secret, has enhanced international marketability of their products and created a competitive advantage for them. However, such differentiation has not been on a scale that could constitute an entry barrier.

Three, *capital requirements* to enter into the industry is relatively low. This is evidenced by the smallness of most of the firms within the industry. Barring the cost of or rent for the land, the minimum capital for starting a horticultural farm is 4,595,450 cedis (approximately, US$ 574 in 2002).[12] Coupled with the relatively low capital requirement, are the opportunities provided for *leveraging financial resources on a small-scale and obtaining technical assistance* through an elaborate institutional framework, which has been established by the Government. The objective for creating this institutional framework, made up of public (i.e. government and quasi-governmental) and private institutions, is to effectively support the development of the export sector (Kuada and Sørensen, 2000, p.140). Institutions that constitute the framework have been classified into (Kuada and Sørensen, 2000, p.138):

Promotional institutions purposely established to create incentives and facilities that motivate firms to engage in exporting. A typical example is GEPC, which provides advisory services on international markets, products, product presentation, export procedures and documentation, suppliers and importers, export financing, and general information on exports.

Facilitatory institutions whose actions directly or indirectly enhance the operational capabilities of firms. An example is Private Enterprise and Export Development (PEED), which promotes the growth of private Ghanaian exporters through the provision of short-term credits to exporters and the provision of technical assistance. Another source of funding worth mentioning is the *Export Development and Investment Fund (EDIF),* which was passed into law in October 2000 to provide funds for the development and promotion of the NTE sector. It provides credit guarantee and insurance support as well as direct financing of NTE activities (*"The Akoben"*, GEPC, 2000).

Regulatory institutions, which ensure that export companies provide the goods and services promised and that their behaviours, in general, conform to established standards in the country and/or abroad. A good example is Ghana Customs, Excise and Preventive Service (CEPS). They have the responsibility for refunding duties etc. paid on imports that are used in production of export products. The scheme through which the refund is effected is known as "duty drawback".

From the foregoing, it is obvious that government policy has promoted entry into the horticultural industry and therefore has contributed towards minimising threats of new entrants and perhaps towards the fragmentation of the industry.

Bargaining Power of Suppliers and Buyers

Porter (1990) argues that powerful suppliers or buyers *bargain* away the profits for themselves, thereby eroding the profit and competitive base of the firm. To neutralise the bargaining power of suppliers, horticultural exporters have resorted to *collaboration* under one umbrella known as the "Horticulturists' Association of Ghana" (HAG). In addition, there are individual product associations, such as Ghana Assorted Foodstuffs Exporters, Ghana Yam Producers and Exporters Association, Vegetable Producers and Exporters Association, and Papaya Exporters Association. All the associations within the horticultural industry are also members of the Federation of Association of

Ghanaian Exporters (FAGE), a mother association that promotes the cause of Ghanaian exporters. Of particular interest is the Sea-Freight Pineapple Exporters Association (SPEG), which organises vessels and negotiates sea-freight on behalf of exporters. This has ensured efficiency in freight services, strong bargaining power and competitive pricing of Ghanaian sea-freighted pineapples. It is not surprising that pineapple exports generate the largest proportion of exports from the industry.

In the international marketplace, however, findings show that most of the firms within the industry have had to *negotiate selling prices individually*. As a result, occasionally, exporters have operated as *price-takers,* which meant responding to changes in industry demand by adjusting their selling prices. In this regard, they lack the capacity to manipulate the level of their supply in order to influence the selling price.

Threat of Substitute Products or Services

Where substitute products or services provided by a firm's rivals meet approximately the same customer needs in the same ways as the products or services provided by the incumbent firm, this may threaten the performance of the firm. In the extreme, they can ultimately replace an industry's products and services (Barney, 2002). Mostly, substitute products are created through research and development (R&D). Such offers limit the *price* the incumbent firm could charge for the authentic product. The effect is reduced competitiveness and reduced profit potential both in normal times and in boom times (Porter, 1998; Barney. 2002).

One factor that weighs heavily in favour of the Ghanaian horticultural industry is that they export farm fresh products, which virtually have no substitutes, except in cases of genetically-produced varieties. However, global demand for *organic products* is on the increase. This phenomenon may be seen as a chance event in the language of Porter (1990), since it involves *an agro-technological move, outside the power of Ghanaian firms and the government.*[13] The phenomenon has influenced a good degree of dynamism in the production techniques within the Ghanaian horticultural industry. Specifically, Ghanaian producers and exporters of banana and papaya are converting from heavy chemical-based production to organic production, in response to this trend in taste/lifestyle in the international marketplace. To ensure successful conversion, those who have seized this "unexpected" opportunity have joined associations like the International Federation of Organic Agricultural Movement (IFOAM) and the Ghana Organic Agricultural Network (GOAN) for appropriate methods and guidelines. Thus, the threat of substitute products or services is reasonably neutralised and the industry is ensured a sustained demand. Furthermore, given Ghana's favourable weather conditions, if all other production and export conditions are competitive, the Ghanaian horticultural sector stands a good chance of gaining sustainable competitive advantage in the global horticultural industry.

Rivalry among the Existing Competitors

Finally, Porter (1990) asserts that fierce *competitive rivalry* erodes profits by dramatically increasing costs of competing. He states that rivalry among competitors take the familiar form of jockeying for position, using tactics like price competition, product introduction and intensive advertising. Attributes of an industry that intensify rivalry are mainly:

Large number of competing firms: Competing firms are the same size and have the same influence/power. Slow industry growth, thereby precipitating fights for market share.

Lack of product differentiation: Thus, forcing firms to compete only on the basis of price. Fixed costs are high or the product is perishable, creating strong temptation to cut prices. As would be expected in any environment where individual units have goals, which they expend effort and utilise resources to achieve, resulting in different levels of performance, there is rivalry.

Considering the variables that intensify rivalry, all seem to apply to the Ghanaian horticultural industry. As shown earlier, there is a *large number of competing firms,* rendering the industry fragmented. Most competing firms are of the *same size and have nearly the same degree of influence/power.* However, a few, which are endowed with unique and superior resources and leveraging capabilities are relatively larger and more influential in their specific product sub-sectors. For instance, in cases where the management profile in terms of educational background, previous work experience and the like give the firms a greater leverage vis-à-vis risk, network of contacts, understanding of the operational environment and business management skills (Kuada and Sørensen, 2000, pp. 109-111). These capabilities, thus, enable them to gain some competitive advantages and emerge as award winners within the industry. Also, one particularly large banana producer has unusual power with *first-mover advantage.* The firm is the *first* within the Ghanaian horticultural industry to implement on a large-scale an *asset- and skill-generating strategy* in relation to banana production and exports. Indeed it is the only *Fair Trade Producer* in Africa.[14] Although the firm in question has been recently hit by a natural disaster, it still is the largest banana producer in the country.[15]

Furthermore, rivalry is rife by virtue of the fact that government recognises superior performance, although there is collaboration through product associations. Even common available support such as production and marketing assistance (e.g. through Technoserve, a facilitatory institution) does not eliminate rivalry. Government's recognition of superior performance is evidenced by the annual *National Award for Export Achievement,* which was instituted in 1989 as a component of Ghana Government's overall plan and effort to boost exports from the NTE sector. The awards, which are administered by the GEPC, are conferred on exporters who have distinguished themselves in export performance. Categories of award include the following (*"The Akoben"*, GEPC, 2000):

Exporter of the Year Award is conferred on a company with the highest earnings in US dollars and has at least 75% of earnings repatriated for the year under consideration.

Roll of Honour for Export Achievement for retired companies still performing creditably.

Akoben Trophy, which is the gold medal, is conferred on the exporter with the highest total score in a product group, with export proceeds exceeding US$200,000 and has repatriated at least 75% of the exported amount for the year under consideration.

Certificate of Recognition is conferred on the second best performer and/or exporter with earnings of US$150,000 and above and has repatriated at least 50% of export proceeds for the year under consideration.

In addition, companies that show appreciable diversification in the number of products exported with satisfactory total value are also selected for consideration. The selection for awards is done by an inter-institutional committee comprising representatives of the Ministry of Trade and Industry, Ministry of Food and Agriculture, Ghana National Chamber of Commerce, Federation of the Associations of Ghanaian Exporters, Bank of Ghana, Association of Ghanaian Industries and Ghana Export Promotion Council (i.e. the technical advisors). The basic benchmark for products and product groups selected for consideration is a total value of US$150,000 and above. Source of data is the Non-Traditional Export Performance Statistics compiled by the GEPC as a record of exports obtained from utilised Ghana Export Form (Non-Traditional Products) submitted to GEPC by Ghana Customs, Excise and Preventive Service. However, local rivalry has not yielded the desired international competitiveness. This assertion is supported by the fact that Ghana's NTE's still fall short of the economic redeeming figure of $11.6 billion.

Linkages

The above discussions show that linkages exist between the horticultural firms and (1) financial institutions (for financial leveraging), (2) government institutions (e.g. GEPC, MFA and MOTI) for information and positive policy leveraging, (3) sub-sector associations (e.g. Horticulturists' Association of Ghana) and product associations (e.g. Papaya Exporters' Association) to create avenues for dialogue with (quasi) governmental institutions in order to promote their cause and enhance export performance (Kuada and Sørensen, 2000, p.140).

Linkages also exist within the industry's value systems. Firstly, there are linkages between both local and offshore suppliers of raw materials. For instance local suppliers of packaging materials include, Polykraft, Packrite Industries, Paper Conversion, and Ghana Cartons Manufacturing Company. Other relevant local linkages exist between *out-growers*, for supply of exportable farm produce.[16] Internationally, firms purchase supplies such as fertilisers, pesticides, equipment and even seeds (e.g. Tropical Fruits and Seed Centre by Kabety in Côte d'Ivoire). Secondly, linkages exist between firms and channel members, mostly located in the international marketplace and responsible for offshore marketing of the industry's products. Prominent ones are *AgroFair* for banana, GBC Frutta, Switzerland for pineapples, Sainsbury, U.K. for assortment of products, and Amex International. Thirdly, there are linkages with carriers and shippers. The fourth identified linkages are between producers/exporters and the local fresh fruit retailers as well as the food processing industry. After farm produce of exportable quality has been selected, the residues, which are edible but did not satisfy, for example, the required size criterion, are channelled into the local fresh fruit market or the food processing industry.

These linkages are crucial in-as-much as they connect various firms within the industry to sources of resources such as *money, men, markets, machines, methods, material and even minutes (i.e. 7Ms),* which are deployed during a firm's strategic management process for value creation and goal achievement. Firms within the industry can therefore create competitive advantages by optimising or co-ordinating these links to the outside. For example, an exporter may save on *time (or minutes), management effort and farming expertise* otherwise required for farming its total export volume by linking up with *out-growers*. By so doing it may achieve superior performance through increased total export volume, total income and total profit. Also just-in-time delivery by suppliers (e.g. packaging boxes from local manufacturers) can save warehousing cost and improve cost advantage. Additionally, linkages with local retailers and food processors can help mop up export "residue", avoid waste, create jobs in the fresh-food-retailing sector, increase food supply and generally *improve national income and social welfare*. To illustrate, the production of bananas for export has created a booming banana retail sub-sector in the country within the past six years. In the case of pineapples, as stated earlier, 60% of the industry's production is exported and 40% goes into local consumption or processed for export.

Notably, these linkages portray the value system[17] of the industry and the interdependencies between firms' value chain and those of suppliers and institutions, such that through co-ordination and optimisation of links competitive advantages may emerge for firms and the industry as a whole.

Clustering

A good degree of clustering of farms is evident within the Ghanaian horticultural industry. This clustering is geographically and climatically determined. Most of the farms are located in towns with favourable conditions for horticultural farming, but close to the capital, Accra, to ensure proximity to the international airport of the country, because of the perishable nature of the products.

This location strategy also ensures access to other infrastructural facilities such as telecommunications, healthcare and road transport. Table 3 indicates the geographic concentration of some horticultural farms within the industry. The cluster area of these farms has been encircled in the map titled *"Ghana Administrative Map"*. The locations include Nsawam in the Eastern Region and its surrounding towns and villages located in the Eastern Region as well as the Central and Greater Accra Regions. There are also some horticultural farms in Mampong, Ashanti Region, which mainly supply the local market with Asian vegetables; but not the export market because of the distance from the international airport.

Table 3: Geographic Concentration of Horticultural Farms

Pineapple:	Nsawam and surrounding towns and villages. E.g., Bawjiase, Aburi, Amasaman, Samsam, Midea, Obomu, Kasoa, Dobro. Central Region is noted for the "sugar loaf" variety.
Pawpaw:	Same as pineapple
Banana:	Akrade (south of Akosombo) in the Eastern Region
Mango:	Dodowa and environs. Also in pineapple areas.
Asian vegetables:	Mainly located around Accra (e.g. Nsawam and Kasoa)

Clustering of the farms probably engenders *quick diffusion of production knowledge, benchmarking*[18] *and even casual human resource mobility*. Through research and field trips by small teams of workers, firms could compare their farms with those of competitors for benchmarking. Firms may also collaborate to solve problems, especially with respect to outbreaks of natural disasters, like plant disease.

Although these factors may appear to reduce competitive advantage at firm-level, they could generate competitive advantages for the industry as a whole vis-à-vis international competitors. For instance, if the industry as a whole has very high knowledge absorption capacity, through interaction with the international market there will be inflow of knowledge and intense learning, culminating in collaborative innovation to satisfy identified international market needs. This will reduce industry dependence on *static efficiency*[19], propelling a move towards *dynamic efficiency*[20] within the industry.

However, the clustering bias in favour of proximity to Accra may have limited the effective utilisation of Ghana's natural resources in the horticultural sector. Furthermore, the regional imbalances limit the *competitiveness of the country as a whole.* Therefore, there is a need for balanced infrastructural development in the country to facilitate cultivation of fertile parcels of land located in regions removed from the national capital. This would extend the country's horticultural production frontier and increase its competitive potentials.

Summary

The chapter has attempted to provide some answers to *how characteristics such as industry structure, dynamics (e.g. threat of new entrants), linkages and geographical clustering influence the generation and sustainability of competitive advantage for Ghanaian horticultural exporters.* To this end, the chapter has provided an overview of the Ghanaian non-traditional horticultural export industry. Highlights of chapter discussions have revealed the potential of the industry to contribute significantly to national NTE earnings. The dynamics, linkages and geographical clustering that could shape competition and influence the generation of competitive advantage(s) have also been considered.

It was realised that the industry has no entry barriers. On the contrary, Government policies tended to promote entry. This factor, coupled with relatively *low initial capital requirement, minimal product differentiation,* and *low level of trust* appeared to have contributed to fragmentation of the industry. The fragmented nature of the industry tends to *increase transaction cost and hamper companies' growth and innovation,* which could impede competitiveness and the creation of sustainable competitive advantages. The conclusion drawn was that, consolidation of the industry is imperative to increase firms' capitalisation, to further improve capabilities and competencies to promote innovation for the creation of sustainable competitive advantages.

The industry does not suffer any serious threat of substitute products because output is marketed in the natural form, which adequately satisfies consumers' preference for natural fruits and vegetables. Thus, the industry is ensured sustained demand; and attempts to generate sustainable competitive advantages could yield good dividends. Government's national recognition of superior performance within the local industry has promoted a good degree of rivalry. Such rivalry has evoked the application of firm-level competencies and capabilities (e.g. management educational background, experience and networks) to gain competitive advantages for national award winners. However, international competitiveness is still a big question, since performance of the NTE sector is still below target.

Further, although exporting firms collaborate through associations (e.g. HAG and SPEG) to create a strong bargaining frontier (particularly, with suppliers), individual firms are left to their own devices when negotiating with offshore buyers and occasionally these buyers have demonstrated greater bargaining power. This could sometimes reduce the profit margins of Ghanaian exporters.

The chapter identified linkages within the horticultural value system. Particularly, linkages were discerned between horticultural export firms and suppliers, out-growers, channel members, local retailers and the local food processing industry. These linkages present opportunity for the development of external resource leveraging capabilities, as well as other capabilities for crafting and sustaining competitive advantages.

Finally, geographical clustering of horticultural farms in close proximity to the national capital was empirically confirmed. This was mainly due to imbalanced infrastructural development within the country. Diffusion of infrastructural development is, therefore, recommended. The objective is to encourage cultivation of fertile parcels of land all over the country. The ultimate goal is to improve sustainable competitive potentials through large-scale production; and through the benefits that accrue from clusters, including *quick diffusion of production knowledge and benchmarking*.

Notes

[1] The Economic Recovery Programmeme (ERP) was supported by the International Monetary Fund (IMF), the World Bank and other multi-lateral and bi-lateral donors. The ERP was made up of a comprehensive set of policies to reform the fiscal, monetary, and trade sectors. It remained in force for at least 15 years.

[2] NLC stands for National Liberation Council, which was the then the ruling government.

[3] For example, in February 2000 a seminar was organised to teach exporters the techniques of effective trade fair participation. In August during the same year, a National Workshop on Sectoral Export Strategy Formulation was organised to increase export competitiveness (Buame, 2000). This was attended by forty participants.

[4] For example, in February 2001, the Japanese fruit juice market was identified as an export opportunity for Ghanaian exporters. This was done through the collaboration between GEPC and the Japan External Trade Organisation. The information at the time was that Japan imported approximately US$2 billion of fruit products annually, and Ghanaian exporters were urged to secure a share of this market.

[5] The GFZ derives its legal origin from the passage of the Free Zone Act (Act 504), which became a law in August 1995 (Asenso-Okyere and Asante, 1997). Specific economic development strategies of the GFZ programme include, attraction of foreign direct investment, creation of employment opportunities, increasing foreign exchange earnings, transfer of technology, and enhancement of technical/managerial skills and expertise of Ghanaians (MOTI, CEPS, GEPC and TIP, "Ghana Export Bulletin", 1997). Incentives given by the Free Zone Act include: duties, taxation, zone ownership, capital/profit repatriation, and sales to the local market (Asenso-Okyere and Asante, 1997).

[6] According to Bank of Ghana figures, earnings from NTEs in the year 2000 represented 13.6% of total export earnings.

[7] The present government, which succeeded the National Defence Council (NDC) Government on 7th January 2001, is the New Patriotic Party (NPP).

[8] According to a study conducted by the Government of Ghana and USAID in North Carolina in 1997, Ghana's exports must grow to about US$16.3 billion by the year 2020 if the middle income objective is to be achieved. The report of the study stipulated that of this figure NTEs are expected to account for US$11.9 billion (about 73% of all exports) (Opoku Agyeman, 2001). This motivated the setting of a Vision 2020 target by the erstwhile National Defence Council (NDC) Government.

---

[9] Fragmented industries are industries in which a large number of small- or medium-sized firms operate, and no small set of firms has dominant market share or creates dominant technologies (Barney, 2002).

[10] To a firm seeking competitive advantage and above-normal profit **environmental threat** is any individual, group, or organisation outside the firm that seeks to reduce the level of that firm's performance (Barney, 2002).

[11] The term **structure** in the **S-C-P model** refers to industry structure measured by such factors as the number of competitors in an industry, the heterogeneity of products, and the cost of entry and exit. **Conduct** refers to specific firm actions in an industry, including price taking, product differentiation, tacit collusion, and exploiting market power. **Performance** has two meanings: the performance of individual firms and the performance of the economy as a whole. (See Barney, 2002)

[12] The estimate of minimum capital for starting a horticultural farm was obtained from the Ministry of Food and Agriculture (MOFA). For a farming venture, land is usually leased for 30-50 years and farming machinery may be leased by small farmers; but this creates difficulties that hamper growth and resource accumulation.

[13] Porter (1990) explains **chance events** as occurrences that have little to do with circumstances in a nation and are often largely outside the power of firms (and often the national government) to influence. In relation to creating competitive advantage, there could be a wide variety of examples including pure invention, technological discontinuities, surges of world or regional demand, and wars. Chance events can create discontinuities that allow shifts in competitive position. Such events can nullify the advantages of previously established competitors and create the potential for a new nation's firms to supplant them to achieve competitive advantages.

[14]According to the firm, **Fair Trade** concept means ensuring environmentally and socially sound production. Specifically, the producing firm is required to ensure availability of water in growing areas, the absence of major banana pests (or diseases), and environmentally friendly farming practices. Additionally, workers' rights must be fully respected; they must be decently paid and not exposed to toxic agro-chemicals. (cf. Liddell, 2000)

[15] The firm in question had cultivated approximately 800 hectares of bananas and employed about 700 people. On 12th October 2002, a storm destroyed approximately 380,000 banana plants. As a result, 280 workers have been laid off. The firm needs $1.3 million to return to profitability (Daily Graphic, March 3, 2003).

[16]**Out-growers** are farmers who cultivate exportable fresh agricultural products and supply exporters with their output. By this system, horticultural exporters are also relieved of some of the responsibilities related to the cultivation of their export products and are able to broaden their supply base. In that capacity, therefore, the out-growers (i.e. farmers) only act as ***indirect exporters***. In some cases the out-growers are pre-financed by the exporters, who also monitor the

---

farming techniques of the out-growers to ensure required standards are being met.

[17] Porter (1985, 1990) argues that the ***firm's value chain*** for competing in a particular industry is ***embedded*** in a larger stream of activities, which he calls the "**value system**". The value system is the interaction between suppliers' value chains (upstream value), firm's value chain, channel value chains (downstream value), and buyer value chains (downstream value).

[18] Benchmarking is a process, whereby companies find out how others do something better than they do and then try to imitate or improve on it (Daft, 1998, p.306).

[19] **Static efficiency** involves using resources that can be copied or duplicated e.g. land and labour. Such resources are location specific and have no unique regeneration ability, but can reduce cost as long as competitive environmental conditions remain static, with zero innovation.

[20] **Dynamic efficiency** relates to self-organising and self-generating resources. These are inimitable and usually, core to the organisation. For example, knowledge regenerated through innovation.

References

Akyea, Tawiah (1993): "Production for Exports", *The Journal of Management Studies,* 3rd Series, Vol. 9, January-December, School of Administration, University of Ghana, Legon.

Amenuvor, Eric D.K. (1993): "Export Promotion in Ghana: The Policy", *The Journal of Management Studies,* 3rd Series, Vol. 9, January-December, School of
Administration, University of Ghana, Legon.

Asenso-Okyere, W.K. and F. Ankomah Asante (1997): "Recent Performance of The Non-Traditional Export Sector in Ghana", *Legon Export Outlook,* Vol. 1, No.1, School of Administration, University of Ghana, Legon.

Barney, J. (2002): *Gaining and Sustaining Competitive Advantage,* 2nd Edition, Prentice Hall, New Jersey.

Buame, Samuel C.K. (2000): "Export-Related Events in Ghana from 2000 to 2001", *Legon Export Outlook,* Vol. 1, No. 3, School of Administration, University of
Ghana, Legon, .pp. 104-114.

Buckley, Peter J., Christopher L. Pass and Kate Prescott (1988): "Measures of International Competitiveness: A Critical Survey", *Journal of Marketing Management,* Vol. 4, No. 2, pp. 175-200.

Daft, Richard L. (1998): *Organisation Theory and Design,* 6th Edition, South-Western College Publishing, Cincinnati, Ohio, U.S.A.

Daily Graphic Newspaper (2003): "Banana Industry Still in Crisis" in *Monday, March 3, 2003 Issue,* Graphic Corporation, Ghana

Ghana Export Promotion Council (2000): "The Akoben: Export Awards Ceremony, 2000", GEPC, Accra, Ghana.

Institute of Statistical, Social and Economic Research, University of Ghana, (1994): "The State of the Ghanaian Economy in 1993", Wilco Publicity Services Ltd., Accra.

Institute of Statistical, Social and Economic Research, University of Ghana, (2001): "The State of the Ghanaian Economy in 2000", Wilco Publicity Services Ltd., Accra.

Kastner, Adelaide Naa Amerley (1995): "Development of Ghana's Non-Traditional Export Sector: The Behaviour of the Firm", Paper presented at the First Ghana Export Sector Development Forum at the University of Ghana under the theme, "The Internationalisation of Ghanaian Enterprises and Export Promotion", July 25-26, 1995.

Kastner, Adelaide Naa Amerley (1996): "Internationalisation of Ghanaian Companies: The Non-Traditional Export Sector (Motivations and Strategies)", MBA Thesis, University of Ghana, School of Administration, Legon, Ghana.

Kuada, John and Olav Jull Sørensen (2000): *Internationalisation of Companies from Developing Countries,* International Business Press, New York

Liddell, Ian (2000): "Unpeeling the Banana Trade", Paul Donovan (Ed.), Fairtrade Foundation, August 2000, http://www.fairtrade.org.uk/unpeeling.htm

Ministry of Trade and Industry (MOTI), Customs, Excise and Preventive Service (CEPS), Ghana Export Promotion Council (GEPC) and Ghana Trade and Investment Programme (TIP) (1997): "Ghana Export Bulletin: Annual Report, 1997" Ghana

Opoku-Agyeman, Edmund (2001): Paper presented at the 5th Ghana Export Sector Development Forum at the School of Administration, University of Ghana on 2nd August, 2000.

Porter, Michael E. (1985): *Competitive Advantage – Creating and Sustaining Superior Performance,* The Free Press, New York, N.Y..

Porter, Michael E. (1990): "The Competitive Advantage of Nations", Macmillan Press Ltd., Hong Kong.

Porter, Michael E. (1998): *On Competition,* Harvard Business School Press, Boston.

Sey, Esi (1997): "Export Development in Ghana: An Overview of the Institutional Framework", *Legon Export Outlook,* Vol. 1, No.1, School of Administration, University of Ghana, Legon, pp. 6-10.

Sørensen, O. Jull and V.K. Nyanteng (2000): "Ghana's Exports to Neighbouring Countries", *The Journal of management Studies,* Vol. 15, No. 1, School of Administration, University of Ghana, Legon, pp. 52-75.

Sørensen, Olav Jull (2001): "Innovation and Internationalisation of Companies: Barriers to and Opportunities for Innovation in Ghana", Paper presented at the 6th Ghana Export Sector Development Forum at the School of Administration, University of Ghana on 25th July, 2001.

3

LINKAGES AND UPGRADING IN GHANA'S EXPORT PROCESSING ZONES

John Kuada

Introduction

The contemporary literature advances the view that export-led growth strategy in general, and foreign involvement in export processing zones (EPZs) in particular, inheres the potential to accelerate the process of economic growth in the developing economies (Kusago and Tzannatos 1998). The literature argues that under propitious circumstances and good management, EPZs can achieve the three basic goals of creating employment, increasing foreign exchange earnings and improving the potentials for innovation and learning within local industries through linkages with foreign firms located in the export zones.

The understanding is that foreign companies can enhance the leadership of EPZs, foster inter-firm linkages and boost upgrading through positive spillovers. Furthermore, since foreign technology requires higher skilled employees for their effective usage, foreign firms would train local employees. If such workers then move to local firms or establish their own firms in order to supply inputs to the foreign firms, the skill upgrading gets transferred to other sectors of the economy. Governments in developing countries are therefore advised to formulate policies that stimulate foreign investment inflows into export zones. The 1970s therefore, saw the EPZs boom, mostly in developing countries of Latin America, the Caribbean, Asia and to a lesser extent Africa (ILO 1998). A common characteristic of EPZs is the provision of special incentives to attract (mostly foreign) investment for export production. These incentives range from tax holidays, duty-free export and import to free repatriation of profits.

Despite its popularity as an economic growth instrument, EPZs have received limited academic interest. Thus after a recent review of the available evidence, Cling and Letilly (2001) called for more intensive research into the phenomenon in order to produce a more informed basis for policy and strategy. Empirical investigations so far undertaken focus attention on the employment generation aspects of EPZs (ILO 1998, Cling and Letilly 2001) and have neglected the expected local upgrading and competence development dimensions. The present paper seeks to contribute to our understanding of the role of EPZs in technology and knowledge advancement in Ghana. This is done by discussing the results of an exploratory study of the impact of government policies on foreign investment inflows into Ghana's free zone and the resultant dynamism within the economy. In specific terms the paper addresses the following research questions:

1. To what extent has the export zone policy resulted in linkages between local and foreign firms?
2. What has been the impact on learning and competence development within the local firms?

Answers to these questions are expected to provide knowledge bases for revisions in the country's economic policies and strategies and to serve as pointers to future research.

Methodology and data sources

Records from the Free Zone Board showed that eighty-six (86) projects have been licensed under the free zone since its establishment. Fifty-two (52) of them are currently in operation while the rest are in a start-up or build-up stage. The total investment in the free zone projects stood at a meagre US$405.16 million by 2001. The firms can locate in any part of the country[1], but 80% of them are located within the Accra-Tema metropolis due to the infrastructural advantages of the metropolitan area. The firms are engaged in a widely diversified range of businesses including furniture/wood products; garment and protective clothing; petroleum products; food processing; rubber/plastic products; cosmetics; coconut fibre extraction; pharmaceutical; trading; logistics (warehousing and packaging); telecommunication; and fibre glass manufacturing.

The empirical results reported in the paper are based on survey data, interviews with the top executives of the Free Zone Board as well as reports written by the Free Zone Board. Questionnaires were sent to all the 52 firms operating under the free zone provisions by the end of 2002. But after a series of follow-ups through personal visits and telephone reminders, only 20 usable questionnaires were returned[2]. But since the 20 firms cover all the major sectors within which the free zone companies are represented, we consider the information reliable enough to provide us with good insight into types and contents of linkages initiated as a result of the free zone initiative.

Literature Review and Propositions

The literature presents EPZ establishment as an indication of a country's decision to move away from import substitution towards an export-oriented economy. EPZs stimulate economic growth directly through investment/capital inflows, technology transfer and employment generation (ILO 1998, Kusago and Tzannatos 1998, Cling and Letilly 2001) and indirectly through linkages and spillovers. Such a policy has been associated with the significant industrial development in such countries as Singapore, the Republic of Korea, Taiwan (China), Hong Kong (China), Panama, the Dominican Republic, and Mauritius.

A key component of EPZs is the provision of various kinds of incentive packages to attract foreign firms from developed and/or middle-income countries. These incentives are usually divided into "hard" and "soft" ones. Hard incentives include specific centralized infrastructure: industrial zones equipped with water, electricity, communications, and in some cases, industrial buildings and good transport links. Soft incentives are varied, and according to Kusago and Tzannatos (1998) they include the following:

- A simplification of administrative procedures, both for investment and for enterprise creation, and for production.
- Duty free imports of machinery and equipment, raw materials and intermediate goods necessary for the production of goods to be exported.
- Tax advantages for the enterprise (company taxation) and for the expatriate workforce employed.
- Waivers to the application of national employment laws.
- Special foreign exchange arrangements, frequently granting total liberty regarding the transfer of funds.

Following the available evidence, the decision of foreign investors to locate their businesses in developing countries may be guided by one or a combination of the following motives:

Resources-seeking: Those which seek to access local resources that are either non-available in their home countries or are found to be cheaper in the host country.

Efficiency-seeking: Those which seek to relocate to countries that provide them with cheaper factors of production such as labour.

Market seeking investments: Those, which seek to relocate in the host country in order to bypass present or potential trade barriers that would normally restrict their market expansion.

Upgrading of technological and managerial capabilities of local firms has been presented in the literature as one set of benefits that foreign firms bring to developing countries. The benefits arise partly through demonstration effects and partly through spillover effects (Driffield and Taylor 2002). The argument of the "demonstration effect" is that since the products and technologies that foreign firms bring in have already been tested in foreign markets, their mere presence in the developing countries, can inspire and stimulate local innovators to develop new products and processes. That is, the trial-and-error process that usually characterizes innovation of local firms will be shortened when innovative efforts are built on the proven methods of the foreign firms. Spillovers take place through vertical and horizontal linkages between foreign and local firms. Vertical linkages motivate the acquisition of improved technology, the transfer of technological know-how through staff training and the adoption of managerial behaviours that enable local firms to satisfy the contractual obligations that they may have with the foreign firms.

Having said that, it must be noted that the spillovers from the foreign firms would depend on the capacity of the local firms to absorb the new technology and competencies that linkages with foreign firms would entail. Said differently, the higher the resource position of the local firm prior to the linkage the more upgrading will take place. Furthermore, the deeper the relationship (in terms of content and commitment), the better the prospects of upgrading. It must also be noted that upgrading is a process and time-dependent. That is, the longer the duration of the relationship between local and foreign firms the greater the upgrading is likely to be.

Technology absorption relates to another important concept in management literature: organisational learning. Building on insights provided by such organisational learning scholars as Argyris and Schön (1996), Senge (1992), Nonaka, (1994), it can be argued that linkages between local and foreign firms, enhances learning in local firms by ``short-circuiting'' the learning process. Huber (1991) refers to the process by which firms internalize knowledge not previously available within the organisation as ``grafting''. But as the benefits associated with cooperative relationships and alliances do not accrue automatically to the firms involved, but require conscious management action to ensure that useful knowledge is actually integrated into the firm's activities. Following Cohen and Levinthal (1990) the internalization of new knowledge by local firms will depend on the absorptive capacity of these firms. That is, their ability to recognise and value new knowledge, ability to assimilate the new knowledge, and ability to apply the new knowledge to solve existing and novel problems. Other scholars, leaning on the resource-base view of a firm, argue that the difficulties of knowledge transfer lies in the fact that a great deal of the knowledge firms have are so deeply embedded in the fabric of the firms that it is difficult to codify and communicate to outsiders. Alternatively, local organisations may deliberately refuse to absorb the new knowledge, due to cognitive dissonance, i.e. if the new knowledge is found to be inconsistent with received wisdom or accepted rules of behaviour in the community.

A recent study of Export Processing Zones indicated a very high concentration of zones in few regions of the world. The most reliable estimate to date indicates that there are some 850 EPZs worldwide which employ some 27 million people (1997). This includes 20 million people employed in foreign-owned enterprises established in the 100 or so EPZs in China. Excluding China, EPZs established in developing countries are estimated to account for some 4.5 million employees in 1997 (Kusago and Tzannatos 1998). The Latin American export zones employ 48% of these workers while the Asian countries (excluding China) account for 42%. Africa represents barely 5.5% of the total (250,000 employees in 1997). Apart from Madagascar and Mauritius, all African countries have largely failed in such ventures.

Academic assessments of the performance of the EPZs have produced mixed conclusions. In a study of Malaysia, Johansson and Nilsson (1997) also found that EPZs could have an export

"catalyst" effect; that is, foreign firms attracted to the EPZ may encourage local firms to export. Other scholars argue that the incentive packages offered to attract foreign investments into the EPZs are welfare reducing for the economy as a whole (Hamada 1974, Hamilton and Svensson 1982, Young 1992).
Building on the prior literature, we expect the free zone policy in Ghana to stimulate foreign investment, and enhance competence and technological capacity upgrading of local firms. As far as linkages are concerned, we expect firms to form vertical linkages with local firms since this will be consistent with the resource motives of the location of foreign affiliates in Ghana.

Results

Following the reports of the Free Zones Board, the cumulative amount of investment capital in the free zones from 1996 to 2001 amounted to US$405,161,092.00. The 52 firms in operation employed 7,745 persons in 2001, 39% female and 61 % male. Expatriate employees constituted approximately 1 percent of total number of employees. The remainder of this section presents an analysis of the responses from the 20 free zone firms that participated in our investigation.

Business Activities within the Free Zone

Table 1 provides an overview of the composition of the firms. Ten are local firms, four are joint ventures and 6 are foreign firms. This composition provides us with an opportunity to compare the perceptions of the local firms with those of the foreign firms, and also to examine the extent to which ownership influenced the types and intensity of linkages as well as linkage governance. Eleven of the firms are engaged in processing of local raw materials (most of the Ghanaian firms are in this line of business), while 4 are engaged in processing imported materials and 5 are engaged in trading. This composition also reflects the motives underlying the location of the firms. While 2 of the joint ventures are engaged in local raw material processing ventures (i.e. reflecting resource seeking motive), only 1 of the six wholly owned foreign firms are engaged in local raw material processing. Three of them process imported raw materials (for both local and export markets) while 2 are engaged in trading within the domestic market (i.e. reflecting market seeking motive.)

Table 1: Business Activities of Firms Located in the Export Zones

Ownership of Firms	Nature of Operation			
	Local material-based processing/ manufacture	Imported material-based processing/ manufacture	Commerce and service-oriented firms	Total
Ghanaians	8	-	2	10
Foreign-Ghanaian Joint ventures	2	1	1	4
Wholly foreign owned	1	3	2	6
Total	11	4	5	20

Upgrading

In terms of upgrading the respondents were requested to indicate whether or not their firms have acquired new production or information technology, or have engaged in new product development in recent years. If they have undertaken any of these activities, they were then required to indicate whether they have received assistance from local and/or foreign firms and organisations in the performance of these activities. The results are reported in Table 2. Nearly all the Ghanaian firms have acquired new technology in recent years, none of the joint venture firms did while 2 of the wholly owned foreign firms did. Similarly, most of the Ghanaian firms have acquired new information technology such as computers while only 2 foreign firms did. The picture for product development was similar.

Judging from the results of this analysis, the degree of technological upgrading resulting from the foreign investment inflows is surprisingly low. This is a reflection of the nature of business in which the three categories of companies are engaged.

As indicated above, two of the foreign companies are engaged in trading while three are engaged in processing/manufacturing using imported materials.

Table 2: Contents of Upgrading

Dimensions	**Ownership of Firms**					
	Ghanaian		**Ghanaian-Foreign Joint ventures**		**Wholly owned Foreign Firms**	
	Yes	**No**	**Yes**	**No**	**Yes**	**No**
We acquired new production technology (n =16)	8	2	1		2	2
We acquired new information technology (n = 11)	5	2	-	-	2	2
We have engaged in new product development during the past 3 years (n = 16)	5	5	1	1	2	2
We have received assistance abroad with respect to new product development (n = 16)	1	9	-	2	1	3
We have been in link with local firms or institutions with respect to new product dev. (n = 17)	2	8	1	2	3	1

Type and Extent of Linkages

Respondents were asked to indicate whether or not their companies have any relationship[3] with the following five categories of firms and organisations: local suppliers, customers, technical service providers, business management service providers, and industry associations. They were also required to provide an assessment of their degree of satisfaction with these relationships on a 5-point Likert scale. The results are reported in Table 3.

The evidence shows that 15 firms had relationship with their local suppliers, 13 were linked to customers, 12 with technical service providers, 15 with management service providers and 12 with industry associations. As would be expected all the Ghanaian firms had links with their suppliers since they are engaged in processing local raw materials. They also reported a fairly high level of satisfaction with the local suppliers. Similarly, the joint venture firms were all linked with local suppliers and report fairly high level of satisfaction in this relationship. Surprisingly, 4 of the 6 the foreign owned firms have local suppliers, providing them mainly with packaging items mostly of imported origin.[4]

With respect to relationship with customers, the picture remains much the same. Nine of the Ghanaian firms are in link with their customers, but have expressed some dissatisfaction with this relationship. The four joint venture firms on the other hand are quite satisfied with their customers while three of the foreign firms are very dissatisfied. The low level of satisfaction may also be a reflection of the power asymmetries within the vertical chain. The firms within the export zone appear to have greater power over local suppliers and are disadvantaged in their relationship with their foreign customers.

Geographical proximity has apparently strengthened their ability to effectively govern their relationship with local suppliers while geographical distance makes the effectiveness of governance arrangements more difficult with respect to foreign customers. Only the Ghanaian and joint venture firms have relationship with technical service providers.

Close examination of these "relationships" reveals that they are dormant. The service providers are called upon when the needs arise. In-house personnel undertook normal machine maintenance. One joint venture firm had a foreign consultant who was sent down by the foreign partner when the firm's equipment runs into technical difficulties. This consultant was at the same time responsible for training the local staff. All the three categories of firms made some use of local business management service providers (including accounting services and management training). But the level of satisfaction with these relationships is relatively low. Respondents were however not specific about what they considered dissatisfactory with these services. One major complaint voiced by the foreign firms was that the services were not delivered on time and were therefore not reliable. Industry associations are not considered as offering any substantial services to the firms.

Table 3: Assessment of Relationship with Intermediaries and Agencies

Dimensions	Ownership of Firms /Scale								
	Ghanaian			Ghanaian-Foreign Joint Ventures			Wholly-owned Foreign Firms		
	1-2	3	4-5	1-2	3	4-5	1-2	3	4-5
Local suppliers of materials and components (n =15)	2	4	4	-	1	3	2	1	1
Customers (n = 13)	4	1	4	1	-	3	3	-	1
Technical service providers (n = 12)	2	2	2	1	-	-	3	-	-
Business/ management service providers (n = 15)	6	-	3	2	-	1	3	-	1
Industry associations (n = 12)	4	1	1	1	-	1	3	-	-

1-2 = Not satisfactory, 3 = Satisfactory, 4-5 = Very satisfactory

Learning and Knowledge Management

Respondents were also required to state whether or not their firms have established in-house training centres, whether they have a training department or whether they send their staff to off-the job training. Table 4 presents the results of the analysis. Out of the 17 firms who answered this question only 2 had their own training centres, 5 had a training unit within the personnel department while most of them assigned their training duties to a specific staff member. Off-the-job training methods were used by 7 of the 16 firms whose respondents replied to this question. There are no major differences between the three categories of firms with respect to their human resource development strategies.

Table 4: Internal Learning Arrangements within Firms

Dimensions	Ownership of Firms					
	Ghanaian		Ghanaian-Foreign Joint Ventures		Wholly-owned Foreign Firms	
	Yes	No	Yes	No	Yes	No
We have our own training centre (n = 17)	2	8	-	3	-	4
We have our own training department (n = 18)	2	8	1	3	2	2
We have assigned training duties to our staff (n = 18)	7	3	3	1	2	2
We send our staff out for training (n = 16)	5	5	1	2	1	2

Governance and Inter-firm Knowledge Transfer

As shown in Table 5, the free zone firms adopted two main methods in the governance of their relationship with local suppliers. Sixteen firms conducted regular inspections of the products supplied and rejected those that proved to be of unsatisfactory quality. Added to this 3 of the 4 joint venture firms and the foreign-owned firms threaten to withdraw from relationships with local suppliers whose product qualities failed to satisfy specified quality standards.

Standards are communicative instruments. They communicate customers' expectations to their suppliers and ensure stability in the quality of inputs received. It is intriguing to note that none of the Ghanaian firms adopted this approach. Only 4 firms gave any training to their local suppliers, and 2 assisted the local suppliers in acquiring ISO certification or encouraged them to receive such a certification.

Table 5: Quality Assurance Mechanisms (Firm-Supplier Linkages)

Dimensions	Ownership of Firms					
	Ghanaian		Ghanaian-Foreign Joint Ventures		Wholly-owned Foreign Firms	
	Yes	No	Yes	No	Yes	No
We inspect and reject poor quality inputs supplied (n =16)	8	-	4	-	4	-
We trained their producers/workers(n = 16)	2	8	1	3	1	1
We cancel/threaten to cancel orders (n = 16)	-	10	3	1	1	1
We assist them in acquiring/ implementing ISO certification (n =16)	-	9	1	2	1	3
We test their staff/workers (n =16)	1	9	-	3	1	2

Discussions

Three major observations can be made from the evidence reported above. First, the inflow of foreign investments into the free zone is disappointingly low when seen in terms of the benefits that the government has provided in the free zone package. Second, there has been a limited degree of linkages between the firms within the free zone and local firms. Not only that, the contents of the linkages have been limited and the intensity of interactions between the firms has been very low. Third, the degree of knowledge transfer initiated in these inter-firm linkages has been very low. Thus taken together, the free zone experience has so far belied the expectations of Ghanaian policy makers.

Taking the low foreign investment inflows first, it must be noted that the free zone evidence is consistent with the general pattern of foreign investment flows into the rest of the Ghanaian economy and into other African countries.

According to the latest Ghana Investment Promotion Centre (GIPC) report, 1,084 FDI projects have been registered in Ghana since 1994. Their breakdown in terms of sectors was given as follows: 314 in the service sector, 300 in manufacturing, 129 in tourism, 92 in building and construction, and 87 in agriculture. There were 763 joint foreign-Ghanaian and 321 wholly foreign-owned projects, valued at US$1,209.64 billion and US$398.88 million respectively.

Previous studies have also shown that African countries' share of foreign investment inflows has remained relatively small, despite the fact that investments in developing countries as a whole have increased. A recent report by Sauvant (2001) showed that in contrast to the experience in most other parts of the world, inflows of foreign direct investments to Africa (including South Africa) declined in 2000 (for the first time since the mid 1990s), from $10.5 billion to $9.1 billion. As a result, the share of Africa in total FDI flows fell below 1 per cent. For example, Asiedu (2002) provided corroborating evidence in a separate study, which showed that while foreign investment inflows into European and Central Asian countries increased by 5,200% between 1980 and 1998, Sub-Saharan African countries registered a modest increase of 59%. She therefore argued that there is an adverse regional effect on investor's perception of the attractiveness of SSA countries as investment targets. That is, being an African country is itself enough to be excluded from foreign investors' radar.

A number of tentative explanations can be provided for the low level of inter-firm linkages reported. It is argued in the literature that the propensity of foreign firms to establish linkages with local firms may depend on their motives for relocation in the country. Affiliates established through joint ventures or mergers and acquisitions have been found to be more likely to source their inputs locally than wholly owned foreign companies. The reason is that joint venture firms can take advantages of the supplier relationships of the acquired firms or the local partners. It takes the wholly owned firms a lot more effort and resources to develop linkages with local suppliers and this may deter them from doing so.

The limited flow of knowledge from the free zone firms to local firms is partly an outcome of their preference for transactional governance mechanisms rather than relational and collaborative mechanisms. The evidence here is therefore consistent with earlier studies. For example Lall (1982) noted that linkages between Multinational Corporations (MNCs) and local firms are usually of a contractual nature. We may have to turn to the concept of bounded rationality popularly adopted in Transaction Costs Economics to understand this preference for transactional governance mechanism. Crudely stated, the concept of bounded rationality acknowledges that there is a fundamental uncertainty among economic actors concerning future contingencies of their action. Said differently, when one firm is unilaterally dependent on another firm, it is assumed that the partner firm may be tempted to take opportunistic advantage of the dependence and extort a greater share in added value. Prior empirical evidence on supplier-customer relationship in Ghana suggests that there are good justifications for such opportunism or non-adherence to agreements regarding quality and conditions of delivery (Fafchamps 1996).

This uncertainty may be managed through direct observation, measurement and monitoring. Alternatively, one may relinquish such centralized control, and try to settle risks of transactions through knowledge sharing and mutual trust building mechanisms, or what Nooteboom (2001) refers to as "relational governance mechanisms". As indicated above, the free zone firms have chosen the former approach to governance, i.e. close supervision of goods delivered and threatening to cancel orders. Presumably, this is an indication of their inability to identify the transactional hazards that linkages with local suppliers entail and the limited trust in the public systems to intervene with reasonable promptitude in events of breach of contract.

Conclusion

The research presented in this paper aimed at exploring the extent to which the export zone policy adopted in Ghana has resulted in linkages between foreign and local firms and competence development within the latter. The evidence suggests weak linkages and limited stimulus of competence development within the local firms. The results are therefore consistent with views expressed in prior literature. In their review of the performance of EPZs Kusago and Tzannatos (1998) noted that linkages from the zones to the domestic economy are often weak, and the use of domestic raw materials by EPZs has not been significant. But the fact that the free zone has been established in the country would have indirect benefits to the economy in the form of changes in government officials' attitude to private business. This appears to be the case judging from comments from managers during our interviews. They reported on changes in bureaucratic procedures and removal of restrictions.

Granting that this is a widespread observation within the business sector, it is fair to argue that the most significant contribution of EPZs may not be seen in the anticipated direct effects within the enclaves and the spillover effects on local firms outside the zones, but from the creation of a more liberal and business friendly operational environment for both local and foreign investors. Additional research is required to establish the validity of this observation.

It is, however, debatable whether the incentives offered to attract investments into the free zones is socially acceptable to a developing country that requires all the resources that it can marshal in order to fulfil its social responsibilities. Benefit cost-analysis is required to provide policy makers with justifications for further improvement in the incentive packages, as far as this is deemed necessary in order to attract a greater number of foreign investors.

Notes

[1] The notion of a free trade zone operating in a defined geographic area is gradually disappearing to the profit of "free enterprises" or "free points" scattered throughout a territory.

[2] The researcher and one other research assistant administered some of the questionnaires. This offered us the opportunity to gain deeper insight into some of the key issues addressed in the questionnaire through the interviews conducted to fill in the questionnaires.

[3] Relationship is defined in the questionnaire as "having regular transaction with the firm or organisation". The term "regular" is left to the interpretations of the respondents. But since most of the questionnaires were administered, the terms "regular" and "frequent" were used synonymously to emphasise that simple occasional transactions must be excluded in the definition.

[4] Further investigations revealed that there exists what may be termed *second order linkages* within the agricultural chain. That is the initial linkage between a fruit processing firm and a local commercial farmer would encourage the Ghanaian farmer to establish linkages with one or several other Ghanaian farmers. The so-called *out-grower* relationship is a case in point. The farmer supplying the processing firm is then linked up to several independent Ghanaian farmers who then grow fruits and vegetables based on specifications and inputs as well as technical support of main supplier. This phenomenon has, however, not received specific analysis in the present study.

References

Aitken, B.J., Harrison, A., (1999): "Do domestic firms benefit from direct foreign investment? Evidence from Venezuela" *American Economic Review* 89 (3) pp. 605-618

Argyris, C; Schön, Donald A (1996): *Organisational Learning II*. Reading Massachussetts: Addison-Wesley Publishing Company.

Asiedu, Elizabeth, (2002): "On the Determinants of Foreign Direct Investment to Developing Countries: Is Africa Different?" *World Development* Vol. 30 No. 1 pp. 107-119

Cling, Jean-Pierre and Letilly, Gaëlle, (2001): "Export Processing Zones: A Threatened Instrument for Global Economy Insertion?" *Document de Travail* DT/2001/17 pp.1-50

Cohen, M.D. and D. A. Levinthal (1990): "Absorptive capacity: A new perspective on learning and innovation", *Administrative Science Quarterly* 35, 128 - 52.

Driffield N and Karl Taylor (2001): 'Spillovers from FDI and skill structures of host-country firms.' Birmingham Business School, Working Paper Series 2001-01.

Driffield N and Karl Taylor (2002): "Spillovers Domestic wage determination: Spillovers and inward investment." University of Leicester, Working paper 2002 02/012.

Ghana Investment Promotion Centre (2002) *Investment Report* (Accra)

Haddad, M. and A Harrison, (1993): "Are there foreign positive spillovers from Direct Foreign Investment: Evidence from panel Data for Morocco" *Journal of Development Economics* 24 (1) pp. 51-74

Hamada, K. (1974): "An Economic Analysis of the Duty-Free Zone," *Journal of International Economics* 4, 225-241.

Hamilton, C. and Svensson, L.E.O (1982): "On the Welfare Economics of a Duty-Free Zone," *Journal of International Economics* 20, 45-64.

Huber, George P. (1991) "Organisational learning: the contributing processes and the literatures", *Organisation Science,* Vol. 2, no 1., pp 88-115

ILO [1998], 'Export Processing zones: Addressing the social and labour issues', available on the Internet [www.ilo.org].

Johannsson, Helena and Lars Nilsson (1997): "Export Processing Zones as Catalysts," *World Development,* 25, 12, 2115-2128.

Kusago, T., Tzannatos, Z. (1998): 'Export processing zones: A review in need of update', *World Bank Discussion Paper* No. 9802, January.

Lall Sanjaya, (1982): "Export Orientation versus Import Substitution: A review Article", *Journal of Development Economics.*

Nonaka, I. (1994): "A dynamic theory of organisational knowledge creation, *Organisation Science* (5)1, 14-37.

Nooteboom, B. (2001): Learning and innovation in organisations and economies. Oxford: Oxford University Press

Senge, Peter M. (1992): *The Fifth Discipline: the art and practice of the learning organisation.* Repr. London: Century Business.

Rolfe, Robert J., Woodward, Douglas P., and Kagira, Bernard (2003): "Footloose and Tax Free: Incentive Preferences in Kenyan Export Processing Zones" Paper presented at the Biennial Conference of the Economic Society of South Africa, Somerset West, South Africa, 17-19 September 2003.

Young, L. (1992): "Unemployment and the Optimal Export-Processing Zone," *Journal of Development Economics* 37, 369-385.

Appendix 3A:

List of All Enterprises Covered by the Study

Name Of Enterprise	Nationality of Enterprise
Lewadis Limited	Foreign
Pioneer Food Cannery Ltd	Foreign
Lewancs FZE	Foreign
Acs-Bps (Gh.) Ltd.	Foreign
Tatcol Sagr	Foreign
Nourex Limited	Foreign
Comet Gh. Limited	Foreign
Carnuad Metal Box	Foreign
Najabsco Ltd.	Foreign
Top Industries Co. Ltd.	Foreign
Socomex Ghana Ltd.	Foreign
Ghana Printing & Packaging Ind	Foreign
Ghana Biscuit Co. Ltd	Foreign
Edward Snell (& Co. Africa) Lt	Foreign
Scanstyle Mim	Ghanaian
Gelina Packaging Co. Ltd.	Ghanaian
Airways Catering Ltd.	Ghanaian
Weitnau & Gtdec Ltd.	Ghanaian
Machine Wood Ltd	Ghanaian
Standard Wood Processing	Ghanaian
Tatlock Ltd.	Ghanaian
Ghana Cotton Co. Ltd.	Ghanaian
West Africa Mills Co. Ltd.	Ghanaian
Fruits Of The Spirit Company L	Ghanaian
Great Imperial Co. Limited	Ghanaian
Quality Food Processing	Ghanaian
Gafco Fish Cannery & Smoking L	Ghanaian and others
Carson Products	Ghanaian and others
Managecraft	Ghanaian and others
Blue Skies Products	Ghanaian and others
Crystal Auto Ltd.	Ghanaian and others
Wienco Fibre Ltd.	Ghanaian and others

Phyto Riker Pharmaceuticals Lt	Ghanaian and others
Fpi (Gh) Ltd.	Ghanaian and others
Sixteen 47 Gh. Ltd.	Ghanaian and others
Slid Industries Ltd.	Ghanaian and others
Arrow Network Systems Ltd.	Ghanaian and others
A-Q Solutions	Ghanaian and others
Ktk Manufacturing Co. Ltd.	Ghanaian and others
First Catering Limited	Ghanaian and others
Lakshimi	Ghanaian and others

KEY F= Foreign, F/GJV= Foreign/Ghanaian Joint Venture

4

INTERNATIONALISATION AND MANAGEMENT OF GHANAIAN EXPORT FIRMS

K. A. Ofei

Introduction

One of the most important forces changing and challenging Ghanaian businesses is globalisation. Falling trade barriers have opened new business opportunities. As a result domestic businesses have embarked on the exportation of various goods. These firms are subject to a wide spectrum of environmental challenges. The firms have to do business in many different economic, political, and cultural environments, and must meet intensive challenges from other global competitors.

In order to adequately respond to the environmental pressures, the exporting company must develop some strategic competencies so as to overcome the liability of its foreignness. It must also have some organisational capabilities so as to get better returns from leveraging its strategic strengths internally rather than through contractual relationships with outside parties (Levitt 1983). Ghanaian export firms will therefore have to develop organisational structures and associated management processes. By choosing an appropriate organisation structure and management processes, an organisation can develop the relevant strength to face environmental challenges.

Organisational structure concerns the shape adopted by a business in the pursuit of its strategic objectives. According to Selznik (see Badran/Hinnings, 1980), the organisational structure is the "institutionalized patterns and procedures bringing resources to bear on the goal attainment processes and regulating the commitment of participants to the organisation". Badran/Hinnings (1980) have also indicated that the importance of structure "lies in the fact that structuring of activities of organisations is an institutionalization of the control process in organisation".

For international businesses, the importance of structure is brought into focus because of the distances between the various parts and the need to co-ordinate activities between them. It also ensures that all different value adding activities are coordinated and controlled in a way that enables the organisation to achieve its goals. Hence, an appropriate structure should ensure effective and efficient use of resource so that the level of resource utilization matches the level of activity, and resources are only deployed on what needs to be done (Bartlett/Ghoshal 1995).

The organisational structure, as a static set of roles and responsibilities, is a powerful but blunt instrument of strategic change. The company's entire management - the administrative system, communication channels and interpersonal relations become the tools for managing such a change (Bartlett/Ghoshal 1995). The development of management processes can therefore be seen as complementing choices about a firm's structure in that they further delineate specific patterns of executive interaction and behaviour with the basic organisational framework. Management processes therefore provide a flexible mode of a firm's ability to integrate its activities and otherwise adapt to its environment.

Though structure and management process are highly interrelated, there are still important differences among these complementary tools. Structural choices tend to lead to a more discrete and finite attempt by an organisation to adjust to its environment, a change in structure signifies a major shift in an organisation's ability to deal with its strategic challenges (Lorange/Chakravarthy 1991)

Our interest in the structure and management processes of non-traditional Ghanaian exporting firms comes from research evidence suggesting that structures of exporting firms change in accordance with their degree of internationalisation.
More formally internationalisation is defined as "a step by step process of international business development whereby a firm becomes increasingly committed to and involved in international business operations through specific products in selected markets" (Luostarinen 1994). In this regard the stages theory has been used to identify organisational changes occurring in the process of internationalisation (Kuada and Sørensen 2000).

The stages theory views the internationalisation of the firm as a sequential and orderly process. It argues that firms proceed in a consistent stepwise fashion along some organisational continuum as they develop their international relationships (Kuada and Sørensen 2000). The overall contention here is that a firm expands its activities either through geographical diversification or increased product lines, and the end use of the products. The firm, to be effective, must change its structure from a centralized, functional form to a decentralized divisional structure. More accurately a firm must forge an organisational structure consistent with its strategy to successfully implant plans through its management system.

Focus of the Study

Our discussions above suggest that by choosing an appropriate organisational structure and management processes an organisation can develop a relevant strength to face environmental challenges in the global market. It also suggests that internationalisation of exporting firms follows certain stages of development, which will alter the organisational structure of the exporting firm.
Given the paradigm of interrelationships indicated by the stages theory the main question to be addressed in this study is

whether the norms of organisational design of Ghanaian exporting firms are subject to the theoretical expectations internationalisation literature or there is a distinctive type of enterprise structure and management practices peculiar to Ghanaian exporting firms.

We pose these questions because the post-war economic success of Japanese firms has highlighted the limited generality of the business strategy–structure relationships identified by Chandler. It has also emphasized the viability of alternatives to American management structures and practices (Whitley 1995, Hamilton/Biggart 1988). This is emphasized in the distinctive nature of firms in other East Asian societies.

The questions actually come from a debate initiated by Kerr (1964) about the logic of management development. Kerr (1964) contended that the imperatives of industrialisation would ensure that managerial attitudes, values and behaviour would become increasingly uniform; the demands of organisational life would be a force for convergence. This has generated two theoretical positions, the cultural free theorists and the culturally specific theorists. A key argument of cultural free theorists is that there is a dominant technical rationality in economic markets, which inexorably leads to a single way of organizing and controlling economic resources. This cultural free theory suggests that "there is a consistency of relationships between the variables of organisation context and organisational structure, and this will hold for all work organisations" (Hickson et al 1974). This relationship is associated with the growth in organisational size (measured by the number of employees), division of labour and formalisation (degree to which rules, procedures, instructions and information in general appear in written form; Hickson et al 1974).

The central idea of the culturally specific argument is institutional divergence, i.e. the rules and controls of agencies in socio-cultural environments will make organisational structures isomorphic with the structures of the external agencies. The cultural specific argument further points out that for organisations to succeed in their environments, they must not only design their structures to suit their environments, but they must also arrange their rewards to suit the aspirations of their members and societies at large.

The purpose of this study, therefore, is to examine the organisational and management patterns of Ghanaian export firms, especially their stages of development as they seek to internationalise.

Key Objectives of the Study

The present study is concerned with the influences hypothesized to be related to the organisation and management of exporting firms. Specifically, the objectives of the study are to:

- Characterize the internationalisation process of Ghanaian firms concerning changes in their strategies, functions and administrative structures, as well as patterns of decision-making authority and processes of managing resources.
- Determine whether they show any distinctive structures unique to the socio-cultural and institutional environment in Ghana.
- Determine which contextual variables are responsible.

Related Literature

This study raises a number of theoretical and epistemological issues about the internationalisation process of Ghanaian exporting firms. The stages theory has itself attracted a number of explanations.

For instance, the Uppsala School considers internationalisation based on market entry and development mode. The process involves: no exports, Export via agents, exports via sales subsidiary and production in a subsidiary abroad (Kuada and Sørensen 2000).

Cavusgil (1984) also operates with a criterion based on export involvement and distinguishes between three phases of internationalisation based on: no involvement, experimental involvement, characterized by those firms which exert little commitment to foreign market development (e.g., passive response, applying domestic market strategies abroad and little financial commitment). The second phase - active involvement, occurs when the managers of the firm are willing to build up and penetrate foreign markets; to adapt the marketing mix according to the specific needs of overseas markets; and to conduct the export activities on a regular basis rather than sporadically. The final stage - committed involvement, characterized by the situation in which the firms search for business activities worldwide, not only through exports, but also through other means of foreign operations such as investment in sales and production subsidiaries broad.

Bilkey and Tesar (1977) also provide a six-stage export development framework based on a mixture of classification criteria. They suggest the following stages:

1. Management is not interested in exporting; would not even fill an unsolicited export order.
2. Management would fill an unsolicited export order, but makes no effort to explore the feasibility of exporting.
3. Management actively explores the feasibility of exporting.
4. The firm exports on an experimental basis to some psychologically close countries.
5. The firm is an experienced exporter to that country and adjusts exports optimally to changing exchange rates, tariffs, etc.
6. Management explores the feasibility of exporting to additional countries that are psychologically far away.

Table 1: Evolution and Growth of International Business and Corresponding Changes in Organisational Structures and Formalisation

Evolution and growth of international business	A. Evolution of organisational structure	B. Other structural characteristics
1. Initial stage	Export department	Loose formal relationships
2. Early production stage	Export dept/International division	More formalised relationships between headquarters and subsidiaries
3. Standardisation of production process- mature stage few products	International division	Increased formalised relationships
4. Product innovations and growth through diversification	Product/area bases for structuring of organisation	Increased formalisation
5.Quest for global rationalization	Product/ area bases for structuring /matrix type organisation	Increased formalisation

Source: A. R. Neghandi (1987)

Table 1 shows that at the earlier stage of development, the firm manages its overseas business through the export department, which maintains loose formal relationships with overseas distributors. By the time the firm has established four to six manufacturing subsidiaries overseas, a more formal linkage with the foreign operations becomes a necessity. The firm therefore establishes an international division within the domestic organisational structure to communicate with and coordinate the subsidiaries operations. At the next stage of expansion the international division becomes extremely overloaded. Its ability to coordinate the subsidiaries' operations becomes insufficient, and some other form of organisational structure to manage the overseas business is now needed. At this point, depending on the nature of the expansion strategies – i.e., either through product diversification or through geographical expansion – the firm will establish a product or a global organisational structure.

Moreover, growth and internationalisation work as strong forces for improving many managerial operations. Therefore when the firm finds it is approaching a certain limit of growth in the current market, it allocates a considerable portion of its staff and resources toward improving the primary production and marketing activities. In addition, such a firm attempts to build new technological capabilities with long-term research and development plans. A formal strategic planning system is often established to provide guidance for overall corporate management.

The stages theory has also attracted a number of criticisms (Strandskov 1993). It has been argued that the stages approach represents an attempt to systematize the development process of firms in some phases, which rely on causal relationships between different sets of variables within the firm's inner or outer environments. The approach also implies not only an attempt to establish certain patterns of causality at specific points in time, but to construct descriptive models which point to the definite direction of changes, i.e. a time-related process also due to causal relations. The theory also applies a linear descriptive mode in the sense that all firms have to go through each stage in a particular manner. This provides a mechanistic explanation of firm internationalisation and prescribes a terminal or irreversible forces reducing the influences of individual and contingency factors.

Formal Organisation Theory and Internationalisation of Firms

The stages theory suggests a process of organisational change in which formal organisational structures, processes, systems, planning and control systems change. It shows how developmental strategies might shape the way in which organisational structures have been designed. Analytical models for this approach have been based on the famous argument of "structure follows strategy" by Chandler (1962). He argues that growth without structural adjustment can lead only to economic efficiency. Unless new structures are deployed to meet new administrative needs which result from an expansion of a firm's activities into new areas, functions, or product lines, technological, financial, and personnel economies of growth and size cannot be realized.

Since the 1960s, there has been a special concern by organisation theorists with the structure and functioning of formal organisations. In a considerable number of studies, they have developed empirically testable hypotheses and concepts for the study of organisational structures (Blau 1985, Pugh 1963). This has made it possible to develop organisation profiles and how they relate to the socio-cultural and institutional environment in which they operate.

The formal organisation structure has primarily been associated with the authority structure of bureaucratic organisations. In such organisations, the authority structure specifies the functional relationship between superiors and subordinates. At the various hierarchical levels of authority are, e.g. managers, supervisors and group leaders. Authority is exercised downward through a hierarchy of full-time officials who influence the behaviour of lower level participants in the organisation. That is, the direction of the initiation of orders is from a higher level to a lower one (Holt 1998).

The framework for the study of organisations suggests that the pattern of authority relationships in organisations will be related to the structuring of activities. The structuring of activities implies the degree to which behaviour is overtly defined. This involves the degree of specialisation in task allocation, the degree of standardisation of organisational routines and the degree of formalisation (extent to which rules in organisation are written down, Pugh 1963, Rollinson et al 1998).

The Configuration Approach to Organisational Design

Mintzberg (1979, 1985) also provides two basic approaches to the formation of organisational structure, the contingency and the configuration approach. Although the factors discussed in the previous section contribute to an understanding of how organisation structures evolve, Mintzberg (1979) points out that any organisation represents a complicated network of groups and individuals, departments and functions, main line activities and support staff, key players and periphery people internal and external stakeholders. According to Mintzberg (1979), organisations must take account of the following design parameters:

Job specialisation – to logically divide up the tasks of the organisation.
Behaviour formalisation – standardisation of work processes.
Training – instruction programmes to provide employees with the skills and knowledge to do their jobs.
Indoctrination – to inculcate organisational norms in workers.
Unit grouping – according to (1) business function (e.g. marketing, finance, production, etc.), and (2) market served. These may conflict with each other as grouping by business function centres on the efficiency of the processes of the organisation while grouping by market increases organisational flexibility but encourages duplication (in turn, reducing efficiency).
Unit size – the number of positions contained in a single unit of the business;
Planning and control systems – used to plan and control the activities of the organisation.
Liaison and integrating devices – devices like task forces and committees can integrate the units of the business. The logical conclusion of such devices is a matrix structure.

The need for centralization or decentralization – the extent to which it is necessary or desirable to diffuse decision-making power.

In addition, it is important to consider both horizontal and vertical communication requirements and systems within the organisation. In an international business unit grouping, planning and control systems, integrating devices, the need for centralization or decentralization and indoctrination are particularly important. The way in which units are grouped is one of the most significant decisions to be made in the design of international organisations. It is not simply a decision of grouping by functional area or by market, but rather how to integrate the two. The structures of global organisations must also take account of the need to co-ordinate and integrate geographically dispersed activities, at the same time as making possible local responsiveness where and when it is required.

According to Mintzberg (1979), these factors should not be picked and chosen at random. Rather they should be selected according to internally consistent groupings. These groupings should be consistent with the situation of the organisation, its age and size, the conditions of the industry in which it operates, and its production technology. He points out that, like all phenomena, from atoms to stars, the characteristics of organisations fall into natural clusters or configuration. When these configurations are mismatched, that is, when wrong ones are put together the organisation does not function effectively and does not achieve its natural harmony. There must therefore be a fit.

According to the contingency theory (as it relates to organisational structure) the most important determinants, the structure of an organisation, will depend upon factors like the following:

- Nature of its business and size.
- The geographical span of its activities.
- Age and history of the organisation.

- The nature of its environment.
- Global strategy of the business.
- The level of technology in the organisation.
- Geographical span of activities.
- Leadership and leadership style.

Pugh (1963) has also suggested that the study of the structure and activities of an organisation structure must be conducted in relationship to its other contextual variables. The contextual variables describe the circumstances or conditions under which an organisation operates. Research has highlighted a number of crucial contextual variables which appear to influence the structure of organisation. These contextual variables include the characteristics of organisations such as technology, origins and history, social functions, and ownership control and the socio-economic context in which the organisation operates.

Transaction Costs and Internationalisation of Firms

Probably the most sustained effort to explain the relationship between structure of the organisation and its performance is the transaction cost theory (Moschandreas 1994). Transaction cost attempts to explain why firms exist (Coase 1937). Its main contention is that efficiency is the motivating force behind the emergence of firms. In its most general formulation, transaction costs theory holds that activities of the firm are organised optimally when they minimize the production costs and economize the transaction costs involved in producing the desired outcomes. The transaction cost reasoning therefore seeks to explain the existence of different organisational forms. Williamson (1985) has been a major developer of Coase's (1937) argument that transaction costs account both for why the hierarchically organised firm even exists, and why particular kinds of hierarchies have evolved in particular kinds of economic environments. Williamson's general argument is that in the pursuit of efficiency, the structure that is adopted should be the one, which will minimize transaction costs for the firm (Hymer 1977). The transaction costs reasoning has therefore been used to explain the existence of different forms of organisations such as peer groups, simple hierarchies and multistage hierarchies.

Peer Groups

A peer group is simply a group of people working together without a hierarchy. In the peer group the most important coordination mechanism is mutual adjustment. There is no boss, so there can be no direct supervision. The peer group sells its output, the proceeds of which are shared among the members of the peer group according to some sharing rule. Examples of peer groups are small partnerships (lawyers, auditors, and doctors).

Peer groups have certain advantages. First, economies of scale may be obtained. This may arise in information gathering. Secondly, a peer group may have risk-bearing advantages over a group of independent persons (Demetz and Alchian 1972).

Simple Hierarchies

A simple hierarchy is a group of workers with a boss. The boss has the right to adjust wage rates, to alter the composition of the group and to tell the workers of the group what to do. Most small manufacturing firms (like the factory making grandfather clocks) are organised as simple hierarchies not as peer groups. In a peer group, all members are equal: they receive the same income and have the same decision rights. In simple hierarchies supervision is an important co-ordination mechanism. Also, in a hierarchy a person's income usually corresponds to his or her performance, either past performance or expected future performance. Williamson stresses hierarchy as the alternative to mutual adjustment within peer groups. Most organisations are of a more complex type involving more coordination mechanisms than mutual adjustment and direct supervision.

Multistage Hierarchy-Form and M-Form Enterprises

In a simple hierarchy there is only one manager who coordinates the work of the other team members. However, because of bounded rationality, single managers can no longer coordinate the work of all team members. Several managers are now needed. This creates an opportunity for division of managerial work so that each manager can specialize. Thus, within the firm, departments along functional lines are created, and each functional department has a manager. A general manager coordinates the work of these functional managers. This organisation form is widely used by medium- sized firms. Williamson calls this the **unitary form** or **U-form** enterprise. Within a U-form enterprise there are at least two layers of managers. It is a **multistage hierarchy** as opposed to a single-stage or simply hierarchy (Rumelt, et al 1995).

In the discussions above we reviewed literature on the nature of organisations and how the institutional and socio-cultural environment might influence its structure. We found that all organisations must divide tasks and activities into well defined operations and delineate authority to co-ordinate those activities. While the stages theory of internationalisation provides universalistic propositions on the relationships between the degree of internationalisation and the structural development of the organisation, the design of organisations will however be contingent upon the constraints of industry competition, technology and the company's markets as well as the socio-cultural and the institutional settings.

The framework for the study is therefore based on the following two assumptions:

- The structure of the Ghanaian export firm is a function of its degree of internationalisation. This involves a form of creeping incrementalism where structures evolve from simple entrepreneurial firms to greater reliance on specialisation and subsequent delegation of authority. A hypothesis on this relationship is that as division of labour increases in number, managers introduce procedures to regulate the activities for which they are responsible, resulting in increased documentation and a larger supportive hierarchy. This suggests that specialisation, formalisation, and centralization will be highly positively correlated.

- The degree of internationalisation will determine the interrelationships among the structural and the management practices of the firm within the constraints of industry competition, technology and markets and the socio-cultural environment.

With growth and/or internationalisation firms face common managerial problems, independent of their nationality. Therefore, we could expect that the managerial sophistication that takes place in response to such common problems would lead to similarities between Ghanaian firms and other foreign firms.

Methodology

The study was based on a comparative study of Ghanaian export firms. This demanded research methods that would produce reliable and valid information and that could be collected quickly and at a relatively low cost.

According to Kast and Rosenzweig (1985), the comparative method deals with the evaluation of variations in organisational design, management practices, employee attitude in different organisations. They contend that it is "a shift from concentrating on unique organisations toward seeking generalizations about patterns of relationships in a variety of facilities".

In our study, therefore, export firms were compared with respect to their structural characteristics. That is, they were being compared on structural factors that we believe will lead to different degrees of internationalisation. It was expected that export firms with similar degrees of internationalisation would also exhibit similar structural characteristics. The significance to this study is that it would not only help to test hypothesis about the relationship between variables, but would also provide a basis for indicating conditions to determine the differences or similarities in the firms

The Sample

Thirty-six of the 58 firms to which questionnaires were sent responded. These firms covered five different industries/sectors. As shown in Table 2, they were seafood 12 (33.3%), clothing and textiles 2 (5.60%), handicraft 4 (11.10%), fruits and vegetables 16 (44.4%), cocoa products 1 (2.80%), and aluminium 1 (2.8%).

Table 2 Industry Sectors

Sectors	**Frequency**	%
Sea food	12	33.3
Clothing and textiles	2	5.6
Handicrafts	4	11.1
Fruits and vegetables	16	44.4
Chocolate products	1	2.8
Aluminum works	1	2.8
Total	36	100

The Data

Three sets of data were used for the study. These are:
(1) Variables describing organisational design norms,
(2) Variables describing the degree of internationalisation of the firms, and
(3) A set of contextual variables.

Variables Describing Organisational Design Norms

Several writers have postulated important organisational design and management style dimensions for cross-national studies. Because our strategy is focused on norms of organisational designs and management, we distilled from those attributes that have been linked to the characteristics of these two dimensions (Pugh et al 1963, Mintzberg 1979, Whitley 1995). In addition, we included information on the contextual variables of the organisation. In general, our selection of variables is based on the conceptual scheme for the empirical study of work organisations from the Aston Programme of Research. The following organisational variables will be measured:

- Formal structure (formalisation, specialisation).
- Differentiation of activities; vertical and horizontal differentiation.

The other set of scales focused on management processes, including:

- Management planning and control systems
- Communication and decision making process

The Degree of Internationalisation of a Firm

The measure of the degree of internationalisation of a firm has attracted a lot of attention in the literature. Over the years, attempts have been made to infer degree of internationalisation by looking at the evolution, structure, and process of relationships among a firm's demographic, strategic, market, organisational, product and attitudinal characteristics of international expansion. Further, measures have included internationalisation of the percentage of sales volume, production, profits, and assets. A recent attempt at measurement is provided by Albaum et al (1998) who have developed a composite measure based on the following factors:

- Foreign sales as a percentage of total sales.
- Foreign assets as a percentage of total assets.
- Overseas subsidiaries as a percentage of total subsidiaries.
- Psychic dispersion of international operations.
- Top managers' international experience

Our main measure of internationalisation was based on foreign sales as a percentage of total sales. The measure was supplemented by the following checklist developed by Piercy (1982). This checklist requires a company to make the following assessments:

- How international it is now.
- How international it can be.
- How international it wants to be.

Contextual Variables

The contextual variables include:
Origin and history: Private versus public funding and history of changes in ownership and location.
Ownership and control: Public versus private ownership and the number and type of owners.
Size: Number of employees, net assets, and market position.
Interdependence: The extent of dependence on customers, suppliers, and national associations

Sources of Information

The primary source of information was interviews with key personnel, that is, management. Another form of data gathering consisted of case studies about strategic decisions made by the firms. These were obtained from interviews and company documents. They serve the purpose of providing a more general perspective about the firm.

Method of Analysis

A number of statistical techniques were employed. Firstly, descriptive statistics such as histograms and frequencies were used to describe the various dimensions of structure. Bivariate and correlation analyses were also used to analyze relationships between the variables. Below the findings of the study are given in three parts. They are:

- Firm demographics and the internationalisation process of Ghanaian export firms.
- Organisational structure of the export firms
- Organisational structure and the management process of the export firms

Firm demographics and the internationalisation process of Ghanaian export firms

In this section we describe the key characteristics of the sample. These include: industry sectors, export percentage, ownership, amount of export and size and type of firm.

Degree of Export

Responses from 23 of the firms showed that the percentage of export to total sales range from 25% to 100%. The firms were equally divided in their export orientation. Eleven firms (30.6%) exported up to 50% of their products and 12 firms exported over 50% of their products. These are shown in Table 3.

Table 3: Export Share Percentages

Categories	Frequency	%
Below 25%	5	13.9
25% to 49%	6	16.7
50% to 74%	3	8.3
75% to 100%	9	25.0
Total	23	63.9
Missing cases	13	36.1
Total	36	100

Ownership of the Firms

The majority of the firms (21 of them) were wholly Ghanaian and privately owned. There were 9 foreign firms and six joint ventures. See Table 4.

Table 4 Ownership of the Firms

Ownership	Frequency	%
100% foreign owned	9	25.0
100% locally/privately owned	21	58.3
Joint venture	6	16.7
Total	36	100

Export Performance

The export performance of the firms is given in Table 5 below. Performance is expressed in terms of the total sales made by the firms by the year 2001. This measure was adopted because it helps indicate the intensity of export activity.

Table 5 shows that more than half (52.8%) of the 36 firms studied made sales under 100 million Cedis. About 22% fell between 100million and half a billion. Only 4 firms (11.1%) could make it between 500million and 1billion. (See also figure 1)

Table 5: Export Performance

Exports	**Frequency**	**%**
Under 50million	15	41.7
51-100	4	11.1
101-200	2	5.6
201-500	6	16.7
501-1bn	4	11.1
Total	**31**	**86.1**

Figure 1: Export Performance

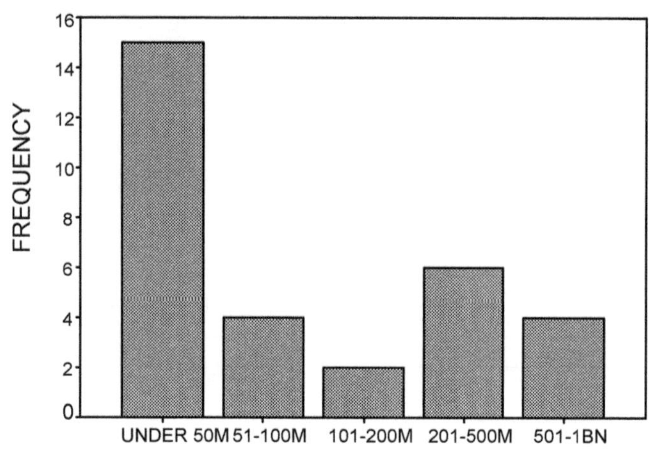

Size and Type of Firm

Table 6 shows the size and types of firms studied. The firms were classified as micro enterprises (1-9 employees), small (10-29 employees), medium-scale (30-140 employees) and large-scale firms (141 employees and above). As Table 4 shows, 27.8% of the firms studied were micro enterprises, while 30.6% were large-scale firms.

An important question to ask is how were the sizes of the different firms distributed among the different industry groups under study. This is shown in figure 2. The figure indicates that the majority (73.4%) of the fruits and vegetable firms were small and medium scale enterprises (SMEs). This is in contrast to the seafood firms, which were mainly large-scale enterprises (72.7%). The rest of the firms - cocoa products and aluminium, were mainly larger scale firms with employees well above five hundred workers.

Table 6: Size and Type of Firm

Sizes	Frequency	%
Micro scale enterprises (1-9)	6	16.7
Small scale enterprise (10-29)	10	27.8
Medium scale enterprise (30-140)	4	11.1
Large enterprise (141 above)	11	30.6
Total	31	86.1
Missing items	5	13.9
Total	36	100

The internationalisation process

Two major questions were of importance here. These were about where Ghanaian firms export their products to and how they did it.

Table 7: Destination of Exports

Destination	No.	%
Japan	0	-
European Union	24	61.8
North America	0	-
African countries	7	19.4
Other countries	5	13.8

Table 7 shows that the majority of firms export to European Union countries, some other African countries and other countries. There was practically no export to the Asian countries. Other countries indicate minor exports to countries along the West African coast.

Foreign Entry Strategies of the Firms

A firm enters an overseas market because it believes that it will be profitable. This assumes not only that the overseas market is attractive, but also that the firm can establish a competitive advantage vis-à-vis local producers and other multinational corporations.

In exploiting an overseas market opportunity, a firm has a range of options with regard to mode of entry. For instance, export via agent, export via sales subsidiary and production in a subsidiary. The modes of entry of the 36 firms are shown in Table 8 below.

Table 8: Foreign Entry Strategies of the Firms

Entry Strategies	Frequency	%
Export directly to clients overseas	13	36
Sell to overseas agent in Ghana	7	19%
Sell to equity partner overseas	0	0%
Other methods	7	13%

Table 8 shows that most Ghanaian firms export through agents, either in Ghana or overseas. None of them has been able to establish its own overseas base. Even the large scale firms we identified above suggested that this approach was easier and less risky since they did not have the capability yet to establish their own outlets.

Relationship with Customers

Two important issues were of concern here. These were about the type of links with the customers and the extent of dependency on them. As shown in Table 9, the majority of the firms (47%) have some kind of contractual relationship with their agents while about 36% had no contractual agreement with their agents. Furthermore, about 58% of the firms indicated that their customers represented their major outlets to foreign markets.

Table 9: Links with Customers

Nature of Contracts	Frequency	%
Regular long term contracts (1 year or more)	8	22.2
Regular short term contract (less than 1 year)	9	25.0
No contractual agreement	13	36.1
Total	30	83.3

Dependency on Customer

The analysis suggests that most of the firms had no overseas outlets and about 58% of the firms were also tied to particular agents. This suggests a strong dependency relationship with their customers. The examination of the mode of externalization suggests that most Ghanaian export firms have little options to develop any strategies for competitive advantage.

Table 10: Dependency on Customers

Outlets	Frequency	%
Sole outlet	4	11.1
Major outlet	17	47.2
Medium outlet	6	16.7
Minor outlet	2	5.6
Total	29	80.6

Organisational Structure of the Export Firms

Organizing is the way in which activities in organisations are divided up, organised and coordinated. Hence, it involves the grouping of activities, the assignment of each grouping to a manager with authority necessary to supervise them and the provision for co-ordination horizontally and vertically in the enterprise structure.

A key argument of this study was that for a Ghanaian export firm to adequately respond to these pressures they will have to develop organisational structures and associated management processes. By choosing an appropriate organisational structure and management processes, an organisation can develop the relevant strength to face environmental challenges. In order to establish structural changes in the Ghanaian exporting firms, we first examined their structural configuration. This was done by the degree to which their activities have been differentiated. That is, the ways in which various activities or tasks were assigned to different departments and or people in the organisation.

In organisations differentiation occurs in two directions:

- Vertical specialisation of activities. This is represented by the organisational hierarchy or the authority system.
- The horizontal differentiation of activities called departmentalisation.

Hierarchical Levels and Authority System

The authority system shows the extent to which firms integrate, coordinate and control resources. Firms in this view function as economic actors by authoritatively directing and organizing economic activities. It is through the power, status, and hierarchical relationships within the organisation that firms add value to human and material resources and function as relatively separate units of economic decisions (Penrose 1959, Whitely 1995). The levels of authority are shown in Table 11.

Table 11: Levels of Authority

Level of Authority	No.	%
Board of Directors	20	55.6
Top Managers	33	91.7
Middle Level Managers	20	55.6
First Line Managers	24	66.7

Table 11 shows that 45% of the firms do not have middle level managers and board of directors. However, almost all of them had put into place top management positions. This means that some of the firms have maintained a well structured hierarchical organisations whereby authority flows from the board of directors, managing director to a deputy and then to departmental managers who directly supervise non-management staff.

Industry Sector and Hierarchical Levels

Analysis of how the industry sector may influence hierarchical levels shows that industries such as hardware, seafood, cocoa products and aluminium are the more organised firms (Table 12). This implies that the coordination of activities in the firm is centralized through managers who issue instructions and monitor work activities.

It is, however, clear from the table that these firms have grown beyond the stage of the traditional family managed farming enterprises, which are a predominant feature of the agricultural and industrial sectors in Ghana (Andrea 1981). In contrast fruits and vegetable firms and clothing do not appear to be well structured. For instance, the most important managerial role in the fruits and vegetables firms is that of the top manager. Other managerial levels appear not to have been given any significant attention

Table 12: Hierarchy by Industry Sector

	Sea food	Clothing and Textiles	Hard-ware	Fruits and Vegetables	Cocoa Products	Aluminium
BOD	10	0	4	4	1	1
TM	12	2	4	13	1	1
MLM	11	0	1	6	1	1
FLM	11	2	3	6	1	1

*BOD = Board of Directors
*TM = Top Managers
*MLM = Middle Level Managers
*FLM = Firs Line Managers

Export Orientation and Authority Levels Hierarchy

In Table 13 we also look at how the export orientation of the firms affects the type of structures put into place.

Table 13: Export Orientation and Authority Levels

	Below 25%	25-49%	50-74%	75-100%
Board of Directors	4	2	0	9
Top Managers	5	6	3	9
Middle Level Managers	4	3	1	9
First Line Managers	4	3	3	7

The table shows that all the firms have put in place a centralized decision making systems and well established role positions. Contrary to expectations the firms exporting less than a quarter of their products appeared to be better organised than even those with more than half of their (50-74%) products in export. This suggests that there might be other types of variables that can determine the hierarchical levels other than the degree of export. This issue may be explained by the differences in hierarchical structures observed among the different industries. As indicated earlier, industry firms within the hardware, seafood, cocoa products and aluminium industries are more hierarchically structured than firms within the fruits, vegetables and clothing industries.

The Horizontal Differentiation of Activities

Whereas vertical differentiation concerns the division of authority, horizontal differentiation (departmentalisation) focuses on the division and grouping of tasks. Horizontal differentiation is a necessity because of the need to perform particular functions effectively and efficiently. Hence, organisations or companies choose a form of horizontal differentiation to match their organisations' strategy.

Primary bases of department are the simple structure departmentalisation by function, product, location and customer service. These are also described as divisional organisations. The simple organisational structure has only two levels - the owner manager and the employees. Firms that produce only one product or service, or only a few related ones usually exhibit such a structure, e.g. retail shops in Ghana. A major advantage of this structure is that it allows rapid, flexible implementation of strategies and strategic changes. This advantage is a primary source of competitive advantage that can sometimes allow small firms to compete effectively with industry giants.

Departmentalisation by function is the most prevalent method of grouping activities in modern organisations. In this method people are grouped in terms of the major functions that must be performed if the enterprise is to accomplish its mission. The major functions that act as basis for dividing activities are for example marketing, production and finance.

The divisional or decentralized structure is the second most common type used by businesses. As a small organisation grows, it becomes increasingly difficult for top managers to manage different products and services in different markets. Some form of divisional structure generally becomes necessary to motivate employees effectively, control operations, and compete successfully in diverse locations.

To examine the extent of horizontal differentiation we first looked at types of departments or divisions created by the firms and their frequencies. Information was obtained by asking respondents to indicate the different types of departments and or divisions in the firm. The results are shown in Table 14.

Table 14: Horizontal Differentiation in the Firms

	Frequency
Quality control department	5
Finance department	23
Human resource	11
Research and development	2
Internal control department	4
Quality assurance dept	2
Operations department	7
Engineering department	5
Security department	4
Production department	8
Marketing department	22
Out grower department	2
Farm administration	9
Shipping department	1
Maintenance department	3
Others	19
Public relations	18
Others	21

Altogether seventeen types of departments were observed. These are shown in Table 14. The table shows that all differentiation of activities in the firms was done on the basis of the functions undertaken by the firms. Furthermore, none of the firms showed any indication of any divisions. The most important functions are the finance and the marketing departments. Another function adopted by the majority of the firms was also public relations.

The majority of the functions do not appear to have been given any attention by the firms. Most of them seem to have been adopted by individual firms. For instance, research and development, quality assurance department, out-grower department and the shipping department are units adopted by only one or two firms. To clearly understand why some units are adopted and others not, it is essential to consider our key independent factors: industries, size of firms, and export orientation.

The distribution of departments among the small scale and the medium scale enterprises shows quite similar trends. Finance, marketing, and farm administrative unit are the key departments among these firms. The key differences between the various sizes are, however, the number of departments adopted by the firms. For instance, the micro enterprises have only eight departments of the 17 units; the small-scale enterprises have (82%), the medium scale 41% and the large scale have 94%. This suggests somehow that growth in the firm enables it to differentiate activities.

Horizontal Differentiation According to Industry Sectors

In the previous section we considered the extent to which activities have been grouped together and the basis of specialisation in the export firms. A key question here is whether the type of departmentalisation is specific to a particular industry sector? Table 15 below provides information on the percentage of firms adopting a particular type of structure.

Table 15: Horizontal Differentiation According to Industries

	Sea-food	Clothing	Hard-ware	Fruits and Vegetables	Cocoa Products	Aluminium
Quality Control Department	2	1	1	1	1	1
Finance Department	8	1	2	10	1	1
Human Resource Department	6	1	1	2	1	1
R&D Department	1	0	1		1	
Internal Control Department	3	0				1
Quality Assurance Department	1	0			1	
Operations Department	2	1	1	2		1
Security Department	3	1		0		
Production Department	4	1	1	0	1	1
Marketing department	7	1	3	9	1	1
Out-grower Department	0	0		1		
Farm Administration	0	0		9		
Shipping Department	1	0				
Maintenance Department	0	0	1	1		3
Administrative Personnel	8	2	2	14	1	
Public Relations Department	7	2	2	6	1	1

Export Orientation and Structural Development

A key question of the study was whether export orientation leads to different organisational structures. In Table 16 we have the degree of export and extent of differentiation.

Table 16: Export Orientations and Structural Development

	Below 25%	25-49%	50-74%	75-100%
Quality Control Department	0	0	1	3
Finance Department	3	6	2	5
Human Resource Department	1	1	2	4
R & D Department		1	0	1
Internal Control Department		1	0	3
Quality Assurance Department		1	0	1
Operations Department	1	1	1	2
Engineering Department	0	1	0	4
Security Department	0	0	1	3
Production Department	0	2	1	4
Marketing Department	2	3	1	9
Out grower Department	0	0	1	0
Farm Administration Department	1	3	0	0
Shipping Department	1	0	0	0
Maintenance Department	0	1	0	0
Administrative Personnel	3	6	2	8
Public Relations Department	2	1	2	9

As with the other tables, we see common departments among the different levels of export orientation. These are again finance, marketing administration, and production. This seems to suggest that firms whatever their size will need to establish basic structures to enable them to operate. As they develop, extra structures are put into place to take care of the new functions.

Extra departments emerging are R & D, internal control department, and quality assurance department.

Structural Dimensions of the Export Firms

So far in this study we have examined the various structural dimensions of the Ghanaian exporting firm. A fundamental principle underlying this research is that organisations are not a random collection of characteristics; they form coherent configurations. Given the paradigm of interrelationships, the following questions were posed in this study:

1. Are the organisational designs of Ghanaian exporting firms subject to internationalisation or trends in the globalisation of industries?
2. Are there any distinctive types of enterprise structure and management practices unique to Ghanaian exporting firms?
3. Is there any proven relationship between the emerging configurations and the export performance of the firms?

This section therefore examines the organisational and management patterns of Ghanaian export firms, and determines the differences in their structure, behaviour patterns and strategic decision-making. The findings are shown in Table 17.

Table 17: Structural Relationships

Export shares		Firm size	Hierarchical levels	Vertical Span	No. of Dept.	Formalisation	Specialisation	Export performance
Below 25%	Mean	2.8000	6.8000	3.4000	1.8000	18.6000	4.8000	120.6000
	Std. Dev.	1.0954	2.6833	1.3416	1.788	9.6073	5.7184	118.1262
25% - 49%	Mean	2.0000	4.6667	2.3333	3.333	6.0000	5.8333	123.8000
	Std. Dev.		3.0111	1.5055	2.160	6.9570	4.8339	184.5595
50% - 74%	Mean	1.0000	4.6667	2.3333	3.333	7.6667	5.6667	105.0000
	Std. Dev.	1.7321	1.1547	.5774	4.163	2.3094	2.3094	.
75% - 100%	Mean	3.5556	7.5556	3.7778	4.222	23.0000	12.0000	492.0000
	Std. Dev.	0.8819	0.8819	0.4410	3.192	8.5586	4.3012	314.5227
Total	Mean	2.2500	5.3889	2.6944	2.944	13.0000	7.2222	203.9677
	Std. Dev.	1.4614	2.6107	1.3054	2.4836	9.8387	4.6360	263.8937

The table provides information on the size and type of firm, vertical span, number of hierarchical levels in the organisations, number of departments, functional specialisation, level of formalisation of activities and sales performance.

Firms Below 25% Exports

These firms are either micro- or small-scale enterprises. These were in the handicrafts and the vegetable industries. In these firms we observed that managerial hierarchy was small. Average hierarchical levels are about three while differentiation of activities is about only two departments. This suggests little specialisation of activities in those firms. Average export performance is about 120 million Cedis. As was observed in planning and control the entrepreneur retains right of control. Every activity revolves around the entrepreneur, the firm's goals are his goal, its strategy his vision. Co-ordination is effected largely by direct supervision and power over all important decisions tends to be centralized in the hands of the chief executive. These observations tie in well with Mintzberg's owner-manager or the entrepreneurial firm, which he described as a one-man strategic apex and an organic operating core. Our observations on the organisation of these firms indicate structures, which are quite similar and distinctive to traditional small-scale enterprise in Ghana. Most of these firms are family owned and owner-managed (Brown 1978). Labour was first and foremost derived from kith and kin. Hence, intermediary management levels and functional departments were not very often used.

26-50% Export

The firms in this sector appear even smaller than those with exports below 25%. From the table they are basically small-scale finance enterprises. Although these firms have fewer levels of hierarchy they however appeared to have a broader level of differentiation. This suggests a greater degree of decentralization. In contrast to the firms with 25% export, they have, however, fewer written down rules. The export performance is about 123 million Cedis.

51-75% Export firms

The three firms in this range are basically micro enterprises with about nine employed workers. Just like the previous group, the firms have the same number of hierarchical levels and differentiation of activities. However, the average level of performance is 105 million Cedis.

76-100%

The firms exporting more than 75% of their products have quite distinctive characteristics. These firms are either medium scale enterprises or large-scale enterprises. Further, they have close to four hierarchical levels as well as higher differentiation of activities. In addition, they have the highest level of export sales, 492 million Cedis. This suggests that these firms are built around routine operating work systems, i.e. they have gone a long way in the regulation of the work of its employers. That is, the intended behaviour of employees has been structured by the specification of their specialized roles, procedures they are to follow in carrying out their roles and the documentation of what they want to do.

Most of the work is simple and repetitive and the work processes are standardized. Such firms have these characteristics:

- Formalised procedures at the operating level.
- Centralization of decision-making.
- An elaborate administrative structure.
- Reliance on functional basis for grouping tasks.
- Relatively centralized power for decision-making.
- Elaborate administrative structure with a sharp distinction between line and staff.

- These characteristics were observed in the large food processing enterprises.

A distinctive feature of the table is that up to a certain level of sales activity or size of the firms structuring of activities does not differ very much. We see quite the same relationship with the level of export sales. Hence, there seems to be little difference between the firms in the first three groups. Although their percentage or degree of export activities may differ, their export sales are almost quite the same. It is only when volume of activities increases (i.e. export sales), that we see more formalised structures being adopted.

Inter-Correlations of the Structural Variables

The discussions above have made it possible to develop profiles of the different export organisations in terms of their degree of export. In this section we explore the relationships between the different structural dimensions and search for underlying similarities. This is given in the Table 18.

Table 18: Inter-Correlations of the Structural Variables

Size and Type of Firm	Size and type of firm	Export share	Vertical span	Hierarchy	Differentiation	Form	Specialization	Export performance
Export Share	.425							
Vertical span	.685	.469						
Hierarchy	.685	.469	1.000					
No. of departments	.279	.341	.294	.294				
Form	.505	.456	.754	.754	.193			
Specialisation	.561	.488	.554	.554	.368	.681		
Export performance	.756	.669	.568	.568	.328	.689	.856	

** Correlation is significant at the 0.01 level (2-tailed).
* Correlation is significant at the 0.05 level (2-tailed).

It is evident from the table that many of the variables are highly correlated. For example, the vertical span has the highest correlation of 1.0 with hierarchical levels. Export performance has a correlation of 0.75 with firm size, of 0.66 with export share, of 0.57 with hierarchical levels and 0.70 with formalisation. Formalisation has also a high correlation with the vertical span (0.750) and hierarchy (0.75). On the other hand, lower correlations were found between differentiation and firm size (0.27), export share (0.34), vertical span (0.29) and hierarchy (0.29). In general, the analysis confirms the broad hypothesis posed at the outset of this study. That is, the organisations are not a random collection of characteristics, but form coherent configurations.

Organisational size, one of the major internationalisation variables, was found to have relationships with principal organisational structure variables. It was found to have a stronger relationship with functional specialisation and formalisation. It had also strong relationship with export share and sales performance.

However, there was some diversity in the pattern of relationships. A distinctive feature of the table is that up to certain level of sales activity or size of the firms, structuring of activities does not differ very much. We see quite the same relationship with the level of export sales.

The question posed earlier in this analysis was whether the norms of organisational design of Ghanaian exporting firms are subject to stages theory internationalisation. This appears to be the case for large-scale firms where most of the work is simple and repetitive and the work processes are standardized and have formalised procedures at the operating level. A hypothesis on this relationship is that as division of labour increases in number, they introduce procedures to regulate the activities for which they are responsible, resulting in documentation and a larger supportive hierarchy. This seems to prove the hypothesis drawn from Weberian tradition that specialisation, formalisation, and centralization will be highly positively correlated. However, those

firms have only been able to establish export units within their marketing departments.
Is there any proven relationship between the emerging configurations and the export performance of the firms? Although this was clearly shown by our tables, by comparing the structural characteristics of the smaller and larger export firms, one could see that export performance of the larger firms was better than the small scale ones.

Organisational Structure and the Management Process

A key argument of this study was that organisational structures provide static set of roles and responsibilities and are therefore a powerful but blunt instrument of strategic change. The management process can help extend a firm's ability to adapt to these pressures. The company's entire management - the administrative system, communication channels and interpersonal relations become the tools for managing such a change (Lorange/Chakravarthy 1991).

Contingency theories assume that internationalisation is a well-planned process. Before a company decides to enter a market, it makes a thorough analysis of –in principle – all potential markets, and on the basis of the analysis it enters an optimal market given the objectives of the company (Kuada and Sørensen 2000). Management's planning activities are more concerned with managers' actions and experience. Theories related to the selection of markets or market entry modes are therefore considered planning tools. Here, the starting point is the totality of markets or market entry modes, the totality being gradually reduced using a stepwise selection procedure.

In contrast, action-oriented theories have the intuitive idea of the businessperson as the starting point. The idea is followed up by immediate actions, which in turn provide the actors with experience. This experience is then turned into knowledge through a process of reflections.

With an increase of internationalisation, a firm has to do business in many different economic, political, and cultural environments, and must meet intensive challenges from other global competitors. Therefore, internationalisation also works as a force for improving a firm's production, marketing, environment intelligence, research and development, and long-term planning activities.

Both growth and internationalisation act as strong forces for improving many managerial operations. Fast growing markets lead to both new entry and expansion of capacity. This can lead to saturation, challenging firms to increasing efficiency and seeking opportunities for growth. Therefore, when the firm finds it is approaching a certain limit of growth in the current market, it allocates a considerable portion of its staff and resources toward improving the primary production and marketing activities, and toward strengthening its environment scanning. In addition, such a firm attempts to build new technological capabilities with long-term research and development plans. A formal strategic planning system is often established to provide guidance for overall corporate management.

Lastly, with growth and/or internationalisation, firms face common managerial problems, independent of their nationality. Examples include intensifying competition with the firm's increasing presence in the industry, difficulty of directing and monitoring the activities of subordinates and difficulty of coordinating the independence between sub-units. Therefore, we could expect that the managerial sophistication that takes place in response to such common problems would lead the management style to have many similarities across nations. Firms would also expect attempts to solve managerial problems by actively imitating practices of other successful organisations that have a similar need for efficient management. These inter-firm imitation and learning activities would eventually make those companies with large size and a high degree of internationalisation have a large commonality in their management systems. A good example of such a trend of convergence is the transfer of advanced managerial methods like multidivisional structure (M-form) from the U.S to European and Japanese multinationals after World War II (Chandler 1962). In summary, centralized planning (integrative) is necessary for those firms facing rapid technological changes and intensive market competition in serving their global customers. Decentralized or adaptive planning is more appropriate for firms producing goods and services for local customers with fewer customers and operating in stable technological fields. As the complexity and instability and competition increases, the greater the need for long range planning by firms. Firms adopt more complete long range planning as complexity and instability of business environments increase. This is actually moderated by size of firm. Large firms facing a high degree of environmental complexity and instability undertook long range planning; smaller firms did not under these conditions (Neghandi 1987).

In the developing countries the existence of seller's market, governmental control of prices, and unavailability of raw materials, inflation, and political instability adversely affect the firm's ability to plan for the long term. For instance, where firms were making high profits regardless of management practices because of inflation, planning was irrelevant. Kigundu (1989) shows therefore that environmental factors causing uncertainty seem to discourage long range planning. In order words when the future is uncertain and unpredictable, the usual tendency is to operate on day-to-day short term tendencies (Neghandi 1987).

The above discussions suggest that planning is a key management process that can help integrate activities in a firm and provide an adequate response to environmental situations. To find out about planning activities, we looked at four major issues: the objectives of the planning, major contents of the plans, organisation of the planning activities, and major forms of control. Since we discovered in the earlier section that a key influence in the structure of the export firms was the size of the firm, we also considered how the planning activities differed in the four types of organisation we identified.

The Planning Activities in the Firms

Table 19 below shows that just 44% of the firms have formal written plans. Many of them utilize plans covering more than one time horizon. The most common planning horizon was three years. During the interviews, some of the participants pointed out that quantified plans are often supplemented by informal plans. Two major objectives of the planning are planning to achieve profit targets and production targets.

Table 19: The Planning Activities in the firms

Planning Activities and Contents	Frequency	%
Formalised corporate plan	16	44.4
Company aims to achieve profit target	28	77.8
Company aims to achieve production target	24	66.7
Company aims to determine future profit	3	8.3
Company aims to determine future production patterns	10	27.8
Plan include annual expense budget and for how long?	26	72.2
Plan include business projections and for how long?	27	74.0
Plan include manpower planning and for how long?	21	58.3
Plan includes assessment of the effect of the external environment	19	52.8
Maximize production sale as an important issue in the plan	19	52.8
Important issue in the strategic plan is to have a market share	17	47.2
Important issue in the strategic plan is to make more profit share	15	41.7
Increase labour skills	11	30.6
Important issue in the strategic plan is to have a market leadership	10	27.8
Is the chief executive involved?	22	61
Do you have a separate organisation unit?	7	19.4
Is a planning committee involved?	8	22
Is the planning manager involved?	2	5.6
Plan encompasses monitoring and control systems	17	47.2
Plan encompasses budgeting system	21	58.3

The questionnaire also asked respondents to indicate the specific topics covered by their strategic plans. The table indicates that more than 70% of the firms included business projections and budgets in their plans. About half of them included manpower planning, assessment of the environment, and production planning. More than 50% were also concerned with market trends and production activities. Our study also indicated that 20% undertook comprehensive planning. The planning activities included all major functions such as finance, sales, and work force. Few of the plans we managed to study were also detailed and systematic.

The table also suggests that the chief executive is very much involved in the planning. Very few of the firms (19.4%) have set up units for planning or have special planning committees to do the planning. This suggests a greater degree of centralization in decision-making and the lack of delegation in the firms.

About 47% of the firms had mechanisms for reviewing their plans. Most of them were reviewed quarterly. Firms used combination of various forms of control such as:

- Budgeting,which involved mostly quarterly and yearly comparisons of budgetary targets and expenditure.
- Periodic statistical reports involving reports relevant to departments. This was mostly used by the fruits and vegetables firms to check stocks
- Performance appraisal involves formal method of evaluating and recording the performance of managers and employees. None of the firms reported of the use of such method.
- Policies and procedures. Most firms reported of the existence of formal policies and procedures. But their use as a basis for control was rather negligent.

Planning and Export Orientation

The table does not really show clear differences with content of plans. It, however, shows that planning activities occurred in almost all the exporting firms. However, intensive planning activities can be observed in firms exporting more than 75% of their products.

Our study also indicated that most comprehensive planning took place in the large firms. The planning activities included all major functions such as finance, sales, and work force. The planning activities included all major functions such as finance, sales, and work force. Planning activities in the small and medium scale enterprises did differ in the concentration on different activities. We find that an area that majority of the small firms paid greater attention to, was improvement in labour skills. On the other hand, interests in the medium scale firms were in budgeting, manpower planning production and sales. Issues like monitoring and control also gained substantial attention.

On the whole, our analysis of content affirms the integrative role planning adopted as the firms grows, especially if one considers the considerable interest shown by the large firms in monitoring and controlling. In general, we find that planning activities increased from the small-scale enterprises to the large-scale enterprises. Key conclusions were that:

- Planning structures of the large companies had been institutionalised.
- The majority of the large firms have formalised plans.
- Planning tends to be centralized and involve chief executives.
- Most of the large firms have established staff units composed of specialists to help top line management with planning processes.

Most small-scale firms appear not to have formalised plans yet they had made budgets to support their activities.

Table 20: Planning and Export Orientation

	Below 25%	25-49%	50-74%	75-100%
Formalised corporate plan	4	2	2	7
Company aims to achieve profit target	4	0	0	7
Company aims to achieve production target	1	1	1	7
Company aims to determine future profit	1	0	0	0
Company aims to determine future production patterns	0	2	2	2
Plan includes annual expense budget	3	0	0	3
Plan includes business projections	0	2	0	3
Plan includes manpower planning	0	1	0	0
Plan aims at maximizing production	4	2	1	4
Plan aims at increasing market share	4	1	1	5
Plan aims at increasing profit	2	0	1	7
Increase labour skills	0	1	2	0
Plan aims at achieving market leadership	4	1	2	4
Plan include annual expense budget	3	5	0	3
Plan include business projections	5	4	3	5
Plan include manpower planning and for how long?	5	3	2	5
Plan includes assessment of the effect of the external environment	5	3	3	7
CEO is involved in the planning	3	3	2	7
Firm has a Planning Department	0	0	0	5
Firm has a Planning Committee	4	0	2	0
Are any others involved in planning?	1	0	2	2

Discussions and conclusions

A key objective of the study was to examine the relationship between the extent of the internationalisation of Ghanaian exporting firms and their mode of organisation. This follows the classic theories of internationalisation suggesting that changes in the firm's international activities will have corresponding changes in its organisational structure.

The key findings of the study are the following:

- Most Ghanaian export firms exported their products through external agents. None of them has been able to establish its own overseas base. In addition they depended on sole agents. As such they have a strong dependency relationship with their customers and have little option to develop any strategies for competitive advantage.
- Firms exporting more than 75% of their product are highly structured. They have centralized decision-making systems and well established role positions. The majority of them are large-scale enterprises.
- The small and medium scale enterprises were not so structured. They lacked middle level managers and only a few of them had board of directors. This suggests that these firms are mostly organised as family enterprises where the owner is the manager.
- There were common departments among the different levels of export orientation. These are finance, marketing administration, and production. This seems to suggest that firms whatever their size establish basic structures to enable them to operate. As they develop extra structures are put into place to take care of the new functions.

Summing up the findings on the relationship between the structural features, management processes and internationalisation, the following conclusions can be reached. Increased internationalisation in activities of the firms do not show a clear transition in their organisational structures as indicated in literature, that is from an international division to a worldwide product/geographic structure (e.g. global matrix organisation). Rather we observed that the marketing departments handled most of export activities.

Organisation's structures are not designed to meet the strategic pressures the firms face in the first place. Most of them have developed functional structures. Furthermore, organisational size, one of the major internationalisation variables, was found to have relationships with principal organisational structure variables. It was found to have a stronger relationship with functional specialisation and formalisation. It had also strong relationship with export share and sales performance. This could be found in the large-scale firms where most of the work was simple and repetitive and the work processes are standardized and have formalised procedures at the operating level. This seems to prove the hypothesis drawn from Weberian tradition that specialisation, formalisation, and centralization will be highly positively correlated. That export performance is also highly correlated to these variables would suggest the adoption of an efficient form of organisational structure.

However, there was some diversity in the pattern of relationships. A distinctive feature of relationship was that up to certain level of sales performance the structuring of activities does not differ very much. We saw quite the same relationship with the level of export sales. Hence, there seems to be little difference between the firms in the first three groups. Although their percentage or degree of export activities may differ, their export sales are almost quite the same. It is only when volume of activities increases (i.e. export sales), that we see more formalised structures being adopted.

Management theory suggests that both growth and internationalisation work as strong forces for improving many managerial operations. This can lead to saturation, challenging firms to increase efficiency and seek opportunities for growth. We observed that an increase in the percentage of exports has made, in particular, the large firms improve their production, marketing, environment intelligence, research and development, and long-term planning activities. A formal strategic planning system is often established to provide guidance for overall corporate management.

In our study we found that most of the firms were involved in a single activity (for example cocoa or food processing) and were organised along functional lines. Hence, they can be described as Williamson's U-form enterprise. It was only the cocoa processing company that has diversified into new products. This could lead to two kinds of disadvantages for the firms. First, in a large U-form firm there are several layers of management. Co-ordination of two functional departments (say marketing and production) occurs mainly at the top level. Thus, information has to be transmitted across several layers before it is used for decision-making. As information is transmitted, there is usually a loss of information. Data are summarised and interpreted as they move upward and instructions are operationalised as they move downward. This leads to cumulative control loss: the corporate board loses control of day-to-day operations as the number of management layers increase. This cumulative control loss is a result of bounded rationality. Only because of bounded rationality do data have to be summarized and interpreted before they reach the top manager, and only because of bounded rationality is the top manager unable himself to give detailed, operationalised instructions.

Secondly, as the U-form firm grows, the characters of the strategic decision- making process alter. The top manager is involved in day-to-day operational coordination to such an extent that long-term, strategic decisions receive little attention. This is another manifestation of bounded rationality.

In a large U-form firm the top manager of a functional department may be more interested in furthering the local interests of his department than in the overall goals for the enterprises. A conflict of interest between functional departments cannot be avoided. In a small U- form firm, this conflict of interest is mitigated because the general manager is still in a position to judge how many functional managers care for and contribute to overall goals. In a large U-form firm, the top manager may find himself/herself to be the only person to attend to overall company-wide goals. The tendency to pursue operational sub-goals simply becomes too strong. Departmental interests voiced by functional managers enter the strategic decision-making process.

To summarize, the large, multiproduct U-form firm faces two problems: cumulative control loss and corruption of the strategic decision-making process. The solution to these two problems is to introduce the **multidivisional** or **M-form** enterprise in the large export enterprises.

References

Albaum, G., Strandskov, J. and Duerr, E., (1998): *International Marketing and Export Management,* (London, Addison Wesley Longman Publishing,)

Andrea, G. (1981): *Industry in Ghana,* (Stockholm, Scandinivian Institute of African Studies).

Badran, M. and Hinings, C. R., (1980): "Strategies of administrative control and contextual constraints in a less developed country: The case of Egyptian public enterprise", *Organisational Studies,* vol. 1, No. 4.

Bartlett, C. A. and Ghoshal, S., (1995): *Transnational Management* (London, Irwin)

Bilkey, W. J. and Tesar, G. (1977): "The Export Behaviour of small Sized Wisconsin Manufacturing Firms", *Journal of International Business Studies,* Vol. 9, No. 1, pp33-46

Blau, P. M. (1965): "The Comparative Study of Organisations", *Industrial and Labour Relations Review* 18, No. 3 pp323-38

Brown, A. W. (1978): Craft Industry and Rural Employment in Ghana, (PhD Thesis, Lancaster Polytechnic, England)

Cavusgil, S. T., (1984): "International Marketing Research: Insights into Company Practices," *Research in Marketing,* Vol. 7, No 2, pp. 261-288.

Chandler, A. D., (1962): *Strategy and Structure* (Massachusetts, Massachusetts, Massachusetts Institute of Technology)

Child, J. (1981): "Culture contingency and capitalism in cross cultural study of organisations", in L. Cummings and B. Staw (Eds.) Research in Organisational Behaviour, pp303-356

Coase, R. H. (1937): *The Nature of the Firm.* 4 pp.386-405

Demetz, R. and Alchian, A. A. (1972): "Production, Information Costs and economic Organisation," *American Economic Review.* LXII95):777-95

Hamilton, G. and Biggart, W. (1988): "Market, Culture and Authority, A comparative study of Management and Organisation in the Far East", *American Journal of Sociology, Supplement.*

Hennart, F (2000): Transaction costs theory and multinational Enterprise, chapter 4,

Hickson, D. J., Hinnings, C. R., MacMillan, C. J and Schwitter, J. P. (1974): "The culture Free Context of Organisational Structure", *Sociology* Vol. 8:59-80

Holt, D. H. (1998): *International Management,* Dryden Press, Hartcourt Brace

Hymer, S (1977): *The International Operations of National Firms: A Study of Direct Foreign Investment.* (Massachusetts, The Massachusetts Institute of Technology)

Kast, F. E. and Rosenzweig, J. E. (1985): *Organisation and Management, A Systems and Contingency Approach,* (New York: McGraw Hill)

Kerr, C., John T. Dunlop, F. H. Harbison and C. A. Meyers (1964): *Industrialism and Industrial Man,* (Oxford, Oxford University Press)

Kiggundu, M.N. (1989): *Managing Organisations in Developing Countries: An operational and strategic* Approach, (West Hartford, CT: Kumarian Press)

Kuada, J. and O. J. Sorensen, (2000): *Internationalisation of companies from Developing Countries,* (NY: International Business Press,)

Levitt, T (1995), "The Globalisation of Markets," in C. A. Bartlett and S. Ghoshal, (Eds.) *Transnational Management (London,* Irwin)

Lorange, P. and Chakravarthy, B. S. (1991): *Managing the Strategy Process: A Framework for Multibusiness Firm,* (London, Prentice Hall)

Luostarinen, R. (1994): Internationalisation of Finnish Firms and their responses to Global Challenges (UNU World Institute for Development Economic Research, Research for Action).

Mintzberg, H. (1979): *The Structuring of Organisations,* (New York: Prentice Hall)

Mintzberg, H. (1985): "The Organisation as Political Arena," *Journal of Management Stuies*

Mochandreas, M. (1994): *Business Economics,* (London: International Thompson Business Press)

Neghandi, A. R. (1987): *International Management, (Boston,* Allyn and Bacon).

Penrose, E. T. (1959): *The Theory of Growth of the Firm,* (New York, John Wiley)

Piercy, N. (1982): *Export Strategy: Markets and Competition.* London, George Allen and Unwin

Pugh, D. S., D. Hickson, D. J. Hinnings, C.R. Turner, (1963): "A conceptual scheme for Organisational Analysis," *Administrative Science Quarterly,* Vol. 8, pp289-315

Pugh, D. S., Hickson, D. J., Hinnings, C. R., and Turner, C., (1969), "The Context of Organisational structures", *Administrative Science Quarterly,* vol. 14.

Rollinson, D., Broadfield, A. and Edwards, D. J. (1998), *Organisational Behaviour Analysis, An integrated Approach,* Prentice Hall, Harlow

Rumelt, R. P., Schendel, D. A., and Teece, D. J Eds...(1995): *Fundamental Issues in Strategy,* Harvard Business School Press

Strandskov, Jesper (1993): "Towards a New Approach for studying the Internationalisation Process of Firms", in P. J. Buckley and P. Ghauri (Eds.) The Internationalisation of the Firm: a Reader, (London, Academic Press).

Whitely, R. D. (1995): "Eastern Asian Enterprise Structures and the Comparative Analysis of forms of Business Organisation", in P. N. Ghuari and S. B. Prasad (eds.) *International Management, London* (The Dryden Press)

Williamson, O. E. (1985): *The Economic Institutions of Capitalism,* (New York, Free Press).

5

SKILLS, STRUCTURE AND LEADERSHIP: CRITICAL VARIABLES FOR SME INTERNATIONALISATION

Bill Buenar Puplampu

Introduction

Few Ghanaian Small and Medium-sized Enterprises (SMEs) have traditionally entered and succeeded in the regional and/or international market. Those, which do, appear to operate in the traditional export sector, selling unprocessed or semi-processed goods. In recent times, however, a number of firms in Ghana appear to have made significant gains in selling their products and services in the larger West African market. Notable among these are companies such as Interplast, famous for its 'Atongo' adverts in Ghana, publicizing PVC pipes, various aluminium products firms which make cookware and other aluminium derivatives, and Network Computer Services (NCS), the computer firm and one of the first Internet Service Providers (ISPs) in West Africa.

Globalisation, e-Commerce and difficulty with penetration of Western markets are, however, progressively creating a situation where more local firms have to look beyond the borders of Ghana to the immediate West African region for sustainable markets as well as sources of raw materials. Within the context of socio-economic development, political pluralism and governmental attempts to improve national fortunes through policy initiatives such as the declaration of the 'Golden

Age of Business', 'Private Sector as the Engine of Growth', the 'Cassava Initiative' or taking advantage of the opportunities offered in such groupings as the Heavily Indebted Poor Country (HIPC), African Growth and Opportunities Act (AGOA) and New Partnership for African Development (NEPAD), it can be suggested that these companies - if they are successful - have potential to progress economic growth through employment creation, use of the financial institutions in the country and generation of hard currency income. It is argued by some, that small businesses and medium sized enterprises provide greater real potential to meet the economic aspirations of national development more than a few large companies, which concentrate capital in the hands of a few people. Indeed, according to Chapman (1998), small firms (employing 50 or less), account for 99% of enterprises in the UK. It is therefore necessary to consider how SMEs can better position themselves internally in terms of their skills and competencies, corporate structures and leader foci (style, background, strategy and vision) in order to enter and successfully operate in the regional and international market place.

This study does not include large businesses since most of such firms which operate in Ghana are multinational in character and are owned and operated by Westerners who already tend to have a significant grasp of international entrepreneurship. This study therefore focuses on the internal workings of smaller Ghanaian firms. It seeks to make comparisons between successful and established SMEs operating in the international/regional market and the- not- so successful or 'struggling' Ghanaian SMEs who may want to, but are yet to enter the international market or those which have done so, but are having a difficult time of it. The aim is to find out whether and what particular skills/competencies, structural arrangements and leadership facilitate regional and international involvement.

The skill and competency sets of any organisation represent the core resource that it can use to engage in the productive process. The link between a company's employee profile in terms of skills, competencies and capabilities and its viability have been documented by several writers. In the same way, leadership researchers have shown that leadership impacts corporate strategic focus and internal climate.

This also has a bearing on viability. Critically, however, the structural arrangements in the company provide the frame for efficiency and effectiveness, a point underscored by organisational design. Conceptually, any business concern, which seeks to make an impact in any sector should theoretically, at least, examine its software (skills and leadership) and hardware (organisational structure and other non-human resources). This research is therefore not aiming to identify any new models in terms of these conceptual links. It rather seeks to confirm and document the nature and content of the independent variables in the case of Ghana by benchmarking between successful and unsuccessful firms. A key issue is that operating in the regional or international context may require peculiar resources such as innovation, product quality and packaging appeal, market sensitivity, determination and international business awareness.

This paper is in five sections. Section 1 is the introduction; section 2 is the review of the literature. At the end of section 2 the essential research questions are stated. Section 3 is the methodology and findings while section 4, covers analysis and discussions. Section 5 concludes and proffers some thoughts and recommendations.

Literature Review

This review of the literature examines four main areas. These are as follows: a limited overview of the literature on SMEs. Secondly, it looks at the area of skill requirements in organisational functioning broadly, and SMEs in particular. It then considers the literature on organisational structures and their impact on effectiveness and finally leadership.

What is an SME?

There is no single, uniformly acceptable definition of a small firm (Storey, 1994). Firms differ in their levels of capitalization, sales and employment. Hence, definitions which employ measures of size (number of employees, turnover, profitability, net worth, etc.) when applied to one sector could lead to all firms being classified as small, while the same size definition when applied to a different sector could lead to a different result. The first attempt to overcome this problem was by the Bolton Committee (1971) when they formulated an "economic" and "statistical" definition of the Small Firm. Under the economic definition, a firm is regarded as small if it meets the following three criteria:

- It has a relatively small share of the market.
- It is managed by owners or part owners in a personalized way, and not through the medium of a formalised management structure.
- It is independent, in the sense of not forming part of a larger enterprise.

The Committee also devised a "statistical" definition in terms of:

- The size of the small firm sector and its contribution to GDP, employment, exports etc.
- The extent to which small firm sector's economic contribution has changed over time.
- Applying the statistical definition in a cross-country comparison of the small firms' economic contribution.

The Bolton Committee applied different definitions of the small firm to different sectors. Whereas firms in manufacturing, construction and mining were defined in terms of numbers of employees (in which case 200 or less qualified the firm to be a small firm), those in retail, services, wholesale etc were defined in terms of monetary turnover (in which case the range is 50,000-200,000 British Pounds to be designated small). Firms in the road transport sector are designated small if they have 5 vehicles or less.

Criticisms of the Bolton Approach

There have been criticisms of the Bolton definitions. These centre mainly on the apparent inconsistencies between defining characteristics based on number of employees and those based on managerial approach (personalized versus structured impersonal), etc. Wynarczyk et al (1993) and Storey (1994) also suggest that market size in itself is an inadequate measure given its suggestion of perfect competition – a factor that does not prevail in many economies.

It was against this background that the European Commission (EC) coined the term 'Small and Medium Enterprises (SME)'. The EC's position is that the SME sector should be defined largely in terms of number of employees as follows:

- Firms with 0 to 9 employees - micro enterprises
- 10 to 99 employees - small enterprises
- 100 to 499 employees - medium enterprises.

This appears to cohere with UNIDO's definitions of the SME sector for developing countries.

The Ghanaian Situation

Attempts to characterize the sector in Ghana have been made by various bodies and researchers. From its Industrial Statistics, The Ghana Statistical Service considers firms with less than 10 employees as Small Scale Enterprises and their counterparts with more than 10 employees as Medium and Large-Sized Enterprises. Interestingly, the GSS in its national accounts considered companies with up to 9 employees as Small and Medium Enterprises. However, the National Board of Small Scale Industries (NBSSI) applies both the 'fixed asset and number of employees' criteria. It defines a Small Scale Enterprise as one with not more than 9 workers, and plant and machinery (excluding land, buildings and vehicles) not exceeding 10 million Cedis (approximately US$ 9,000 based on the ¢ to $ exchange rate in 1994). Revising the definition in 1998, the NBSSI emphasized both micro and macro enterprises. It defined Small Business as 'any business that employs up to 29 people'. It also identified two types of small businesses: *micro* and *small*. The Micro is any enterprise that employs up to 5 people or has fixed assets excluding land and building not exceeding $10,000; the small enterprise is one employing between 6 and 29 people or has fixed assets excluding land and building not exceeding $100,000.

The Ghana Enterprise Development Commission (GEDC) on the other hand uses a 10 million Cedi upper limit definition for plant and machinery. Obviously there are issues relating to which valuation framework to use as well as the continuous depreciation of the Cedi. Steel and Webster (1990), use an employment cut off point of 30 employees to indicate Small Scale Enterprises.

The Ghanaian SME: Its Role and Matters of Concern

Chapman, (1998) indicates that in the UK, small firms (those employing less than 50 people) account for some 99% of enterprises. Many of such firms are owned and operated by entrepreneurs and their families – manager/owner (Chell, 1999; Moran, 1999). Moran suggests that despite the power of global multinational corporations, small businesses are important in providing:

- Diversity of products and services.
- Employment for some 47% of the labour force in the UK.
- Links in the value chain between large companies and the consumer.
- Opportunities for innovation, creativity and for growth of cutting edge firms, which grow to become world leaders.

The Ghanaian situation is not much different. Buame, (2000), suggests that SMEs account for some 50% of GDP in Ghana. The dynamic role of SMEs in developing countries as engines through which the growth objectives of developing countries can be achieved has long been recognised. It is estimated that the SME sector employs about 22% of the adult population in developing countries (Daniels & Ngwira, 1993; Fisseha & McPherson, 1991). The sector employs about 15.5% of the labour force in Ghana. The sector therefore adds more employment growth (5%) than micro and large-scale enterprises.

As far back as 1989, Boon argued that the over-emphasis on large-scale industrial activity to the neglect of small-scale productive activity, has, as a national economic and industrial approach, not worked for Ghana. He notes that this overemphasis on large-scale, capital-intensive urban-based enterprises has created a severe imbalance in the economy, especially since Ghanaians may not own many of such large-scale enterprises, which tend to depend on imported raw materials. Such raw materials are often purchased with hard currency earned from the activities of primary producers. Forstater, MacDonald and Raynard (2002) have argued that SMEs offer a unique opportunity for developing countries to grow. They argue that promotion of SMEs can radically help combat poverty, facilitate more equitable distribution of wealth, provide the transition from agriculture-led development to industrialisation, promote entrepreneurial drive and through the linkages among small firms, and between small firms and larger ones, create more resilient economic systems with appropriate forward and backward integrations.

In this regard, various governmental policies aimed at enhancing economic growth through improved performance of the Non-Traditional Export Sector (NTEs) are a necessary spring-board for looking critically at SMEs. This is so because nearly all NTEs emerge from SMEs and the entrepreneurial activities of small businesses: crafts, pineapple exports, textiles and garments, plastics, furniture etc. This has become the cornerstone of Ghana's private sector export-led growth strategy (State of the Ghanaian Economy Report, 2001). Attempts are being made to take advantage of the US African Growth and Opportunities Act (AGOA), various EU and ECOWAS Trade Liberalisation Schemes by using such bodies as the Ghana Export Promotion Council (GEPC) and the Gateway Programme to facilitate greater international competitiveness of Ghanaian firms in terms of exports and general involvement in the international market.

Given the obvious advantages of having internationally competitive Ghanaian SMEs, a critical set of research issues arise. Apart from the macro efforts at the level of government, donors/development partners and international agencies, what micro efforts at the level of the firm, organisation or business are required to catapult Ghanaian SMEs into the regional and international market?

As discussed elsewhere, (Puplampu 2002), no matter the frantic state of macro level efforts at national development, the real synergy comes from efficient, competitive and innovative firms which are doing what they know how to do and are doing so well. From the literature on Organisational Behaviour and also Human Resource Management, it seems reasonable to surmise that critical to all firm level functioning are three key variables: employee skills, organisational structures and corporate leadership parameters. These issues constitute the core concerns of the research reported in this chapter. However, before examining the firm level issues of skills, structures and leadership, it is perhaps necessary to look a little more closely at the issues confronting SMEs – generally – by asking: what are the constraints and problems of SMEs in Ghana and other developing countries?

Constraints to SME Development

Despite the wide-ranging economic reforms instituted in the sub-region, which aim at empowering SMEs, they still face a variety of constraints such as difficulty of absorbing large fixed costs, the absence of economies of scale and scope in key factors of production, and their higher unit costs of production (Schmitz, 1982; Steel & Webster, 1990). A number of other constraints have been identified. These include input constraints, finances and cash flow (Aryeetey et al 1994); equipment and technology (Parker et al, 1995), domestic demand (Daniels and Ngwira, 1993), access to international markets and regulatory constraints (Aryeetey et al, 1994). Of particular concern for this paper is the area of managerial constraints. Lack of managerial know-how places significant constraints on SME development. Even though SMEs tend to attract motivated managers/entrepreneurs, they can hardly compete with larger firms at the compensation levels demanded by capable managers. Related to this is the slow growth in the consulting services sector dedicated to SMEs. In more recent times, in Ghana, the EMPRETEC Foundation and the African Project Development Facility (APDF) are providing training and various types of support services to SMEs and entrepreneurs. A number of questions arise in this context. For example, are the requisite skill sets for SMEs different from larger firms? Do tertiary level training programmes facilitate SME knowledge in students and young persons such that they are better placed to exploit opportunities based on capacity and competence?

Other Challenges

According to Buame (2000), apart from some of the problems mentioned above, the operations of SMEs are adversely affected by macroeconomic conditions such as: inflation, exchange rate hikes, low interest rates for savings and high lending rates and absence of self-sustaining government initiatives. From the foregoing, there are a number of issues worth investigating in the preparedness and ability of Ghanaian SMEs to engage themselves proactively and profitably in the emerging regional and international markets into which their products and services fit. Carr et al (1998) (of the Afro-centric Alliance) underscore the value of small businesses in the African context in that they help push economic development, while satisfying various cultural value systems such as human relations and extended family connections as well as status, profit and self preservation. There is much to be said for SMEs to be helped to grow and expand. The study reported here focuses on human capacity and organisational dimensions of such preparedness for growth, with particular focus on operating regionally or internationally.

Theories of Internationalisation

What do the theories of internationalisation say about the process of growth into foreign markets? A number of theories have been advanced. Kuada and Sorensen (2000) provide an overview and assessment of three main theories of internationalisation. These are the Stages Models; the Contingency Models and the Action Models.

The Stages Models

There are two theories under this umbrella: the Learning Stages Theory and the Product Life Cycle Theory. The Learning Stages Theory holds in essence that the process of a company's internationalisation is 'orderly and sequential'. The company proceeds from one stage to the next based on the learning and experiences it acquires over time as it engages its customers, products and broader environment with its internal workings. It has been argued that the various Stage Models based on the learning principle only use the concept 'learning' as a platform to point to the 'outcomes' of learning, in this case, development of or greater international involvement. The Product Life Cycle models suggest that the internationalisation process is linked to economic assessments of returns from products at various points in the company's engagement with its market (see Kuada and Sorensen 2000).

Others have described the 'sequential' model of internationalisation which is also 'stage' based. It sees a sequence inherent in the point (in the life of a firm) at which the sets of activities, which characterise first attempts at international operations and high degree of internationalisation. The extent to which a firm (using Western companies as the baseline) travels into and engages its resources in markets outside of its borders depends on its 'cultural' orientation or perhaps its openness to the 'world'. The more ethnocentric the firm's cultural orientation, the more its home culture and ways dominate its operations and therefore the less likely it is to venture outside its borders. Companies with a geocentric cultural orientation tend to grow into international activities because geocentricism is less culturally myopic. It may well be that companies traverse from ethno- to poly- to geocentricism in the transition to international markets. The 'simultaneous' models of internationalisation suggest that rather than a staged progression, internationalisation occurs as a result of the convergence of a number of macro economic and broad market factors (globalisation and world travel; standardised consumer tastes; economies of scale; movements of capital and financing towards areas and regions of maximum returns etc) which propel firms into the international arena – almost by default – if they wish to remain in business.

The appeal of the Stages models – for this study – lies in the recognition of 'learning' as a key tool or leveraging factor. In emerging management thinking, knowledge acquisition, management and knowledge use is a dimension of competitive advantage. Such knowledge leveraging comes only to the learning organisation, which is open to receiving information from its world and adapts itself to the functionally relevant demands that its environment is making on it. A common thread that runs through all learning theories, be they operant, vicarious or classical, is that learning leads to skill acquisition which is deployed through competencies and thereby enable a more productive engagement with one's environment. The contention of this study is therefore that there are identifiable skills and competencies, acquired through learning, which differentiate internationally connected or engaged companies from those that are not.

The Contingency Models

According to Kuada and Sorensen (2000), contingency thinking in internationalisation basically holds that the process is driven by managerial strategy and decisions, which are a response to environmental factors – perhaps a bit like the 'simultaneous' concept. While the simultaneous approach may appear to emphasise more the invisible hand of the market place driving organisations into conformity to global pressures, the contingency approach stresses the rationality of management thinking and decision responsiveness.

From the view of the present study, a definite component here is what Kuada and Sorensen (2000) point out: that analytical capacity (in terms of a firm's in-house ability to recognise opportunities and situational contingencies, analyse implications and alternative courses of action and thereby make informed and strategically sound choices among a set of alternatives) is key to the internationalisation process and experience of any firm, industry, country or region.

The Action (Interaction) Models

The essence of the action models is that by deliberate extension of our humanity, which is primarily gregarious and social, firms engage in relational interactions, which build networks of actors, reactors and mutual beneficiaries.

These interactions help organisations to enlist the capacities, knowledge and economies of other actors with whom they are interconnected directly (through first-order relationships) or indirectly (through second or third order relationships leveraged through first-order ones). This has a natural socio-cultural appeal, especially in developing countries where the business of economics is still very much dominated by direct relationships. Beyond this appeal, however, many cognitive psychologists today subscribe to the network approach to human functioning. This is often referred to as the 'connectionist' model. It emphasises the connections between informational items held by the brain and suggests that often, superior performance can be leveraged from the connectionist interactions between the

various items (and their locations) rather than unilateral processing. In this regard, the larger the network space, the more endowed that network space is and the richer the interactions between the points in the network, the greater the likelihood that internationalisation will occur and increase, as members position and reposition themselves and their firms to respond and benefit.
We will now explore these three concepts.

Skill Requirements

Psychologists suggest that skills refer to the capacity to carry out 'complex, well organised, patterns of behaviour' in an easeful and adaptive manner so as to achieve a goal. Originally, the term was associated with physical/motor activity; however, it has come to refer also to verbal and social capacity. In this regard, however, there is the tendency to see a 'skill' in terms of how it fits into a broader pattern of behaviours aimed at influencing and/or manipulating others. Closely related to 'skill' is the emergent use of 'competencies'. Competencies take the concept of skill further. While 'skill' refers to capacity to carry out complex behaviour, competencies refer to the ability to organise ones skills in such a manner as to perform or accomplish a task. Inherent in this are two related parameters: possession of a knowledge base, as well as behaviour capably deployed, in a flexible manner. In today's technology-driven and globalised economy, a range of skills and competencies are deemed critical for corporate or business success. These include team skills, multiskilled task capacity, impression management and innovation and creativity (Hayes, 1997, King and Anderson 1995). Chapman, (1998), for example, emphasizes that while entrepreneurs find opportunities and make a living or chart new territory, it is the work team which will 'grow' the business.

This calls for possession of team skills in today's SME. Anecdotal evidence suggests that a critical challenge facing businesses in countries like Ghana, is the ability of various employees and officials to function and believe in the team concept. We need management, which works as a team; functional arms of a business, which recognise their interdependency; and individuals who eschew the 'one-man' Tarzan-syndrome in which each person seeks the glory for him/herself alone.

The impact of possession of requisite skills on organisational performance and productivity is perhaps beyond question. It drives much of selection psychology and is the cornerstone of human resource management (Milkovich & Boudreau, 1997). The processes of applicant testing and assessment and job analysis to determine the nature and scope of a job or post as well as the training of staff are all geared towards ensuring that the organisation has an appropriate skill set deployed in, and by its employees. Often, organisations are forced to shed staff because some staff may have become skill obsolete (Ambrose, 1996), highlighting the importance to the organisation, of having the required skills. Raven, (1984) developed an extensive listing of core skills and competencies perceived as critical to modern societal and organisational functioning. His essential thesis was that, organisational progress is impossible, indeed national progress is impossible, if people – the human resources – do not acquire and put to use various skills and capacities such as technical ability, innovation, critical thinking, team work etc. He later developed this thesis into a scathing attack on the skills and approaches of public servants who he argues need to redefine their sense of what is required (economic or psycho-social solutions) to address the problems of society (Raven, 1989).

Drew (2002) argues that it is important for organisations to set up systems by which to constantly monitor, define, redefine and fine-tune competencies and skills in line with particular business contingencies and requirements. In this regard, it is interesting that Loan-Clarke et al (1999) refer to the fact that in the UK, the government is actively making efforts to ensure an appropriate set of skills and qualifications for all, including small businesses which are seen as central to the UK economy. They also note that the most successful SMEs offer significant levels of skills training to their staff (*Competitiveness: Helping Smaller*

Firms, 1995; Competitiveness: Creating the Enterprise Centre of Europe, 1996). Loan-Clarke and colleagues found that despite the possible benefits of various skills training for small businesses (especially given that most of them tend to fill senior vacancies from within) the evidence is that many still do not train and facilitate skill development as much as they possibly could. In a similar vein, Hall (1993) found that employee know-how was rated by chief executives as one of the most important contributors to business success. There is thus a clear requirement to ensure a continuous enhancement in the 'stock of knowledge or know-how' – what we might call skills and competencies – through training and learning.

The point being made is that skills, competencies and general ability to perform as required by an organisation are critical. The question is, for SMEs in Ghana, wishing to expand and take advantage of regional and international possibilities what types of skills and competencies are needed? This question is important. Bartram (1995) found that in the UK, many small businesses used very informal means such as referrals and direct initial contact made by the potential employee as the primary means of recruiting. He also found that many small firms valued personality characteristics such as honesty, integrity, and conscientiousness, interest in the work as key attributes to look for when recruiting. Interestingly, they rated vocational/academic/school qualifications and even work experience as less important than integrity and conscientiousness. Within the Ghanaian setting, what skills, competencies and capacities are needed by an SME, which wishes to grow into and exploit the international/regional market? This research sought to answer this question.
This review now turns to the issue of organisational structures.

Organisational Structures

Organisational efficiency and effectiveness are based on how well designed the organisation is. Design is a matter of the nature and relationship between organisational structure, operational processes, technology in use and people or human capacities. As noted by Scott, (1992) and others, an organisation cannot grow, satisfy its market and achieve its goals if it is run in an ad hoc manner. Systems and structures have to be in place. In the developing world, this is often a problem faced by organisations, especially, small private firms.

Several technical and unpublished reports on salary surveys, HR Reviews and due diligence reviews carried out by consulting firms such as PricewaterhouseCoopers, **P**syconH.R, Deloitte & Touche etc. often show that even many large and in some instances well-respected/known organisations in Ghana have ill-defined structures. This has an impact on effectiveness and efficiency. The question obviously is: how much of an impact? Symon (2000) notes that in today's economy, driven as it were by technology and virtual reality, new forms of organising organisations are necessary, leading to the growth of 'post-bureaucratic' organisational forms, which allow employees what may be called a 'structured flexibility' within which to work and deliver.

Organisational structure provides the architecture through which the tasks and activities of the organisation are grouped, divided and subdivided to create decision and authority centres, processes and linkages which host, support and facilitate the implementation of corporate strategies and goals. Critically, structure constrains human behaviour because it makes it possible for people and systems to interact or not to interact. It affects the way 'people size up situations, the way they interact with others, what they value and believe to be important, time horizons, and even management style…' (Cook and Hunsaker 2001: 87).

It is this constraining influence on behaviour that makes organisational structure such an important variable. The design process involves corporate leaders/managers (and perhaps consultants) deliberately setting up task groupings, information networks, authority and decision centres, procedures for coordination, control and conflict resolution, mechanisms by which to link internal units with each other and with external stakeholders such as regulators, customers and suppliers. These design issues determine how the organisation is led, governed, managed and how it is strategically positioned. The component parts of an organisation, as discussed by Puplampu (1998), are its basic structure, operating mechanisms and decision mechanisms.

Practically, organisational structures must detail the various levels of the hierarchy – the strategic apex, middle management and operating core; the functional parts or departments such as marketing, finance, production etc. as well as the coordinating mechanisms by which the components liase and relate with each other. In this regard, various organisational behaviour specialists (McShane & Von Glinow, 2000 and others) indicated that amongst a variety of structural forms, we could identify the following: hierarchical bureaucracies based on function, product or geography; tall/flat structures; centralized/decentralized; mechanistic/organic and matrixed structures. Blackler and Shimmin (1984) and later writers such as Symon (2000) indicate that the issue is not simply a question of what structural form is 'best', but rather, a range of different considerations are required when designing an organisation or when considering how to set out its component parts.

The different considerations include: how adaptable and flexible the organisation has to be – in for example – responding to change; the organisation's goals; the environment and market the organisation is operating in; the organisation's current stage of growth; how differences are to be resolved; how task instructions are issued and monitored; the arrangements required to facilitate proper relationships with the organisation's external stakeholders and constituencies.

These considerations impact the structural arrangements that any organisation has to make so as to enhance its operations. In this regard, Schermerhorn et al (1994) argues that there is a long tradition and history of research and practice linking firm strategy with its structure. Bresnen and Fowler (1996) however, wonder whether the introduction of more organic structures necessarily facilitate greater autonomy (and perhaps performance) for employees. The work of King and Anderson (1995) shows that the link between structure and performance of an organisation is not as straightforward as one might imagine or wish it to be. In this regard, no simplistic 'best structure' can be concluded as the way forward for organisations, which wish to be innovative, for example.

However, based on the work of writers like Stogdill (1971) it is clear that the processes by which leaders and managers as well as other stakeholders of organisations ensure their effectiveness and efficiency are not accidental but deliberate efforts of crafting and design. Triandis therefore suggests that organisation designers have to ask a number of questions such as

- What are the characteristics of the environment in which the firm is operating?
- What are the characteristics of effective and efficient organisations?

Careful assessment of these design issues points to the need to balance structure with function and with process and people. Hatch (1997) also emphasises the complexity by drawing out the demands of subgroups, strategy, technology and networks. The point of these submissions is that success, in whatever organisational enterprise a firm is involved in, requires a certain level of deliberate structural design, to facilitate conformity with strategic thrust. Studies of firm structure in developing countries like Ghana are, however, few and far between. Munene (1995) has found and discussed issues relating to arbitrariness, lack of standardization and poor reliability of organisational linkages in organisations in African countries such as Nigeria and Uganda.

This study seeks to identify whether there are any pointers to structural forms, which may have relevance for SMEs and contribute to distinguishing between those that are achieving their strategic ends and those that are not.

Corporate Leadership

The array of literature on leadership is certainly too vast to cover in this paper. However, the work of Steers, Porter and Bigley (1996) show that leadership, its legitimacy, style and focus, is of growing concern in organisational existence. Recent work by Puplampu (2003) demonstrates how critical the leadership dimension is to corporate survival and progress.

The personality of an entrepreneur for example, in terms of his/her aspirations, ability to recognise and create opportunities, etc may well have an impact on performance of the business (Chell, 1999). In this regard, where SMEs are concerned, it is not appropriate to separate the type of business owner from the performance of the enterprise. In the same vein, Moran (1999) argues strongly that the personality, style and patterns of leadership of the small business owner-manager appears to have great impact on why some businesses develop and grow whereas others don't. He made a useful distinction between having 'growth-potential' from a market perspective and actually experiencing growth by having a leader with a 'growth orientation'.

He identifies a number of dimensions such as the leader's intentions/plans as to the future development of the business, 4extent of innovation and the leader's power of decision making. Owners who are high in growth orientation tend to want to be in charge, with a firm grip on the business, but with a real sense of their responsibility to others. They tend to have a strategic outlook, which facilitates innovation and empowers their subordinates to explore. Would these leader attributes apply in the Ghanaian environment?

More and more, researchers and organisational practitioners are recognising the distinction between *transactional* and *transformational* leadership (Hartog et al, 1997). Transactional leadership can be described as referring to the process of ensuring that the mundane daily exchanges between a superior and a subordinate are crafted to produce in the end, the requisite results from subordinate work behaviour. Transformational leadership, on the other hand, involves processes by which superiors at the helm of affairs provide vision and draw out their followers and subordinates to engage in behaviours, which go beyond the norm and thereby facilitate transformations, change and visionary progress.

Little (2000) explored the stressors confronting owner-managers of SMEs in the UK. Based on the qualitative evidence that 45% of all new businesses fail in the first 3 years, it is assumed that those who have been trading for more than 3 years are in some measure successful. Owners of such firms demonstrate independence, individuality and a capacity to be a jack-of-all-trades. This tends to produce a whole range of pressures on the owner-manager. Of the 16 stressors identified by Little's study, the 4 most frequently cited were problems with information, communication technology; issues with regulatory agencies such as income tax, value added tax, governmental bureaucracy; pressure to meet deadlines and marketing problems. It seems that being at the helm of affairs of an SME has its own stressors and stresses, which require dogged determination to overcome. Theorists suggest that leadership requires adaptive coping behaviours and styles. These should help the leader overcome the necessary challenges of the job, such as the stresses identified by Little, as well as the limitations and constraints on SME development detailed earlier. Organisational Behaviour writers consistently suggest that the challenge of corporate leadership is to create vision, lead through change and energize employees to reach out and drive the organisation forward in its market.

To achieve this fundamental issue confronting all corporate leadership is survival and 'profitable' progress. To effectively lead an organisation therefore entails the following capacities:

- Being Visionary. This requires a capacity to think strategically, see beyond limitations and seek to chart new ground.

- Being Realistic. This requires that despite the visionary outlook, the leader/entrepreneur or manager has no illusions about possibilities and options.
- Being Ethical and Service Oriented. This suggests that the leader has to operate in a ethically sound manner and focus on providing quality service to customers
- Being Courageous: This suggests the need to recognise that there will be challenges and obstacles, but the leader has to act with sustained initiative and determination.

Skills, Structure and Leadership – the Synthesis

Komache (1996) in discussing the resource capability of the firm notes that in the resource-based view, the firm is seen as a discrete set of tangible and intangible resources and capabilities required for product or market competition (Amit and Schoemaker, 1993). However, the capability-based view of the firm is concerned with actions, processes and related behaviours by which to attain a competitive posture. Pulling the discreet resources of the resource-based view and the process dimensions of the capabilities view of the firm together, we achieve a synergy that goes beyond mere possession of a resource such as skills to be proactive and necessarily relevant deployment of those resources to enhance the goals and operations of the business.

In this regard, structural boundaries clearly set, operational possibilities and flexibilities hosted by the structure, and leadership, which empowers, are all likely to ensure that skills and competencies are appropriately deployed. In other words, it is the thesis of this paper that Ghanaian SMEs need to put in place an orientation to strategy which is not a simplistic single-resource based approach, (which may suggest for example, that what a particular SME needs is 'capital') but, a comprehensive approach which recognises a multiplicity of resources which are not discrete, but interlinked and managed in such a way as to maximise their combined outputs. Schermerhorn et al (1994) therefore argue that the appropriate strategic posture is one in which the firm recognises the need to be market -focused as well as ensuring that its structure and systems harness the unique skills and abilities within its walls.

These three variables are therefore considered critical: skills, structure and leadership. As noted earlier, we live in a present day environment when attempts are being made to assist developing countries to take better advantage of regional and global possibilities. At the risk of sounding opinionated, it can be noted, that NEPAD, AGOA and other initiatives notwithstanding, Ghanaian entrepreneurs and SMEs may well not experience growth, despite the existence of the growth potential, until and unless the requisite synergies are created by the interconnection between the human aspects of corporate progress: skills, structure and leadership. In this regard, how are Ghanaian SMEs positioned to acquire and use relevant skills and resources? How are they to structure their organisations? What type of leadership should be exhibited or initiated? This research seeks to examine how relevant these variables are and assess the nature of their complementary interaction in as far as organisational functioning is concerned. As is the case with many of the human and organisational factors in corporate existence, it is perhaps too early – given the current level of knowledge – to conclude that any one of the factors is more or less important than the others.

Statement of the Basic Research Question

Based on the foregoing, the basic research questions are as follows:

a) What human skills and competencies do employees of Ghanaian (SME) companies that operate successfully in the regional and or international market possess?
b) What leadership foci are required in terms of vision, strategy and style?
c) What corporate structures seem most suited to efforts towards internationalisation in terms of governance and management?

These research questions are deliberately not stated as hypotheses since the research reported here is exploratory and the possibility of poor participation of SMEs could render any test of hypotheses ineffectual. It was considered therefore that an exploratory design was more appropriate at this stage.

Methodology and Findings

Design

This research was originally intended to adopt only an in-depth, comparative and exploratory approach to operationalise the research questions. Interviews were therefore to be the primary approach to data collection. However, as approaches were made to the first 4 companies in the sample, it became clear that a preliminary sweep of the field to ascertain certain basic parameters such as size, prevalent structures, issues and business foci was necessary. A detailed questionnaire was therefore developed (see attached). The design was therefore a cross-sectional approach in which data were sought from and about the employees, leaders and structures of a number of Ghanaian SMEs. In the end, the amount of detail obtained from the questionnaire rendered any further interviews unnecessary at this time.

Sample

The sample was made up of 12 Ghanaian SMEs. The respondents were the 12 corporate heads, managing directors or CEOs and or Human Resource managers of the companies, and in one case, the marketing manager.

Data Instrument

A 4-Section questionnaire was designed and sent to each of the participating SMEs. **Section A** of the questionnaire covered the corporate profile. It had 7 questions seeking information about the companies and their key characteristics such as: main line of business, period of operation, intention to enter the regional market etc. **Section B** of the questionnaire covered the skills profile of the companies with 6 questions on number of employees, educational/experience background of managers and skills thought to have contributed to success or failure. **Section C** covered the leadership profile of the companies. It had 4 questions on the leadership style, vision and management/decision strategy of the company. The last, **Section D**, covered the corporate structure. It had 3 questions on availability of organisational chart, structural bottlenecks and presence of a board (governance systems). The questionnaire ended with an open-ended item asking respondents to expatiate on the internal (strategic or operational) problems which affect the growth of the firm.

Analyses

Given the exploratory nature of this research, and to answer the 3 main research questions, the analyses clustered findings from each question and section. A combination of descriptive accounts of the firms as well as summary statistics in terms of frequencies and percentages are used to examine the findings.

Procedure

Contacts were made with a potential range of companies by the principal researcher in Ghana. The initial contact set consisted of 24 SMEs mostly based in Accra and engaged in business across various sectors, from agriculture through export to manufacturing. Twelve companies responded to the initial contacts made. The questionnaires were then sent to these companies, which had agreed to participate. Appointments were made with the CEOs and Human Resource managers, managers/directors and marketing heads for the retrieval of the questionnaires. Relevant company documents, in the form of Organisational Charts were also solicited. Active data were collected over a 6-month period in 2002

Findings

The findings are presented by Section. As noted above, the data instrument was divided into 4 sub-sections: corporate profile, skills profile, leadership profile and corporate structure. These findings are presented using a combination of descriptive case profiles as well as summary tables. For each sub-section, we present first a summary table followed by descriptive case profiles of all 12 companies. We begin with the corporate profiles.

Corporate Profiles

Table 1 Line of business of organisations sampled

Issue		Number	%
Main line of business	Pharmaceuticals	2	17
	Electrical and telecom cables	1	8
	Fast moving consumer goods	1	8
	Aluminum products	3	25
	Bulk PVC, HBPE pipes & plastic products	2	17
	LPG cylinders and stoves	1	8
	Metal related products	1	8
	Bottling of mineral water	1	8
	Total	**12**	**100**

All the 12 participating SMEs are drawn from the manufacturing sector. This was not a deliberate skew. It was simply the result of willing participation. All the companies, which responded to the invitation came from that sector. This may well mean that the sector is quite well populated in terms of SME involvement. Table 2 below shows the ranges in terms of period in business of the organisations.

Table 2: Period in Business

Issue	Range in years	Frequency	%
Period in business	3-5	3	25
	6-11	3	25
	30-35	3	25
	36-41	2	17
	42 and over	1	8

The highest figure for the period of existence in years was 46 and the lowest is 3 years. This suggests some longevity in the lifespan of SMEs in the manufacturing sector Ghana. Table 3 below deals with the sub-regional presence or intentions of the various firms.

Table 3: SME Sub-Regional Presence and Intentions

Presence in Sub-Region	Companies operating in the Sub region	Frequency		%
		Yes	7	58
		No	5	42
	By exporting (based on the 58% operating in the sub region)	**Yes**	6	100
		No	-	
	Through Subsidiaries/affiliates	**Yes**	2	33

Business	**Where in the Sub Region**
PVC pipes & plastic products	Togo, Benin, Burkina Faso, Mali, Cameroon, Gabon, Kenya
Pharmaceutical	Nigeria, Togo
Metal products	Send supplies to its affiliates in Nigeria & Ivory Coast for marketing.
Plastic Wares	Exports to almost all West African countries. Also has a subsidiary in Gambia.
Aluminium	Burkina Faso, Mali
Cables	Burkina Faso, Togo, Guinea, Niger, Mali

Intention to enter the Sub Regional market based on the 5 companies not operating in the Sub Region		**Frequencies**	**%**
	Yes	4	80
	No	1	20

Markets targeted by firms that want to enter into the Sub Region.

Firms	**Target**
Manufacturer of LPG gas and stoves	Burkina Faso, Togo, Nigeria, Benin
Pharmaceutical	Nigeria, Liberia, Togo, Burkina Faso
Aluminium Products	Nigeria, Sierra Leone and all francophone countries

More than half of the companies in the sample operate in the sub-region through exports and maintenance of a subsidiary operation. Of those, which are as yet not in the sub-regional market, 80% would want to enter and have targeted most of the countries in the region. Table 4 below is a summary of the additional markets targeted by 4 of the 7 industries already operating in the Sub Region.

Table 4: Market Expansion Intentions of SMEs Already in the Region

Industry	Targeted Countries
Pharmaceuticals	Cote d'Ivoire
Plastics wares	Hopes to cover the whole sub region with the shortest possible time
Aluminium utensils	Any West African country
Electricals and.cables	Guinea, Burkina Faso, Mali, Liberia, Sierra Leone, Niger, Togo and Benin

It is significant to note that of the companies already in the sub-regional market, more than half have expansion plans into the countries noted in Table 4. Another area examined was ownership of the SMEs in question.

Table 5: Foreign Interests in Ownership of SMEs in Sample

		Freq.	%
Ownership by foreign interest	Yes	7	58
	No	5	42
Origin of foreign Interest	UK	5	72
	Denmark	1	14
	France-Germany	1	14

Obviously, the UK has a significant presence in the SME manufacturing sector from which the sample were drawn. The study also examined the perceived profitability of the SMEs in the sample, from the perspective of the CEOs and management staff who provided the information.

Table 6: Perceived Profitability of the SME

Issue			
		Freq.	**%**
Perceived profitability	Yes	10	83
	No	2	17

The study could not delve into the actual performance indices of the companies: profit levels, sales margins or sales volume. It is significant to note, however, that 10 out of the 12 see their businesses as profitable and making progress. The summary table 7 below details the reasons given by the companies for this.

Table 7: Perceived Basis of Success or Failure of SMEs

The 2 companies which considered their companies as unsuccessful and unprofitable gave the following reasons: Poor performance due to technical and financial problems and undue pressure from the parent company.	
Reasons given by companies which see themselves as successful & profitable	Sustained expansion and diversification; meeting targets; sustained markets with virtual monopoly; product quality, market awareness & customer satisfaction; increase in production & sales; long existence; steady growth and future prospects; strong nationwide demand for the company's products.

Skills Profile

We now present the findings on the skills profile of the companies. Table 8 below details the establishment numbers in ranges for managers and staff.

Table 8 Establishment Numbers

	Range	Freqs		(Range)	Freqs
Managers	1-4	6	Staff	0-49	4
	5-9	1		50-99	5
	10-14	4		100-149	1
	15-19	0		150-199	0
	20-24	1		200-249	0
				250-299	0
				300-349	2

Table 8 shows that in terms of establishment numbers, 3 companies can be classified as medium sized with over 100 staff. The staff strength for all companies surveyed ranged between 12 (lowest) – 312 (highest) for staff and 2 (lowest) – 24 (highest) for managers. Table 9 below provides a summary of the educational/professional qualifications of the Managers of the SMEs.

Table 9: Educational and Experience Capacity of Management of the SMEs

Position Line of Business	**CEO**	**Finance Manager**	**Marketing Manager**	**Production Manager**	**IT Manager**	**HR Manager**
A. PVC pipes	DNS	B.Com, ICWA 12 yrs	Engineer 10yrs	BE Mech. MBA 15yrs	BSc. Admin 6yrs	HND Business Studies; 30 yrs
B. Pharmaceuticals	NA	AIA, ACCA 17yrs	BSc. Admin 3yrs	Bsc. Mech. Eng. 2yrs.	Higher ACP, A'level; 6yrs	Cert. Personnel Adm. 25yrs
C. Metals	DNS	DNS	DNS	Dip Mech. Eng 18yrs	DNS	BSc Educ 30yrs
D. Plastic products	MBA, BTech 15yrs	CA 12yrs	MBA 7yrs	B.Tech12yrs	NA	BA, 25yrs
E. LPG Cylinders	NA	NA	NA	Bsc. 9yrs	DNS	MPA 22yrs
F. Aluminum products	HND, Mech. Eng. 25yrs	NA	NA	DNS	NA	NA
G. Pharmaceuticals	DNS	ACCA 15yrs	BSc.Phrm 3yrs	BSc.Phrm 32yrs	NA	Same as Fin Mgr.
H. Aluminum products	LLB	PF, A' level 10yrs	NA	NA	NA	NA
J. Aluminum products	BSc .Soc Science 28yrs	ACCA 9yrs	Dip Marketing 10 yrs	A'level 15yrs	NA	NA
K. FMCG	MPhil 30yrs	Chartered Acc 20yrs	BA Hons 9yrs	NA	NA	NA
L. Bottling of mineral water	**BSc Bio Chem.10yrs**		**ACCA 4yrs**		**Quality Control BSc. Chem 9yrs** Plant Eng. Dip in Mech Eng 9yrs (This company had no IT, Production, Marketing or HR Managers)	
M. Electrical and Telecom Cables	DNS					

It is noteworthy that only 5 of the 12 firms have 3 or more apparently well endowed managers in place (in terms of technical ability, experience and education). A set of detailed skill and competence areas were sourced from participating companies in terms of impact on company performance. These are grouped under a number of broad headings.

Staff Skill Requirements

The data suggest that the following attributes of staff are important: honesty, discipline, dedication. These can be grouped together as personal skills. Another set of skills can be grouped under task skills. These are: team building and time management. The final set of skills could be referred to as technical: marketing skills, skills for production and sales, quality control, academic strength, technical expertise.

Managerial Skill Requirements

The SMEs sampled suggested the following attributes for managers: supervisory and leadership skills, coordination, marketing and sales skills, interpersonal and communication skills, strategic planning and a general capacity for effectiveness. These can be grouped together as managerial and leadership skills. Managers should also have a keen understanding of business. Intellectual skills also appear to count in terms of academic strength and analytical ability. Technical and IT skills are also considered important.

Business Growth Skills

The following were identified as key to business growth and success: Open mindedness, dedication, hard work, and commitment. These can be grouped together as personal and or professional skills. Technical ability, managerial and leadership skills, marketing and entrepreneurial acumen are also mentioned and can be grouped together as business skills. Organisational supports such as transfer of training skills to work, on-the-job training and maintenance of quality are also mentioned.

Leadership and Governance

The study explored the approach of the leaders of the SMEs in the sample. The findings are reported below. These refer to the styles in use by the leaders and managers.

Table 10: Style of Leadership

Style of Leadership	Freq.	%
Participatory	7	58
Strict	1	8
Dynamic and democratic	1	8
'Scientific' (mix of autocratic and participatory)	1	8
Visionary (but without managerial skills)	1	8

The leaders and CEOs of these firms articulate a number of vision positions or strategic foci. These include: Focus on customer satisfaction, profitability, market expansion and corporate progress. Others aim to become the market leader, or to double in size by 2005. The vision of others is to ensure continuous growth and progress to satisfy all stakeholders and to become the biggest plastics producing company in the country. What is not clear is the extent to which such visions are owned by employees and whether these visions actually drive the organisation. We sought to establish a number of governance parameters such as decision-making and presence of board oversight. The findings are reported below in Table 11.

Table 11: Governance

Management Meetings	**Occurrence in sample**	**Overall Governance Situation**
Weekly	6	In 2 organisations there are no management meetings at all.
Monthly	2	
Hardly	2	
None	2	
Presence of a Board	**Board Oversight through Regular Board Meetings**	6 SMEs do not have boards or where such boards exist, they do not meet or their meeting schedules are not known.
75% (9 out of 12)	55% (5 out of 9)	

It is interesting to note that in 25% of the sample, there are hardly any management meetings. The data also indicated that where such meetings take place, the issues discussed and decisions taken cover areas such as: strategic planning; review of previous work; problems and performance; production issues, product quality and technical issues; finance and training; problems with salaries and administration; production progress and stagnation; staff activities and other general issues.

Organisational Structure

11 companies supplied their organisational charts. Three of these appeared rather rudimentary and did not reflect the set of anticipated core functions of manufacturing concerns – production, sales/marketing and finance/administration. Three indicated the presence of internal audit departments. We summarise below the situation with organisational structures in Table 12.

Table 12: Nature and Adequacy of Organisational Structures

Structural Parameters in terms of Functions/Departments	Frequency
Corporate structure reported and drawn out	11
Possess core structure (production/ finance and administration/ sales and marketing)	6
Possess advanced structures (Core Plus IT/HRM/Internal Audit etc)	4
Possess weak structures (incomplete core and no or limited additionals)	4

Two companies reported severe structural problems relating to poor capacity at the helm of affairs and poor financing and resource mobilisation. We explored the issues of strategic and operational problems hampering expansion and found 6 companies reporting difficulties as follows:

Table 13: Strategic Problems

Problems	Reported by Companies in
Lack of Finance	Aluminium, Pharmaceuticals, Fabrication
Competition & Market Strength/Share	Aluminium, Metals
Equipment and Human Resources	Aluminium, Fabrication

Finance, market and resource limitations – human and equipment – are obviously the key problem areas for these companies. In order to provide a more detailed understanding of the skill, structure and leadership issues as they confront each SME in the sample, a descriptive profile of each of the 12 companies was developed. These are presented in Appendix 1.

A summary image profile of the sector as represented by the 12 companies in the study was also developed. This is presented as Chart 1 below, and provides a picture of the state of the SMEs in the sample.

Discussions

This research sought to address three main questions. These were that, to enter, operate and achieve success in the international or regional market place, what

a) Skills and competencies should employees of Ghanaian (SMEs) companies have?
b) Type of leadership is required in terms of vision, strategy and style?
c) Corporate structures are most suited to such efforts in terms of governance and management?

This discussion explores the findings with regards to each of these questions. In this regard it is important to note that this research is essentially exploratory in character. Key to these discussions would be efforts to examine the different SMEs on these dimensions – skills, leadership and structures in terms of their perceived success as SMEs as well as their presence and or intention to enter and succeed in the regional market. To assist in the comparative assessments of the firms, the chart below, which is in essence a pictorial profile of the firms, was developed. It is a useful tool in providing a broad view of the state of the company in question.

The legend for the chart is as follows: *Dark Grey* shades indicate that the firm has difficulties in respect of the variable in question. Such difficulties were significant enough for the respondents to mention them as affecting their operations. *Light Grey* shades show that the firm has the appropriate systems in place or is dealing constructively with the variable. Companies **A, B, L, D, E** appear to have the least by way of difficulties – with a profusion of light grey shades.

Chart 1 Summary of Analyses – Corporate Profiling

Differentiating Parameters	**Companies**											
	A	B	L	D	E	C	G	H	J	K	F	M
i. Perceived Success	√	√	√	√	√	√	√	√	√	√		
ii. Present in Region	√	√	√	√	√	√	√					
iii. 10yrs + in Operation	√	√		√		√		√				√
iv. High human and strategic skills	Light grey	Light grey	Light grey	Light grey	Light grey	Light grey	Light grey	Light grey	Dark grey	Light grey	Dark grey	Dark grey
v. Higher level education	Light grey	Light grey	Light grey	Light grey	Light grey	Light grey	Light grey	Light grey	Light grey	Light grey	Dark grey	Dark grey
vi. Strategic/operational problems	Dark grey	Dark grey	Light grey	Light grey	Light grey	Dark grey	Light grey	Dark grey	Dark grey	Dark grey	Dark grey	Dark grey
vii. Appropriate organisational structure in place	Light grey	Light grey	Light grey	Light grey	Light grey	Light grey	Dark grey	Light grey	Dark grey	Light grey	Dark grey	Light grey
viii. Board and meeting schedules known	Light grey	Light grey	Light grey	Light grey	Light grey	Dark grey	Light grey	Dark grey	Dark grey	Dark grey	Dark grey	Dark grey
ix. Management meets regularly	Light grey	Light grey	Light grey	Light grey	Light grey	Light grey	Light grey	Dark grey	Light grey	Dark grey	Light grey	Light grey
x. Leadership style felt to be appropriate	Light grey	Light grey	Light grey	Light grey	Light grey	Light grey	Light grey	Dark grey	Light grey	Light grey	Dark grey	Dark grey
xi. Vision known, clearly stated and strategic	Light grey	Light grey	Light grey	Light grey	Light grey	Dark grey	Dark grey	Dark grey	Light grey	Dark grey	Dark grey	Dark grey

Key: Light grey – acceptable or successful implementation of the variable in the life of the company.
Dark grey – poor performance, non-existence or problems relating that variable in the life of the company.
√ – the firm in question has registered the variable in its existence.

Presence in, and Intention to Enter the Sub-Regional Market

Seven of the firms studied are represented in the sub-regional market by way of actually doing business beyond the borders of Ghana – 5 of them through the business of exports. Only 2 have subsidiaries or branches in countries other than Ghana. The study did not establish whether these branches were production facilities or sales outlets. This analysis and discussion therefore attempts to examine whether there are appreciable or significantly noticeable differences between those firms that are represented in the market and those, which now seek to enter in terms of the dimensions mentioned above. Four of the companies that, as yet, do not operate beyond the borders of Ghana have intentions to do so.

These companies are in the manufacture of LPG Gas stoves, pharmaceuticals and aluminium products and have targeted Nigeria, Burkina Faso, Togo, Liberia, Benin and other francophone countries. Of those companies already dealing in the sub-region, 4 wish to further expand, as shown in Table 4 above. 5 of the companies, which are operating in the sub-region are over 30yrs old in business; 2 are over 7yrs old in business. 3 of the companies not operating in the sub-region are less than 5 years in business. It would appear therefore that on the face of it, sub-regional involvement *seems to be more likely the older a company is*. There are all sorts of possible influencing variables in this regard: greater market confidence, capacity, better finances, improved production processes from several years of refinements, opportunities to explore and innovate etc. It also seems reasonable to suggest that foreign involvement in ownership seems to facilitate regional business operations. This is based on the finding that of the 7 companies in the sub-region, 4 have foreign ownership involvement (part/full ownership). Of the 3 local firms 2 were previously part owned by foreign interests.

Measures of Perceived Business Success

Over 6 of the SME sample had been in existence for over 5 years. Five of the companies are owned by non-Ghanaian investors from the UK, Denmark, France, Germany and the UK. The study did not examine actual performance indices such as sales and volumes; however, 10 of the companies declared that they felt themselves rather successful based on longevity, sustained expansion, product quality and market awareness, steady growth rates and nationwide demand for products. The 2 companies which did not consider themselves to be successful indicated that this was due to poor technical capacity and performance in one case and in the other case, human resource problems which led to the take-over of a major product line by the parent company, thus reducing their profits and operations.

Skills and Competencies Requisite for Success in the Regional/International

Market

The companies, which consider themselves to be successful **(A, B, C, D, E, G, H, L);** those operating in the regional market place **(A, B, C, D);** and those with the longest (over 10) years of operation, **(A, B, C, D, L, H)** describe a set of skills which seem highly relevant. These can be clustered under 4 broad categories as follows: human skills, (26% mention); professional skills, (42% mention); technical skills, (26% mention); academic capacity, (6% mention). By far the greatest weight is placed on professional skills. These are described to include the following: time management, team skills, strategic planning, marketing skills, leadership and managerial, maintenance of quality, seizing the market, business understanding, sales and interpersonal and communication skills. In terms of import, technical skills are described as production, quality control, information technology and analytical skills. Human skills are described to include: honesty, dedication, hard work, discipline, open mindedness and commitment. These two: technical and human skills are next after professional skills. By far the least weight is placed on academic capacity. This refers to educational qualifications and time spent at school. This receives confirmation in that the data in Table 9 shows that of the 'successful' companies only **A, B, D** and **G** have management with a full spread of educational qualifications for 4 or more top positions. This obviously does not necessarily negate the import of education as a variable. What it suggests is the need to move beyond mere possession of qualifications to acquiring and using a range of professional skills in the process of SME management and leadership.

The companies that are doing well mention training, which is carried out (for them) in some instances by British experts; possession of IT skills, professionalism and dedication to quality. Those companies that do not seem to be doing well (**F, M**,) seem unable to harness their human skills (technical, professional, human, academic). They state that their employees are not well skilled, or it appears their management who in some instances have requisite educational qualifications have not been able to tackle the business issues in operating an SME.

The picture which begins to emerge from the data on skills suggests that those firms operating in the sub-region tend to have foreign involvement in their ownership and appear to have an appropriate set of skills and a certain level of educational calibre in place. 4 of these companies have also been in existence for 10 years or more. The mix of these factors offer some confirmation to the views of a number of writers such as Harzing (1995) who indicate the importance of skills in determining the movement of FDI to less developed areas. It would appear that the experience and capacity of the foreign ownership involvement, combined with skills of local employees enhances the possibility of greater internationalisation of SME operations. It may appear that foreign involvement facilitates transfer or complementary possession of the requisite skills set.

Leadership

Nine of the SMEs report a participatory and or other appropriate approach to leadership. The significant issue here with regards to the questions posed by this research relate to the empirical finding that the 2 companies which report themselves as not successful and having problems (**F, M**) are also the ones with difficulties in terms of leadership vision and capacity. It is also interesting to note that none of the companies operating in the sub-region point to any leadership problems. Two however report problems with the extent to which the vision of the leaders are articulated and shared by the employees. That the participatory approach is dominant with 5 of the companies and also that those operating in the sub-region do not indicate any leadership problems as well as the suggestion that for the 'successful' companies their leaders' visions point to progressive growth, profit, doubling of the business etc, confirm the position of various writers (Chell, 1999; Moran, 1999 and others) about the entrepreneurial personality, the growth orientation and its impact on SMEs. The point being that appropriate leadership has a facilitatory impact on business growth. This dimension however, cannot be considered in isolation.

Six of the SMEs studied have weekly management meetings for review and decision-making, 3 meet monthly. Interestingly, the 2 companies reporting severe difficulties report regular managerial meetings. All the companies in the sub-regional market also report regular meetings. Meetings are obviously a forum for managerial discussion and decision-making. The findings suggest that the successful companies as well as those in the regional market make use of this process. That the companies having difficulties also report regular meetings may suggest two things: firstly that meetings per-se would not guarantee corporate success and secondly, perhaps in times of uncertainty and difficulty, the regularity of managerial meetings increase – in the effort to deal with the situation.

Structure and Governance

The picture here is rather indeterminate. Of the 10 firms, which see themselves as successful and the 7 in the subregion, 4 and 1 respectively do not have functioning board oversight. Clearly however, the companies having difficulties do not report any such oversight. Much has been written about the role of boards in ensuring soundness in managerial processes and function execution. There is no real difference between the firms that have international connections and the wholly Ghanaian owned ones in the matter of board oversight. Only 2 foreign owned firms have boards, which meet regularly. Of the 6 firms with over 10 years of business longevity, only 3 have functioning boards.

The skeletal framework of an organisation – as represented by its structure – is considered crucial to efficiency and effectiveness (Symon, 2000). The findings here confirm the anecdotal evidence that many SMEs are rather rudimentary in their structural frame, either by design or by default. The entire sample was from the manufacturing sector. This is a sector driven by production, marking of products and financial management of receipts. These serve as the expected core functional departments requisite for a manufacturing concern. Obviously size and age/stage of growth would serve as mediating variables. However, we found that only 6 had the core functional departments of production, marketing, and finance. Interestingly, all these 6 perceived themselves as successful and 5 of them were all operating regionally. Furthermore, companies **A, D, B, and H**, which possessed advanced structures all considered themselves successful and were all operating regionally, apart from **H.** An advanced structure (for a manufacturing firm) is one, which possesses the core or expected functional departments as well as additional support or assurance functions such as quality control, human resource, internal audit and customer care. Five of the companies, which possessed appropriate structures all, had over 10 years of operational life.

Conclusions

The Synergy of the Skills-Structure-Leadership Framework

This research is exploratory. It is therefore in order to attempt to tease out as much by way of possibilities and linkages in the variables studied and the data obtained and to ask what can be learned about skills, leadership and structure as important variables in the SME regionalization and internationalisation process?

Moving from Simple Structure to Complex Operations – the Skills Link

A close look at the chart above shows that there appear to be real interactions between the three variables:
skills-leadership-structure and the demographic characteristics of the firms such as regional presence and longevity. Many writers discussing strategy of multinational firms as well as their structures stress the importance of internal skills, a learning orientation and the attitude of top management as very critical to the transitional phases of the multinational organisation's growth. The same argument could be extended to SMEs in West Africa and their attempts to internationalise.

The first generation explanation of an organisation's growth necessarily takes place in the basic structural form as identified by Mintzberg (1990) in his example of the old Chinese pottery shop: owner (Apex) and pottery hands (Operating Core). The coordinating mechanism appropriate for this form is, obviously, mutual adjustment. However, with time (longevity, as found by this research is a key variable) the SME acquires the necessary capacity in the form of an appropriate managerial, administrative, technical and market heritage, which can be used to create wider opportunities for itself. This move invariably, cannot be achieved without moderate to major changes in structure and associated coordinating mechanisms. The question is how is structure retrofitted to support more complex or more demanding operations? And how are coordinating mechanisms metamorphosed and transformed to facilitate effective and efficient structural functioning? Paauwe and Dewe (1995) suggest that 'organisations go through a learning process as they move towards becoming international.' (pp: 66). This is perhaps the key: learning. skills. human capacities - appropriately deployed.

The skills and capacities of the sample divide along the following lines: those with regional operations **(A, B, C, D, E, G, L)** who do not report skill deficiencies and those without regional operations **(F, M, H, J, K)** from amongst which **M, J, F** report severe skills deficiencies in the technical, professional and strategic domains.

Another dividing line can also be drawn in terms of those with foreign ownership/involvement **(A, B, C, E, H, J)** and those without **(D, F, G, K, L, M).** Among those with foreign involvements, **A, B, C, D** and E stress that their staff are well skilled, they point to skill transfer as a key element in their growth, they suggest that strategic, market oriented and technical skills are critical to their success. These perhaps confirm a point. Firstly, that, international operations require serious investments in skills and secondly, that perhaps interactions with overseas players facilitates skill transfer or skill acquisition.

There are obviously a number of interaction dynamics in the alliances between partners, firms and resources originating from different countries and cultures, which must be taken into account when assessing the usefulness of such alliances (Kumar & Nti, forthcoming). That, however, falls outside the scope of this paper.

Those companies with the requisite skill mix seem better poised to 'reap' the benefits of regional operations. They seem better able in capacity and structure to engage the regional market. Such engagement can only take place if the people who operate the company have the requisite skills to manage various components of the structure (e.g. finance, production) as well as have the capacity to coordinate complex or demanding operations and processes (strategy, linkage, marketing and sales activities, dealing with regional regulatory agencies etc). Skills create (or enable) structures and once created, structures host skill deployment. How and where does leadership come into the equation?

The Facilitatory Role of Leadership: Creating Skill-based Regional Opportunities while Securing the Centre through Structural Dynamism

Peters and Waterman, (1984), present a theme for corporate leadership which is picked up by Puplampu (2003). The essence of the arguments advanced by both sets of writers is that organisations, be they MNCs or SMEs, local or international, can only do as well, grow as far and achieve as much as their leaders and leadership processes allow them to. Of the 8 variables set out in Chart 1 against which the companies were profiled, 3 dealt with leadership (directly or indirectly): governance/board oversight; leadership style and vision/strategy. It is the leadership of the organisation, which will craft a strategy and policy framework, which will enable employees to effect the goals and aspirations of the firm. It is the behaviour of leaders and their willingness to use appropriate structures, which will hold the organisation together through its learning cycles.

Leadership is in essence a facilitator. The list of skills the companies sampled include business growth skills such as commitment, hard-work and entrepreneurial acumen. These are skills, which in large measure are not transferred or acquired from the formal educational system, but rather from the energising capacities of business leaders who draw their employees along. It is therefore significant that the 'successful' firms suggest that participatory leadership has been a significant enabling tool.

The West African Context

West Africa is a region with immense possibilities and potential. It is however, also a region beset with numerous problems typical of any developing area. Political leaders of the 15 key states in the region have since 1975, through the Economic Community of West African States (ECOWAS), sought to facilitate regional trade, interaction, business and opportunities. But the schisms between espoused policies and ideals and practical encumbrances have meant that despite many trade and integration protocols discussed and signed by political leaders and bureaucrats alike, regional trade is still very difficult: road blocks, customs barriers and stultifying formalities, informational bottlenecks etc all make regionalization of business rather difficult. The potential, however, exists, as can be attested to by the success of the only purely African owned regional financial house: the Ecobank Group, which in the last 12 years has grown tremendously and has become a major provider of financial services to businesses across the region, disregarding the traditional francophone and Anglophone divide with possibilities in even the Lusophone (Portuguese) countries.

The growth of this Bank, regional setbacks notwithstanding, is testimony to strong leadership (which is presently symbolised in the leadership of Dr. Jean Aka, the Ghanaian Executive Chairman of the Group); appropriate structural arrangements – it has banking operations in each of the 15 ECOWAS member states structured in such a way as to maximise national autonomy, while maintaining a strong regional overarching coordination and high skill levels – the staff of the Ecobank Ghana, as an example, are some of the most able, forward thinking and skilled professionals in the region. Interestingly, and significantly, all these have been achieved without the involvement of Western business concerns, suggesting that it is possible for West African firms to regionalize and internationalise on their own, if the appropriate frameworks are put in place by these firms.

The Overall Picture: The Skills-Structure-Leadership Model

The questions, which guided this research sought to make the case that possession of the appropriate skills, leadership and structure would have an enabling impact on SME functions. It was also implicitly suggested that these variables point to the internal resource arrangements and requirements for effective regional involvement and internationalisation. Much as this was an exploratory study, the findings appear to confirm the importance of the three variables in SME operations. A pictorial overview of the Corporate Profile Chart (chart 1 above) shows that the section of the chart occupied by the strong companies (**A-E**) has far fewer dark grey shades. The dark grey shades indicate problem areas, lapses and gaps in the functioning of the organisation being profiled. The picture suggests that in interaction, these three variables: leadership, skills and structure do contribute to or differentiate towards an enhanced and healthy state of corporate life (Puplampu, 2003). Further research is needed to quantify the correlations, determine the significance of these interactive effects and determine the applicability of these considerations to other SME sectors outside of manufacturing.

From the literature on internationalisation briefly reviewed earlier, it seems quite clear that the theoretical frames lend credence to the three-concept approach of this study as follows: the action approaches strongly suggest *structuring and configurations* (although their focus is on action models speak of networks outside of the firm), in this instance we speak of in-firm structural configurations which allow for responsive interaction. The contingency models, as well as the simultaneous approaches suggest strategy, which is in many instances a matter of *leadership*. The stages models point to cumulative learning, which builds *skills and capacity*.

How do these 3 variables come together and interplay? We now suggest a model, which is based on the literature on entrepreneurial growth, internationalisation as well as the findings of this research.

Figure 1: The Leadership, Skills and Structure Model of Internationalisation in the Developing World

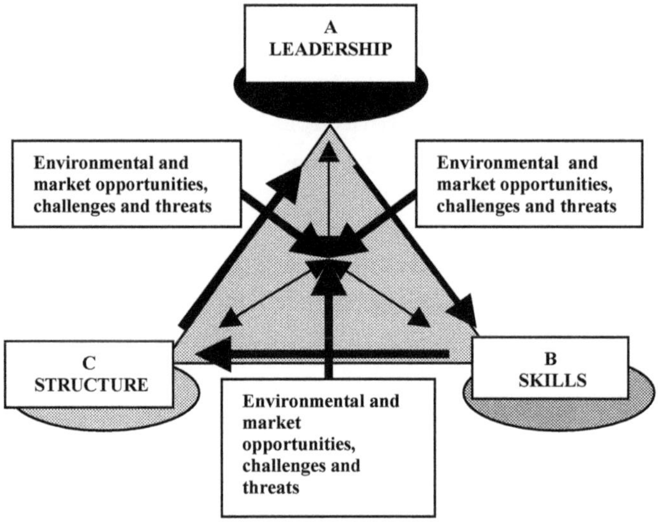

A. Leadership is the initial point of the model. It is composed essentially of entrepreneurial and strategic leadership, which requires an entrepreneur to recognise an opportunity and pursue it domestically. This leadership creates or 'takes advantage' of opportunities. In taking advantage of opportunities it builds skills, which impact task execution.

B. Skills is the dimension, which buttresses or supports the strategy, vision and push of the leader/entrepreneur. This refers to the skills of employees as well as that of the leader. The skills dimension presupposes the dynamism of a learning organisation. The skills developed become the means by which the organisation as a whole can leverage its vision/strategy within its environment/sector under its leadership. Leadership can become severely compromised where its drive is not matched or responded to by the capacity and ability of implementers (employees). Developing or grafted skills enable a relevant structure to be put in place.

C. Structure is the third and final arm of this model. The structure is a response to market demands, which requires certain internal configurations of position, authority, decision-making and functional capacity. The move towards a structural form which is adequately aligned to and with market demands, opportunities and challenges is without a doubt closely tied to the type of leadership and the level of learning/knowledge acquisition and management that the organisation has been able to acquire. In other words, structure cannot be implemented without the say-so of management, which sees its need, and, appropriateness of structure cannot be realised without the skill set, which identifies what structural components are needed and how to implement and internationalise them to good use.

While not suggesting that the more elaborate a structure, the better, it can be seen that the organisations sampled in this study divide clearly along two structural lines **A, B, L, D, E, C, G** seem to have structures which detail functionally relevant components. The rest of the organisations seem to have rather rudimentary structural forms. The concept 'structure' here, subsumes within it the coordinating mechanisms which represent the software by which the structure works.

This model therefore incorporates stages, actions and contingencies. Critical to all these is a responsiveness and reflexivity, which drives or propels the emerging organisation into a particular type of international activity which satisfies the needs and aspirations of both the market as well as organisational principals/stakeholders/owners. In sum, the internationalisation of the SME, seems to depend on having leaders who recognise the regional/international opportunities and strategise towards that. It also depends on possession of skills (whether by transfer, acquisition, association or interaction), which support the strategy, and the development of appropriate organisational structures, which allow a constructive engagement with the market.

It seems that the deployment of the leadership-skills-structure mix may be sequential, staged, simultaneous (or perhaps even ad hoc!), whichever approach the deployment takes, the interplay must create a synergy which enables the SME to enter and stay in the international domain.

References

Afrocentric Alliance (Suart Carr & Co) (1998): Groups at work in East and Central Africa. In Perspectives in Malawian Psychology- A Reader for Students. MacLachlan M. & Carr, S. Eds. Zikomo Press. Zomba.

Ambrose, D. (1996): *Healing the Downsized Organisation (NY,* Three Rivers Press).

Amit, R. & Schoemaker, P.J. (1993): "Strategic Assets and Organisational Rent" in *Strategic Management Journal,* 14, 33-46.

Aryeetey Ernest et al, (1994): "Supply and Demand for Finance of Small Enterprises in Ghana". Discussion Paper No. 251. Technical Department, Africa Region. Washington, D.C.: World Bank.

Adedeji, A. (1981): Indegenization of African Economies (New York, Africana)

Agamah, G.K (1985): "New Directions in Economic Policy for Ghana". *The Journal of Management Studies*

Amin, S. (1973): *Neo-Colonialism in West Africa* (New York, Monthly Review Press).

Aryeetey E, Baah-Nuakoh A, Duggleby T, Hettige H & Steel W.F (1994): 'Supply and Demand for Finance of Small Scale Enterprises in Ghana', *World Bank Discussion Paper No. 251.*

Aryeetey E, Hettige H, Nissanke M & Steel W (1997): 'Financial Market Fragmentation and Reforms in Ghana, Malawi, Nigeria, & Tanzania', *The World Bank Economic Review*, Vol. 11 No. 2 PP 195-218.

Brigewater, S. (1971): "The Internationalisation Process and Types of Firms" in **Bolton J.E (1971)**: *Report of The Committee of Inquiry on Small Firms (London,* HMSO)

Buame, S (2000): "Managing Small and Medium Enterprises" (Unpublished Working paper, SOA UG.)

Buame K.S (1996): *Entrepreneurship: a Contextual Perspective* (Lund, Lund University Press).

Buame, S (2000): "Managing Small and Medium Enterprises" ((Unpublished Working paper, SOA UG.)

Buame K.S (1996): *Entrepreneurship: a Contextual Perspective* (Lund, Lund University Press).

Bartram, D. (1995): "The recruitment and selection of young people by small businesses" in *Journal of Occupational and Organisational Psychology*, 68, 339-358.

Blackler, F. & Shimmin, S. (1984): *Applying Psychology in Organisations* (London, Methuen).

Bresnen, M. & Fowler, C. (1996): "Professionalisation and British Management Practice: Case Evidence from Medium-sized Firms in Two Industrial Sectors" in *Journal of Management Studies*, 33, 2, 159-182.

Chapman, M. (1998): "Small firms: Overlooked or Misunderstood? Reflections on an emerging field in work/organisational psychology" in *The Occupational Psychologist*, 34, 44-47.

Chell, E. (1999): "The Entrepreneurial Personality – Past, Present and Future" in *The Occupational Psychologist*, 38, 5-12.

Cook, C. & Hunsaker, P. (2001): *Management and Organisational Behaviour* (Boston, McGrawHill).

Daniels, L and Ngwira A. (1993): "Results of a Nation-wide Survey on Micro, Small and Medium Enterprises in Malawi", *GEMINI Technical Report No 53.* (New York, PACT Publications).

Dawson J (1990): "The Wider Context: The Importance of The Macroenvironment for
Small Enterprise Development", *Small Enterprise Development,* Vol 1 No. 3

Dawson J (1992): 'The Relevance of The Flexible Specialisation Paradigm for Small Scale Industrial Restructuring in Ghana', *IDS Bulletin* Vol. 23 No.3.

Dordunoo C.K (1994): 'The Foreign Exchange Market and The Dutch Auction System in Ghana', *AERC Research Paper* No. 24.

Dummet, R.E (1983): "African Merchants of the Gold Coast: 1860-1905" in *Comparative Studies in Society and History.* Vol. 25 (4): 661-693

Forstater, M., MacDonald, J. & Raynard, P. (2002): "Business and Poverty: Bridging the Gap" in *Folium* (London, The Prince of Wales International Business Leaders Forum).

Hatch, M.J. (1997): *Organisation Theory (Oxford,* University Press)

Hartog, D., Van Muijen, J. & Koopman, P. (1997): "Transactional vs transformational Leadership: An Analysis of the MLQ" in the *Journal of Occupational and Organisational Psychology,* 70, 1, 19-34.

Hall, R. (1993): "A framework for linking intangible resources and capabilities to sustainable competitive advantage" *Strategic Management Journal,* 14, 607-18.

Fisseha Y & McPherson (1991): "A Country-wide Study of Small Scale Enterprises in Swaziland', *Gemini Technical Report No. 24,* (Washington D.C., Development Alternatives Inc.)

Hand book on Made in Ghana Solo Exhibition in Burkina Faso, August 2002.

Harris, N (1987): *The End of the Third World: Newly Industrialised Countries and the Decline of an Ideology* (London: Penguin).

Hopkins, T. (1973): An Economic History of West Africa. London: Longman.

Kayanula & Quartey D (2000): "The Policy Environment for Promoting Small and Medium-Sized Enterprises in Ghana and Malawi" in *Finance and Development Research Programme* (Paper No 15, University of Manchester).

Komache, K. (1996): "Strategic Human Resource Management within a Resource Capability view of the Firm" in *Journal of Management Studies,* 33, 2, 213-233.

Kuada, J. & Sorensen, O.J. (2000): *Internationalisation of Companies from Developing Countries* (New York, IBP)

Kumar, R. & Nti, K. (2004): "National Cultures and the Evolution of Process and Outcome discrepancies in International Strategic Alliances" *Journal of Applied Behavioural Science.* (Forthcoming).

Leff, N.H (1978): "Industrial Organisations and Entrepreneurship in Developing Countries: The Economic Groups" in *Economic Development And Cultural Change.* Vol. 26:661-675.

Levy B (1993): "Obstacles to Developing Indigenous Small and Medium Enterprises: An Empirical Assessment", *The World Bank Economic Review*, Vol. 7 No. 1 PP 65-83.

Loan-Clarke, J., Boocock, G., Smith, A. & Whittaker, J. (1999): "Management Standards and Management National Vocational Qualifications – Awareness, Attitudes and Activity in Small Businesses" in *The Occupational Psychologist*, 38, 22-27.

Little, J. (2000): *Stress and SMEs* in *The Occupational Psychologist*. 39, 44-47.

McShane, S. & Von Glinow, M. (2000): *Organisational Behaviour* (Boston, McGrawHill)

Moran, P. (1999): "The Growth-Orientation of the Small Business Owner-Manager" in *The Occupational Psychologist*. 38, 13-21.

Milkovich, G. & Boudreau, J. (1997): *Human Resource Management* (Boston, Irwin/McGraw-Hill).

Peters, T. & Waterman, R. (1984): *In Search of Excellence* (NY, Warner Business Books)

Puplampu, B. (2002): Towards a Theory of Work and Citizenship. 25th ICAP 2002 Proceedings. Singapore.

Puplampu, B. (1998): "Of Tea Talk and the Human Condition. An Investigation into the Committee System of Decision Making and Administrative Procedure". *Management Monograph Series* 10 (Accra, Afram Publications).

Puplampu, B. (2003): "Understanding the Distressed Organisation" in *Consulting Psychology Journal* (Forth coming).

Raven, J. (1984): "Competence in Modern Society: Its Identification, Development and Release" H.K. Lewis & Co. London

Raven, J. (1989): "Democracy, Bureaucracy and the Psychologist" in *The Psychologist*, 2, 11, 458-466.

Robertson I, & Smith, M. (2001): "Personnel Selection" in *Journal of Occupational and Organisational Psychology*, 74, 441-472.

Schermerhorn, J., Hunt, J. & Osborn, R. (1994): Managing Organisational Behaviour. 5th Ed. Wiley. New York.

Scott, W. (1992): *Organizations – Rational, Natural and Open Systems* (New Jersey, Prentice Hall).

Storey D.J (1994): *Understanding the Small Business Sector* (London, Routledge)

Stogdill, R. (1971): *Dimensions of Organisation Theory. In Organisational Design and Research* (Pittsburgh, University of Pittsburgh Press).

Symon, G. (2000): "Information and Communication Technologies and the Network Organisation" in *Journal of Occupational and Organisational Psychology*, 73, 4, 389-414.
McDale, B.E (1993): "Characteristics of Small-Scale Enterprises. Entrepreneurship and Determinants of Business_Success Among Africans in a traditional crafts industry in Ghana". PhD Dissertation. University of Texas, Austin.
Mosley P & Hulme D (1998): 'Micro enterprise Finance: Is There a Conflict Between Growth and Poverty Alleviation?' *World Development* Vol. 26 No.5, PP 783-790.
Opoku-Afriyie K.J (1997): 'Promoting Enterprises in The Wood Products Sub sector in Ghana' in *Small Enterprise Development,* Vol. 8 No. 1.
Osei B, Baah-Nuakoh A, Tutu K.A, & Sowa N.K (1993): 'Impact of Structural Adjustment on Small-Scale Enterprises in Ghana', in Helmsing A.H.J and Kolstee T. H (eds): *Structural Adjustment, Financial Policy and Assistance Programmes in Africa,*(Nairobi, IT Publications .
Parker R.L, Riopelle R, Steel W.F (1995): "Small Enterprises Adjusting to Liberalisation in Five African Countries", *World Bank Discussion Paper* No. 271, (African Technical Department Series).
Ray D.N (1991): "Venture Capital and Entrepreneurial Development in Singapore", *International Small Business Journal,* Vol. 10 (1) PP 11-26.
Ray, D.I (1986): *Ghana: Politics, Economics & Society* (London, Frances).
Robson G & Gallagher C (1993): "The Job Creation Effects of Small and Large Firm Interaction", *International Small Business Journal,* Vol. 12 PP 23-37.
Rotchchild, D (1991): *Ghana: The Political Economy of Recovery*: (London, Lynne Reinner Publishers).
Sandbrook, R. (1985): *The Politics of Africa's Economic Stagnation* (Cambridge University Press, UK).
Schmitz Hubert (1982): "Growth Constraints on Small Scale Manufacturing in Developing Countries: A Critical Review." *World Development*. Vol. 10,6:429-450.
Schmitz Hubert (1989): "Flexible Specialisation - A New Paradigm of Small-Scale Industrialisation?" *IDS Discussion Paper* 261
Schmitz Hubert (1991): "Small Shoemakers and Fordist Giants: Tale of a Supercluster", *IDS Discussion Paper* No. 331
Schmitz Hubert (1998): "Fostering Collective Efficiency" in *Small Enterprise Development* Vol. 9 No. 1

Schmitz Hubert (1995): "Collective Efficiency: Growth Path for Small Scale Industry", *The Journal of Development Studies,* Vol. 31 No. 4 PP 529-566.

Steel W.F (1977): *Small Scale Employment and Production in Developing Countries: Evidence from Ghana*, (New York, Praeger)

Steel & Webster L (1990): "Ghana's Small Enterprise Sector: Survey of Adjustment Response & Constraints" in, *Industry Series* Paper 41, (Washington DC., World Bank, Industry and Energy Dept)

Steel & Webster L (1992): "How Small Enterprises in Ghana Have Responded to Adjustment", *The World Bank Economic Review*, 6(3): 423-438.

Storey, D (1994): *Understanding The Small Business Sector,* (London, Routledge).

The Wall Street Journal's (1995) reports on small business: "Avoiding the Pitfalls" (May)

Wynarczyk P, Watson R, Storey D.J, Short H & Keasey K (1993): *The Managerial Labour Market in Small & Medium Sized Enterprises (London,* Routledge)

Company A

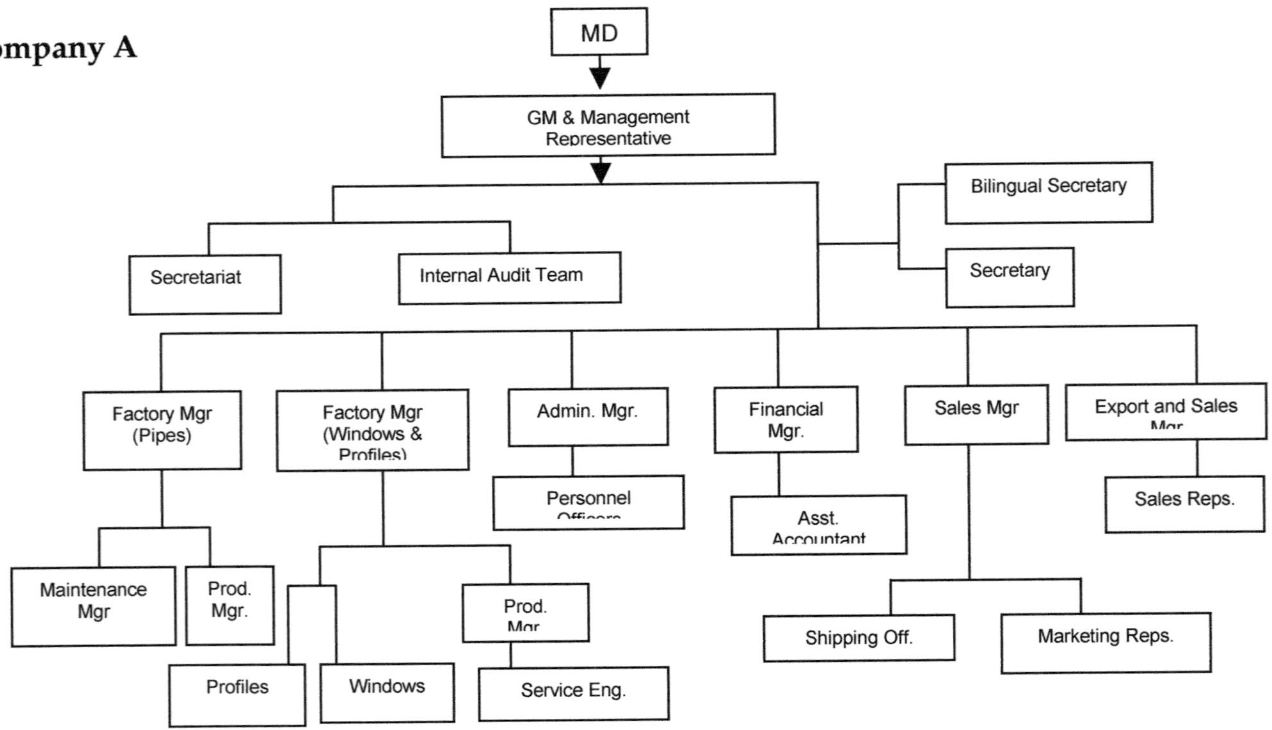
MD
GM & Management Representative
Secretariat
Internal Audit Team
Bilingual Secretary
Secretary
Factory Mgr (Pipes)
Factory Mgr (Windows & Profiles)
Admin. Mgr.
Financial Mgr.
Sales Mgr
Export and Sales Mgr
Personnel Officers
Asst. Accountant
Sales Reps.
Maintenance Mgr
Prod. Mgr.
Prod. Mgr
Shipping Off.
Marketing Reps.
Profiles
Windows
Service Eng.

Company B

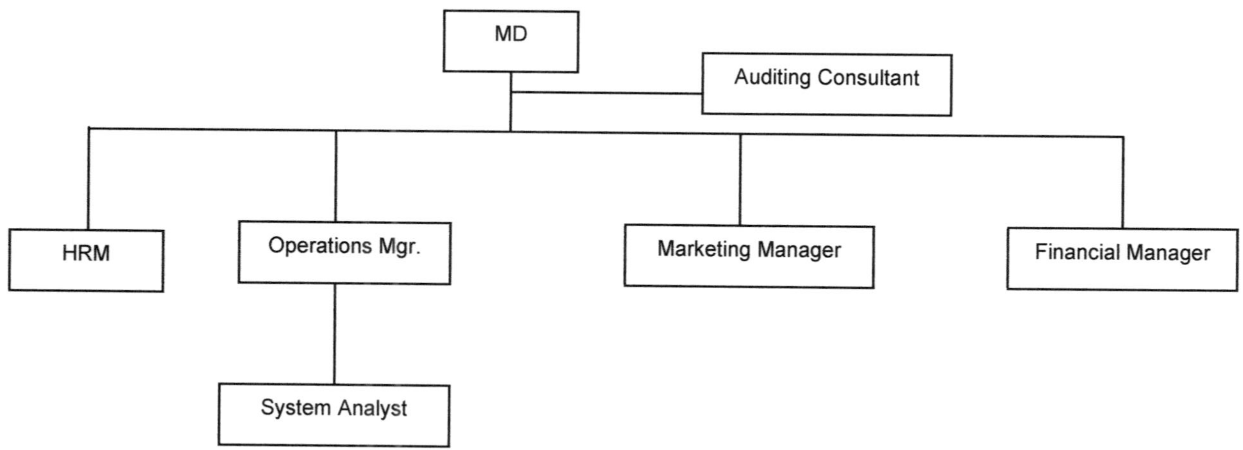
MD
Auditing Consultant
HRM
Operations Mgr.
Marketing Manager
Financial Manager
System Analyst

Company C

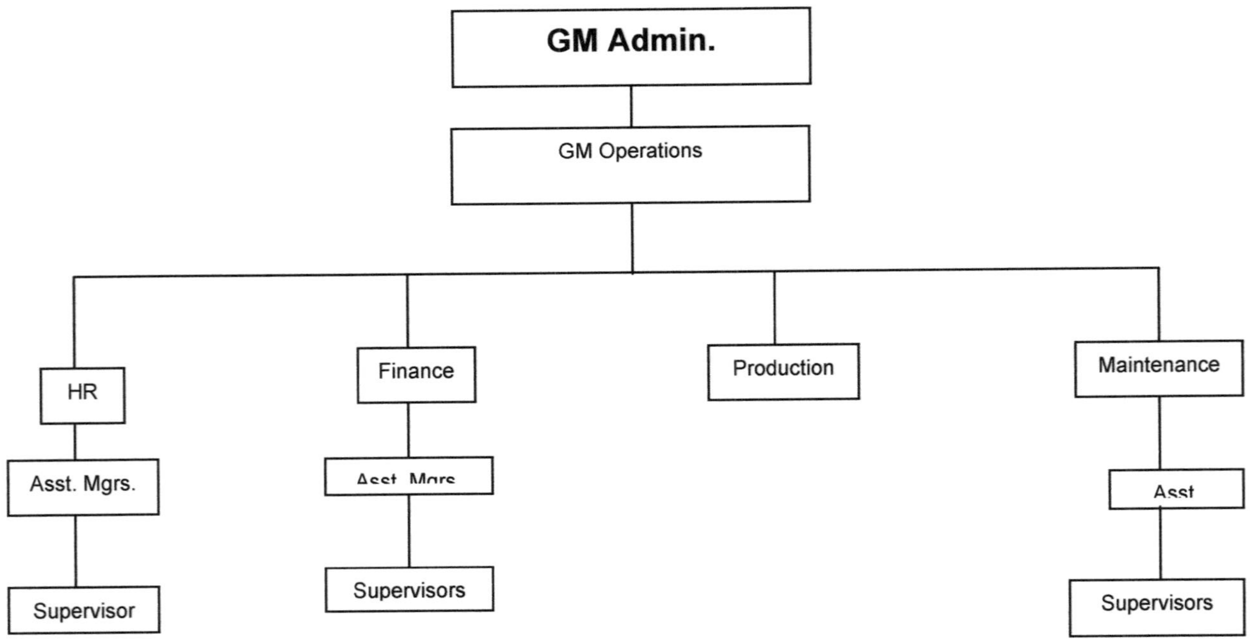
GM Admin.
GM Operations
HR
Asst. Mgrs.
Supervisor
Finance
Asst. Mgrs
Supervisors
Production
Maintenance
Asst
Supervisors

Company D

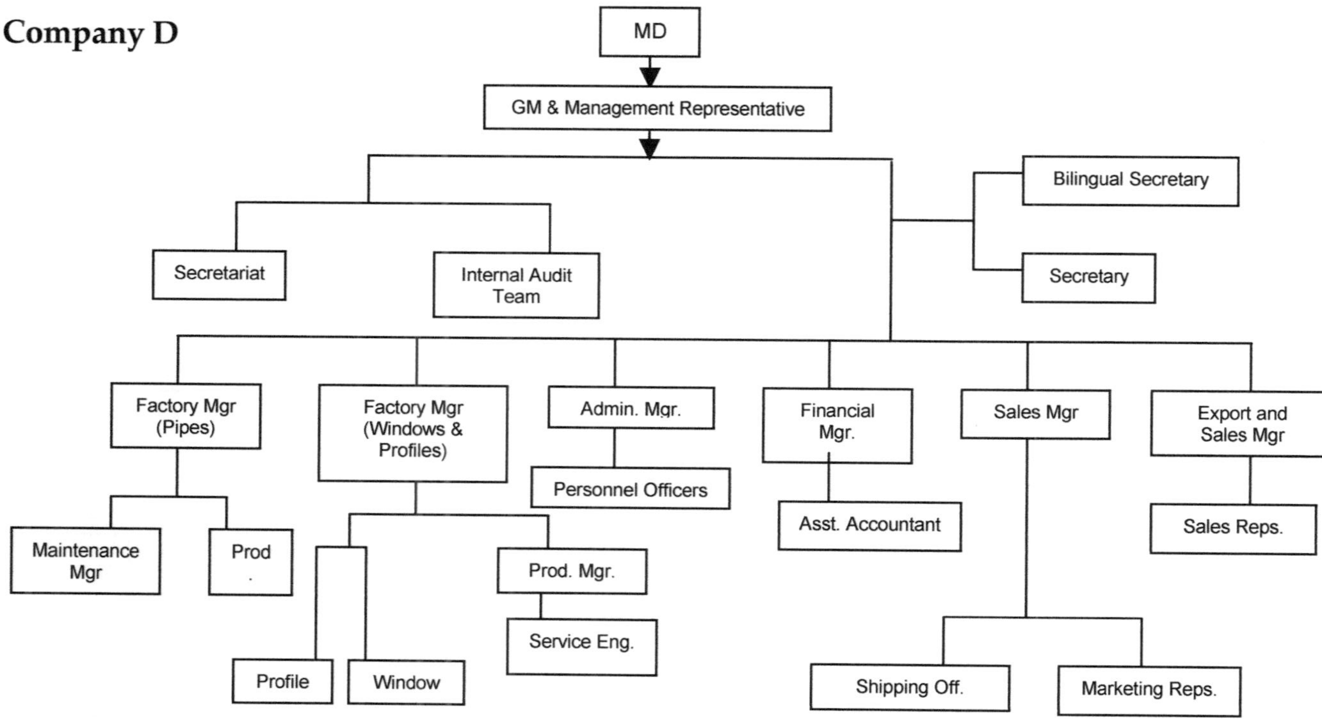
MD
GM & Management Representative
Secretariat
Internal Audit Team
Bilingual Secretary
Secretary
Factory Mgr (Pipes)
Factory Mgr (Windows & Profiles)
Admin. Mgr.
Financial Mgr.
Sales Mgr
Export and Sales Mgr
Maintenance Mgr
Prod
Personnel Officers
Asst. Accountant
Sales Reps.
Prod. Mgr.
Service Eng.
Profile
Window
Shipping Off.
Marketing Reps.

Company E

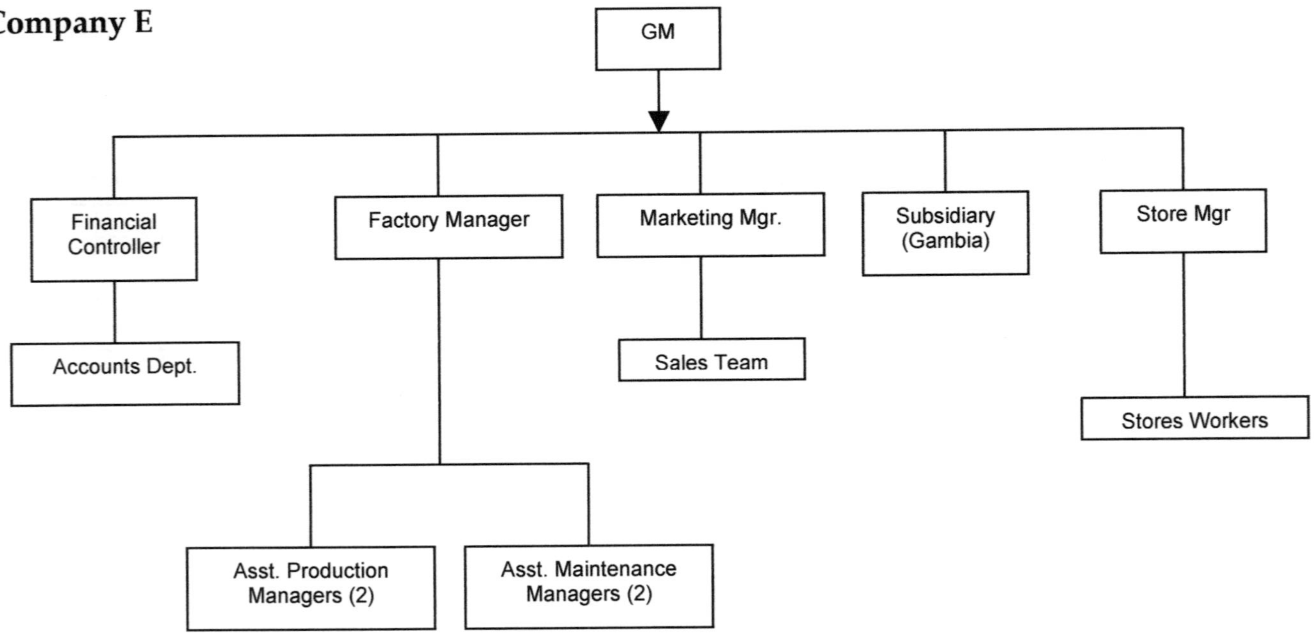
GM
Financial Controller
Factory Manager
Marketing Mgr.
Subsidiary (Gambia)
Store Mgr
Accounts Dept.
Sales Team
Stores Workers
Asst. Production Managers (2)
Asst. Maintenance Managers (2)

Company G

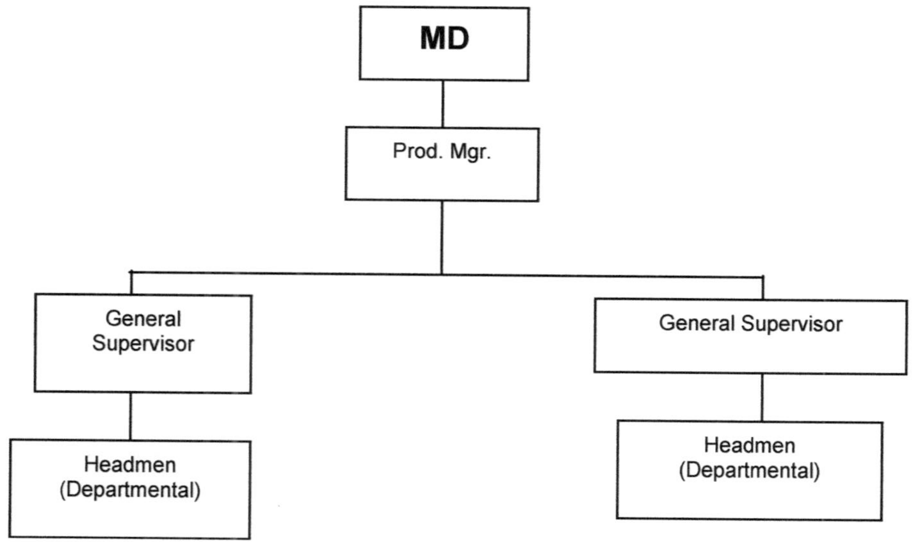
MD
Prod. Mgr.
General Supervisor
Headmen (Departmental)
General Supervisor
Headmen (Departmental)

Company H

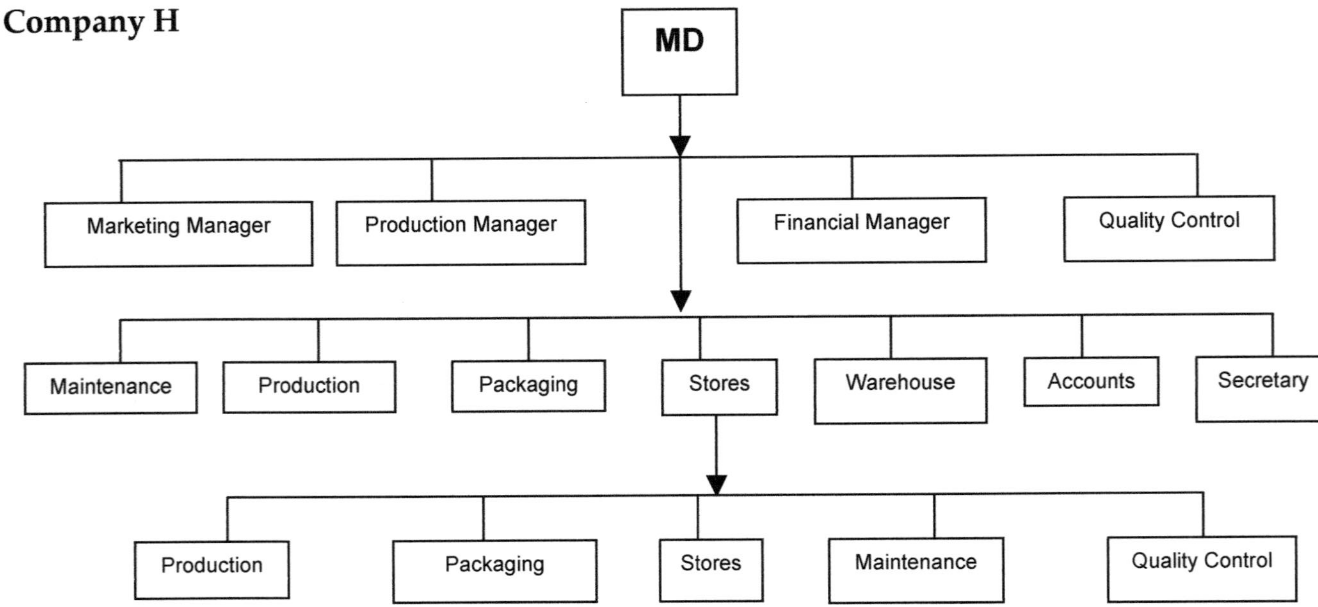
MD
Marketing Manager
Production Manager
Financial Manager
Quality Control
Maintenance
Production
Packaging
Stores
Warehouse
Accounts
Secretary
Production
Packaging
Stores
Maintenance
Quality Control

Company J

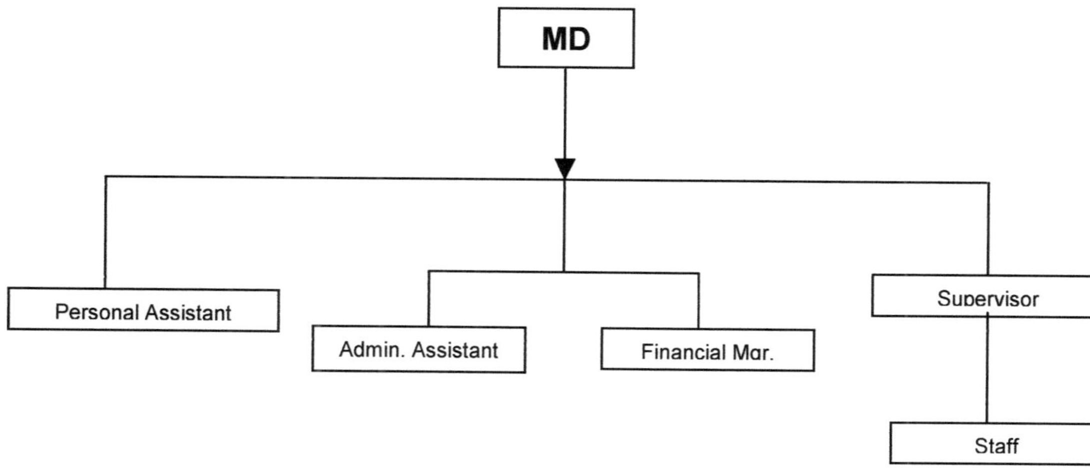
MD
Personal Assistant
Admin. Assistant
Financial Mgr.
Supervisor
Staff

Company K

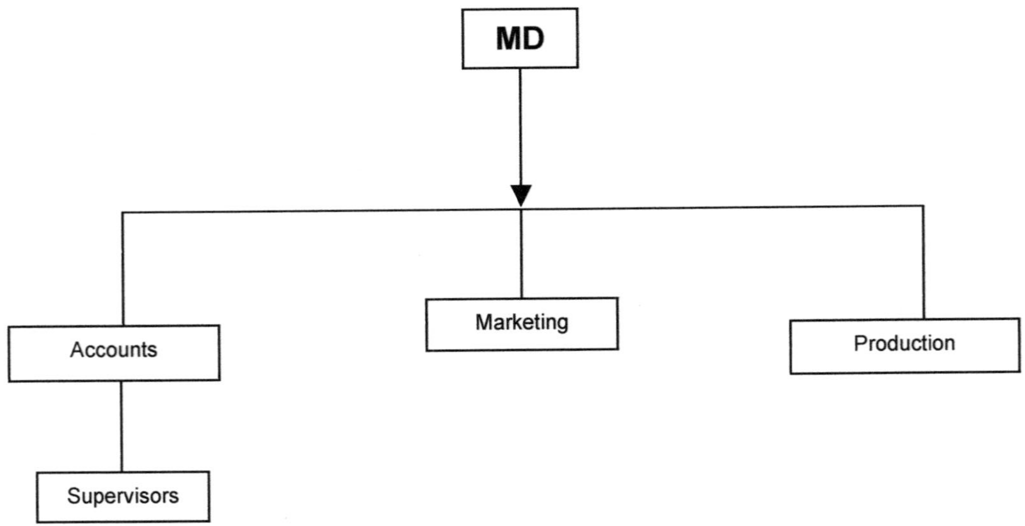

Company L

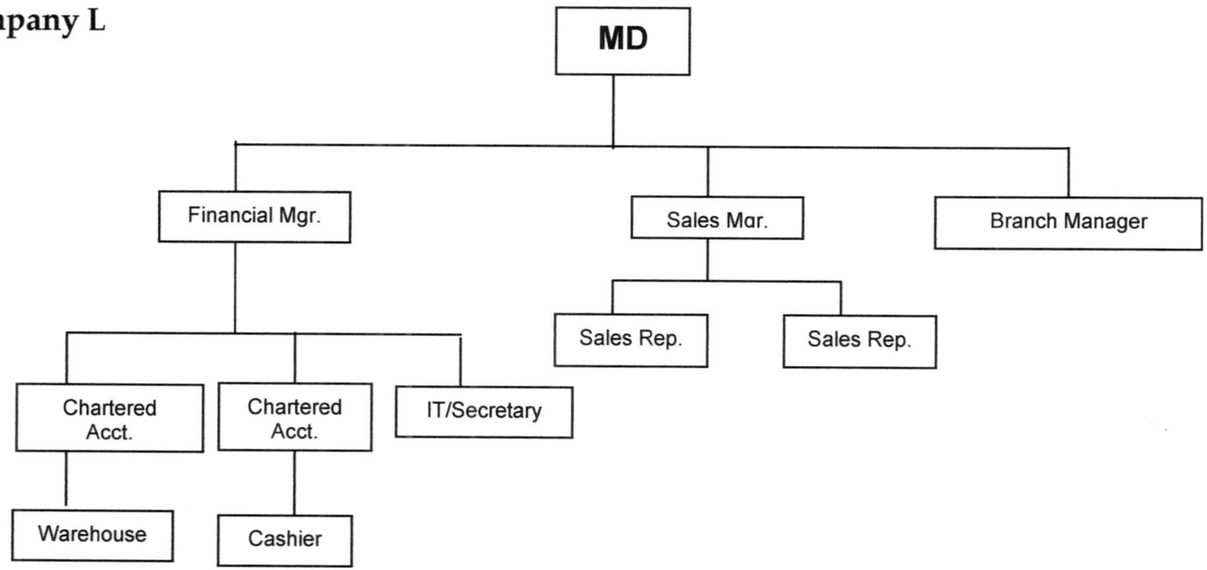
MD
Financial Mgr.
Sales Mgr.
Branch Manager
Chartered Acct.
Chartered Acct.
IT/Secretary
Sales Rep.
Sales Rep.
Warehouse
Cashier

Company M

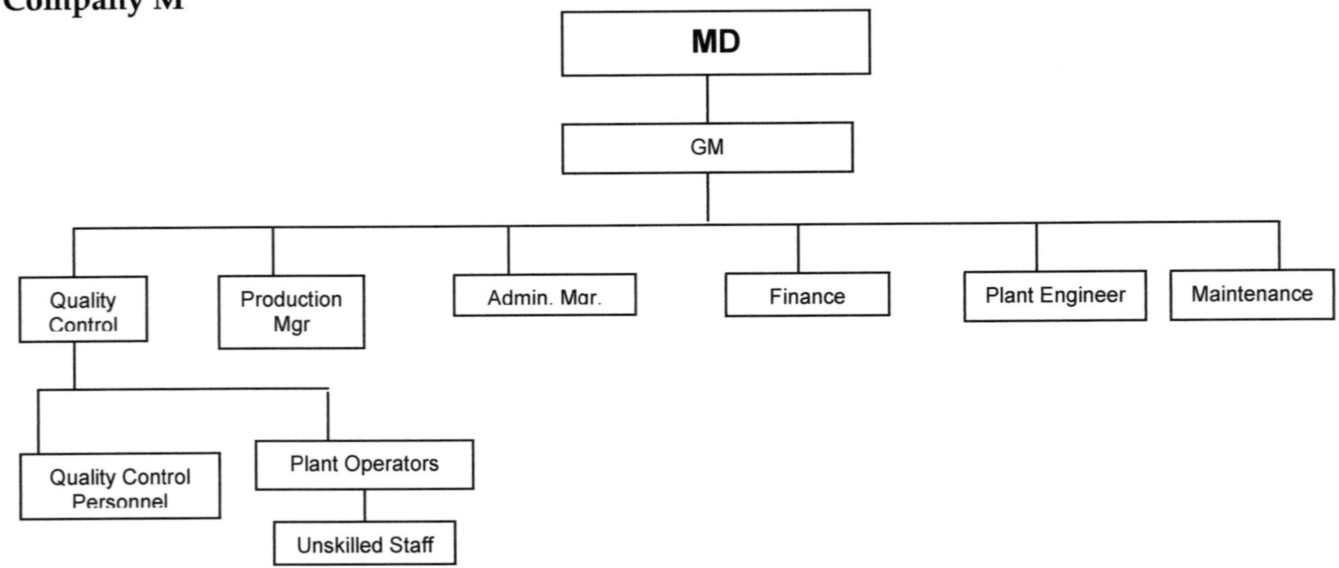
MD
GM
Quality Control
Production Mgr
Admin. Mgr.
Finance
Plant Engineer
Maintenance
Quality Control Personnel
Plant Operators
Unskilled Staff

6

CROSS BORDER INTER-FIRM COLLABORATION: DANISH-GHANAIAN EXPERIENCE

Bedman Narteh

Introduction

International strategic alliances or cross-border inter-firm collaborations have become a major way of organising economic activities. Studies have shown that there has been an exponential growth in their use since the 1980s. Reasons such as market access, access to technology, economies of scale and opportunities for organisational learning have been cited to be responsible for their continued use in the business landscape (Child & Faulkner 1998, Hamel 1991, Killing 1983, Bleeke and Ernst 1993).

Various interpretations have been given to the concept of strategic alliances, but suffice here to say that they are long term co-operation between firms for the purpose of development, manufacture and sale of products and services for their mutual benefit. If the partners are from different countries, the venture is termed an international strategic alliance (ISA). Broadly speaking, ISAs have been grouped into equity and non-equity alliances (Das 2000, Inkpen and Dinur 1998, Mowery et al, 1996). An equity alliance involves equity participation by the partners and is divided into joint ventures and direct investment. Non-equity alliances do not involve equity participation and includes sub-contracting, licensing, R&D collaboration, just to mention a few.

Studies on ISAs have taken various dimensions. Some researchers focus on developed-developed country alliances with particular reference to the triad (Hamel 1991, Inkpen and Crossan 1995, Inkpen and Dinur 1998, Inkpen and Currall 1998, Bleek and Ernst 1993). Mostly these alliances are between competitors in the developed world, which pool their complimentary resources together in order to achieve higher competitive positions within their respective markets. The failed alliance between Volvo and Renault, (Bruner & Spekman, 1998) as well as the much talked about NUMMI alliance between General Motors and Toyota (Mahoney & Deckop, 1993) are examples worth mentioning. Alliances can also occur when firms operating in different sectors realise the synergy in pooling their complimentary resources together. For instance, Siemens and Corning brought their complimentary synergy in telecommunication and glass technology into a joint venture called "Siecor" that provided enormous market power for both partners in their respective markets (Inkpen & Beamish 1997).

A significant feature of developed-developed country alliances is that they provide the platform for learning and exchanging of new skills and technologies. Hamel (1991) described such alliances as "learning alliances" because the focus of the partners is to acquire the skills of the other partner, and therefore the partner who learns faster wins the learning race.

A second group of researchers focus on developed country-transitional economies or country alliances as well as developed-developing country alliances. (Child and Yan, 2003, Child and Marckozcy 1993, Lyles 1988, Lyles and Salk 1996, Lane et al 2001, Kuada 2002). These are alliances that have taken place between the west and transitional economies such as China and Hungary. In such alliances, the local partner is said to provide local knowledge and fixed assets such as land and building while the foreign partner brings in technology, capital and managerial acumen. Unlike the learning alliance this type of alliance provides what Tsang (1999) called asymmetric learning because the partners learn with different objectives. The local partner is interested in learning the skills and technologies of the western partner while the foreign partner learns about the "alliance experience"(Tsang 1999). The alliance experience deals with installing the technology and managing the alliance. Such experience is likely to be transferred into the formation of future alliances (Gulati 1995, Child and Yan 2003).

This paper deals with the second type of alliances, developed-developing country alliances. Developed-developing country alliances face different and unique challenges. There is normally high expectation from the local partner about the capability of the foreign partner to supply modern technology; unlimited cash investment, foreign market opportunities and above all the managerial expertise that would transform the alliance into a viable business venture overnight. The developed country partners, usually from the triad, enters the alliance with a foreign mindset, believing that economic conditions would be stable and transparent, (Lane and Beamish 1990) and partners would keep to their promises made prior to the alliance (Kuada, 2002), but often this is not so. As a result of these perceptual gaps, developed-developing country alliances have been described as unstable (Inkpen and Beamish 1997). They offer asymmetric learning opportunities (Tsang, 1999), and are affected by wide cultural gaps between the partners (Lyles and Salk 1999, Kuada 2002). They perform better only when there is a shared management control (Beamish 1988 and 1993, Child and Yan 2003).

In spite of the fact that alliances between developed countries and Africa in general and Ghana in particular have received interest from scholars in recent years (Kuada and Sorensen 2000, Boateng and Glaister, 2002, Kuada 2002) the area still remains under researched. For instance, little has been done to explore the learning potentials of these alliances and how the knowledge gained is managed to the benefit of the participating firms. The purpose of this paper is to contribute to this knowledge gap using Ghana as a case study. The study draws on the experience of Danish-Ghanaian alliances promoted and supported by Danida under its private sector development programme (PSD). The study reports on the perceptions of the Ghanaian partners on pre as well post alliance outcomes. Perceptual data has been used in previous studies to understand alliance dynamics (Child and Yan 2003, Kuada 2002).

The rest of the paper is divided into three parts; the first part deals with the methodology for the data collection. The second part deals with the findings of the perception of the Ghanaian partners on some key alliance issues, such as the role of the catalyst, performance of the alliance, and their perception of the Danish partners' contribution to the alliance. The last part deals with the managerial implications of these alliances.

Methodology

The method of data collection was field interviews conducted in Ghana in 2001. The interviews were conducted with top management, such as CEOs and general managers of the alliances. Senior managers are well placed to provide information on key issues about alliances and have been used consistently in the literature (Child and Yan 2003, Inkpen and Dinur 1998, Lane and Lubatkin 1998, Geringer and Hebert 1991). In all, five equity alliances were interviewed out of the list of ten provided to me from the PSD office. The five agreed to grant interviews within the limited time available. The remaining five were not ready or failed to honour the appointment dates. Equity alliances have received wide research attention in the literature in the context of developed-developing or transitional economies (Lyles and Salk 1996, Lyles 1988, Lane et al, 2001).

The interviews were conducted in the offices of the managers and therefore afforded the researcher the opportunities to visit the plant sites and inspect some of the new products that were manufactured after the alliances were formed. In one particular case, the new products were displayed with the old products in a show room directly at the entrance of the factory.

In one interview, a panel consisting of the CEO who also doubles as the Ghanaian partner, the general manager and the financial controller were interviewed together. This gave us the opportunity to obtain information from multiple respondents at the same time.

The alliances in question were brokered through the Danida Private Sector Development programme[1]. Therefore, to understand the rationale and dynamics of the programme, we also interviewed the co-ordinator of the PSD programme for Ghana in his office. All the interviews lasted between two and three hours with the interview scripts written within 24 hours after the date of the interview.

Limitations of the Study

The study is based on the perception of the Ghanaian partners or general managers' perception of the alliances. One can therefore not rule out the problems of perceptual biases. This I tried to minimise by interviewing the co-ordinator for the PSD programme for Ghana so as to obtain multiple data source to help cross check for accuracy where necessary. The study also failed to obtain the perception of the Danish partners on the alliances. Future research must also consider the other side of the coin by obtaining information from the Danish partners as well.

Moreover, the study also relied on the personal interview as a method of data collection. Such qualitative studies, though useful in obtaining deep insight about a phenomenon, cannot form good basis for generalisation.

The characteristics of the alliances under the study are given in the Table below.

Table 1: Profile of Firms

Characteristics	No. of Cases
Sectors	
Manufacturing	3
Wood treatment and processing	1
Solar Energy	1
Ownership: Ghanaian Partner's Share	
29% and below	1
30 – 39 %	3
40 - 49%	1
Operational History	
7 years	2
5 years	1
4 years	1
2 years	1

The firms were selected from different sectors, three within the manufacturing sector, and one each from solar energy and wood treatment and processing sectors. The Ghanaian partners took minority equity positions in all the alliances, ranging between twenty-four and forty per cent. However, in three of the alliances, they had sub-clauses in the contracts that allowed them to renegotiate and buy more shares from their Danish counterparts. The alliances were relatively young, with an average age of five years, and relatively small in size, employing an average of forty-five employees.

The data analysis was done to reflect some of the main themes within the ISA literature. Themes that relate to motivation, culture, organisational learning, alliance performance and the role of the catalyst were carefully noted because they form the conceptual bases for exploring the perception of the Ghanaian partners in the alliances.

Motivation

Motivation deals with the reasons why the firms entered into the alliances. The following motivation has been found; economies of scale, access to new market, technology and raw materials, competitive advantage, learning from partners' technological and managerial skills (Mowery at al 1996, Zinn and Parasuraman 1997, Beamish 1987, Hamel 1991, Inkpen and Crossan 1995). The assumption is that if firms have well defined motives, they will see the alliances as "strategic", as it will help them in achieving their stated objectives. On the other hand, lack of clearer objectives will imply that the partners entered into the alliances without a clear plan and therefore it may not be strategic to them. The interview indicated that the Ghanaian partners entered into these partnerships with clearly defined motives, since they were mostly responsible for initiating the alliances. Kuada (2002) corroborated this in a study of different sets of these alliances. Clearly, the Ghanaian partners entered into these alliances with three motives, to get access to finance, technology and managerial capability. These, they believed, would improve the competitiveness of their firms.

Partner Selection

ISAs bring partners from different countries and cultures into a working relationship. The choice of the right partner is important as it can yield competitive advantage while failure to land the right partner can lead to many operational problems (Ducin and Hitt 1977). Partner selection in ISA has also been seen as a critical issue because the partner selected influences the mix of resources that is available to the partnership (Glaister and Buckley 1996, Killing 1983, Harrigan 1988, Bo 2003). The literature has identified factors such as strategic fit as well as cultural fit, (Lorange and Roos 1988), strategic compatibility (Doz and Hamel 1998) personal chemistry, Kuada (2002), identical firm size, and complimentarity of resources (Harrigan

1998, Das 2000) as some of the factors influencing partner selection in alliances.

The Ghanaian partners mentioned criteria such as personal chemistry, resource position, and firm size as some of the factors they considered in selecting their Danish counterparts. Personal chemistry appeared significant because most of the firms prior to the alliance were privately owned and managed by the owners and therefore the personality of the owner would be crucial to the success of the alliance. As a result, they would want similar firms that go through similar decision-making process. They also believe that when the partner owns the firm, personal relationships can easily be developed since the key figures of the alliance would naturally be involved in the discussions. It is also assumed that there will be high commitment on their part and to work at all times in the interest of the alliance. One Ghanaian CEO of a 40-60 equity alliance, who took over from his ageing dad and was instrumental in the formation of the alliances, had this to say about the personal chemistry between himself and his Danish partner:

> I enjoyed an excellent working relationship with my partner who also happens to be the CEO of his company. We are both young men in our middle forties and want to achieve something for ourselves. When we started, we were ready to forgo many luxuries, we shared the same office, drove in the same car, and ate lunch together. As such we were able to cut down on our cost and to plough our profit back into the business. We also discussed most of our problems on and off the office.

Culture

Culture has generally been treated as a barrier within the ISAs (Kuada 2002, Lane and Beamish 1990, Meschi and Roger 1984) which must be overcome if the venture is to achieve any degree of success. The cultural problem is said to magnify when the partners are from different cultural environments, such as between developed and developing country partners. Lane and

Beamish (1990) for instance stated " Most western companies see joint ventures as a quick fix to global competitiveness without understanding the relationships being established and the behavioural and cultural issues involved".
Kuada (2002) also found that cultural differences among the partners may effect the valuation of resources into the alliances, fuel suspicion of each other and prolong the negotiation process. Child and Faulkner (1998) however argued that culture could be a barrier as well as a resource that can be used as a tool for competitive advantage by the partners. They suggested that the key to cultural adaptation is to find the relative strength in each partner's culture and harmonise them for the benefit of the alliance.

Was there any cultural clash among the partners? Different views emerge with regard to the cultural problem. Most of the partners argued that they did not know their Danish counterparts or heard of their businesses prior to the alliance. To make matters worse, they had little information about the Danish culture beyond the few initial visits to Denmark during the partner search phase before they entered into the alliances. They were therefore very suspicious of their Danish counterparts because they feared their businesses would eventually be acquired.

However, the Ghanaian CEO of one of the joint ventures had his education in England and was used to the western way of running businesses, their punctuality and a relatively high degree of honesty in business dealings. Therefore, when he met his partner, he had enough knowledge about Danish work culture which he assumed would not be too different from what pertains in England. It also emerged that there was no programmed intercultural competence development to prepare the managers for the alliances with the Danish partners.

One can also argue that cultural clashes were minimal after the negotiation stage because the Ghanaian partners mostly managed the alliances while the Danish partners made inputs at the board level. The Danish partners were actually the chairmen of the board of directors in four of the alliances, but the Ghanaian partners had casting votes to protect their interest.

Performance and Stability

Measuring performance of ISAs has been very difficult so a lot of approaches have been used in the literature. Usually, a combination of factors has been used. Some of these factors have been grouped in terms of objective–subjective dimensions, (Harrigan 1998, Killing 1983), and instrumental-expressive dimensions (Gronroos 1994, Kuada, 2002).

Instrumental measures relate to the physical activities performed under the alliance such as the technology transferred, products produced and the profit realised. Expressive measures deal with the social dimensions of the personal relationships, which develop among the partners and consist mainly of the quality of interaction (Kuada, 2002) among the partners. The objective measures use economic indicators such as profit, market share, survival, duration, and market value of shares among others to measure alliance performance. The subjective measures use the subjective opinion of the partners as well as the alliance management to assess performance. It has also been argued in the literature that the subjective opinion of the alliance management or partners normally corresponds to the objective performance measurement criteria.

In the area of alliance outcome, the perception of the Ghanaian partners was obtained on profitability, product quality, and learning. The assumption is that if they had acquired enough finance, technology and managerial skills, it should reflect in quality products, learning of new skills and knowledge as well as profitability of the alliance. Moreover, learning is being used as a proxy of the extent to which the technology transfers were successful.

Profitability

One of the indices that has been used to measure the performance of business enterprises is their degree of profitability (Tomlison 1970). Profitability attests to an index of managerial efficiency and lays the grounds for survival and future growth of the alliance. Surprisingly, despite the fact that businesses exist to make profit among others, there is a decline in the use of profitability index in measuring performance of alliances. Apart from the difficulty of obtaining financial information on profitability, there are also problems associated with transfer pricing and creative accounting (Child and Yan, 2003). As a result, perceptual measures of profitability have been used since it has been proved to correlate with objective measures of profitability (Beamish and Delos 1997). As a result, the partners were asked whether their alliances were making profit or not. Only one out of the 5 alliances was making profit and was pleased with the performance of the alliance.

This alliance was also singled out by the co-ordinator of the programme as well as two of the participating firms as the most successful of the PSD alliances. Three of the alliances said they were making consistent loses over the past four years, even though the quantum of losses kept declining on yearly basis. The alliances reported lack of working capital, poor managerial practices, unfavourable economic conditions especially the weakened value of the local currency to the major foreign currencies as well as opportunistic behaviour of a Danish partner among others to be responsible for the losses. One alliance manager reported that exchange losses accounted for as much as 74% of the total losses recorded for 2000.

One of the alliances was not operating at all due to conflict between the partners. The Ghanaian partner accused the Danish partner of bringing obsolete equipment to the alliance which did not conform to the requirements of the regulations of Ghana's Environmental Protection Agency, yet he managed to get the PSD to approve payment to him out of the loan granted to the alliance by the PSD. He felt cheated by his Danish partner and betrayed by the PSD staff. The furious Ghanaian partner had this to say about his Danish partner:

> My partner came here to sell his equipment and not to do business. He brought old machines from his sister company in Asia and managed to obtain payments for it through the PSD loan facility without my approval. The machines did not conform to EPA regulations and were not inspected before being shipped. He has since refused to attend all arbitration meetings arranged by the PSD or answer to my phone calls. I am saddled now with a huge debt as a result.

As a result of this opportunistic behaviour, the project came to a standstill while the interest on the loan granted to the alliance by the PSD kept mounting daily. Apart from applying for waiver of the interest, the Ghanaian partner was in the process of seeking redress in the courts to enable him take full control of the alliance.

Learning

The alliances in question were essentially technology transfer alliances. In such alliances, the capability for manufacturing a product is transferred from one firm to another. As such, one can assume that implicit in the objectives of the Ghanaian partners is learning. Learning within the alliance context has been treated in the literature differently. While some authors (Hamel 1991, Inkpen and Beamish, 1997, focused on competitive learning, others (Inkpen and Crossan 1995, Kogut 1998, Doz and Hamel 1998), focus on inter partner learning as a key condition for the success of alliances. The above alliance learning modes seem to be the features of learning within developed-developed country alliances.

Tsang (2002) has argued that alliances between developed and developing countries exhibit asymmetric learning features. While the later will be learning from the alliance experience, the former would be learning the skills and technologies from the foreign partner.

The alliances interviewed fell into the category discussed by Tsang above. The Danish partner is assumed to have among others the technology, which is urgently needed by the Ghanaian partners to replace their obsolete machines and equipment on the production floor. Therefore, the Danish partners assumed the role of teachers while their Ghanaian counterparts became the students. In this circumstance, one expects a high degree of absorption capacity (Cohen and Levinthal, 1990) on the part of the Ghanaian partners for the transfer and learning to become effective. Absorption capacity has been defined as the ability of a firm to recognise the value of external knowledge, internalise it and apply it to viable commercial ends (Cohen and Levinthal 1990). Lyles and Salk (1996) and Lane et al, (2001) later expanded this concept of absorptive capacity and hypothesised that different sets of factors will affect the three absorptive capacity constructs. They applied the models to joint ventures within the Hungarian context and found support for their hypothesis.

Lane and Lubatkin, (1998) also extended the concept further and argued that the firm's ability to realise the value of external knowledge would be related to the characteristics of both the teacher firm and the student firm. This they called *relative absorptive capacity*. They further argued that knowledge relatedness between the student and teacher firms, similarity in compensation practices as well as organisational structures among others would affect learning and knowledge acquisition by alliance partners. They applied their framework to alliances between biotechnology and pharmaceutical firms and found support for their hypothesis. (For details, see Lane and Lubatkin, 1998). The conclusion one can draw from these studies is that a firm's ability to learn from its alliance partner will be affected by factors within the firm itself as well as factors pertaining to the teacher firm.

The Ghanaian partners were asked whether they had learnt from their Danish counterparts. The answer was overwhelmingly "Yes" among all the five firms. In all the alliances, there were detailed programmes, supported by Danida by which the Ghanaian partner sends staff to Denmark to be trained by the Danish partner. Training took the form of classroom discussions, demonstrations and on the job practice. To save cost, time and make the training more effective, Danida requires the Danish partners to document their technology in detail as well as the plan for teaching. Consultants have been hired by Danida to help the Danish partners do this effectively. This helps to make the knowledge embedded in the technology explicit to be absorbed. Nonaka and Takeuchi, (1995) have argued that the biggest challenge facing companies is the conversion of tacit knowledge into explicit knowledge. When asked of the impact of learning on their operations, two of the alliances demonstrated this with improved quality of their products to show that they have actually acquired new skills and knowledge from their Danish counterparts.

In one of the alliances, a manufacturer of wheelbarrows, the old products as well as the new products were displayed in their showroom to demonstrate their new level of production capability and confidence. Significantly, in the two alliances where transfer and learning has been effective, the Ghanaian partners were in the same line of business as their Danish foreign partner prior to the alliance. This implies that the Ghanaians were already familiar with the basic knowledge in the field thereby making learning easy. The ease with which the Ghanaian partners and staff absorbed the technical training materials supports findings in the literature that prior knowledge permits the effective utilisation of new knowledge (Cohen and Levinthal, 1990) because what can be learned is effected by what is already known or learning performance will be enhanced when the object of learning is related to what is already known and when there is a common language as the bases for interpreting experience (Grant, 1996).

However, the interview also indicated that the Ghanaian partners did not acquire managerial skills because they were not taught at all and the opportunities for learning through practice were also not exploited. Managerial skills such as marketing and financial know-how are assumed to be tacit and ambiguous (Simonin, 1999) and therefore difficult to make explicit to be transferred. It is argued that tacit knowledge is better transferred through working with the knowledge holder such as through apprenticeship (Kogut and Zander, 1995). In the alliances I interviewed, three had no Danish permanent staff, two had one Danish expatriate each. This might have constrained the processes of managerial skill transfer to the Ghanaian firms.

Impact of Learning on Performance

Despite the different approaches used in measuring performance, it has been suggested in the literature that a firm should translate its learning and knowledge into products, markets as well as financial performance (Lyles and Salk 1996, Cohen and Levinthal 1990). The argument is that the firm should be able to exploit its knowledge obtained through learning into viable commercial ends (Cohen and Levinthal 1990). However, Lane et. al. (2001 p: 1145) have argued that the acquisition of valuable knowledge by itself is not enough to influence the performance of an organisation unless it is backed by an efficient business strategy and training competence development by the organisation. In their view, there is always a time lag between the acquisition of knowledge and its application to commercially viable ends. Within this time lag, firms must develop appropriate business strategies with this new knowledge as well as train its own personnel to utilise the new knowledge. Inkpen & Crossan, (1995) have also argued that learning should not be equated with improved performance.

As already stated, the interview data provided mixed results. While skill acquisition is effective in all the alliances, the financial results rather paint a bad picture. Only one of the alliances was making consistent profit in addition to improved product quality. Out of the remaining four, two have shown improvement in product quality without any profit while the remaining two showed neither improvement in product quality nor profit. This perhaps shows that acquisition of technical skills from a partner might not be enough to ensure superior organisational performance.

Role of Catalyst

The role of a catalyst is beginning to emerge within the alliance literature both within developed–developed country context and developed–developing country context (Kuada and Sorensen, 2000, Kuada 2002.). Peikkeri and her colleagues who studied technological collaborations sponsored under the European Commission's Espirit[2] programme concluded that where partners are imposed on collaboration ventures, the issue of trust suffers, thereby affecting the success of the programme. However, Kuada and Sorensen (2000) have justified the role of Danida as a catalyst in facilitating partner search, contract negotiation and implementation between Danish and Ghanaian companies. They argued that the two countries are separated by geo-cultural differences in terms of psychic distance, technology, business systems and communication. Moreover Danish companies would naturally not fancy Ghanaian companies as partners due to their location, since they fall outside their search net for potential alliance partners.

In that circumstance, they argued that to facilitate any collaboration between business partners on a scale witnessed under the PSD programme, a *catalyst* (Danida) would be vital in linking up the partners and facilitating interactions, contract negotiations, implementation and subsequent management of the collaborations. They defined the catalyst as "an actor (person, company, institution) who supports and facilitates the identification of partners, the formation, and management of an alliance without becoming an alliance partner himself". From the two arguments above, it appears the role of a catalyst is valued differently depending on the context.

The Ghanaian partners were asked about their impression of Danida and the PSD programme. Over all, all the partners were unanimous in praising the role of Danida as a catalyst in facilitating the alliances. They argued that it has helped them identify partners, supported them with funding to help the collaborations take off, and above all continue to act as an arbitrator which help to nip potential conflicts in the bud. In spite of the overwhelming support for the role of the catalyst, one partner was quick to add that it must perform its watchdog and monitoring role properly.

Conclusion

Developed-developing country alliances are known to face unique challenges and the alliances interviewed were no exception. We sought to understand the perception of Ghanaian partners in alliances with their Danish counterparts on pre as well as post alliance issues. The study concludes among others that with the widening of wealth between developed and developing countries, and the failure of countries in especially Africa to attract the needed foreign direct investment to boost their economies, programmes such as the PSD offer an alternative option for attracting foreign partners into the investment arena in Africa in general and Ghana in particular.

Apart from offering employment, it brings with it the skills and technologies needed for transforming the industrial sector. As the interview data show, three of the alliances were into the manufacturing sector. With the contribution of the manufacturing sector to GDP dropping from 15% in the early seventies to about 4% in the 2000s, the PSD programme offers hope to the Ghanaian economy as it continues to attract more partners into the manufacturing areas. As the co-ordinator of the programme was quick to point out, success was achieved in alliances that married Danish technologies to exploit the raw materials available within Ghana.

To ensure efficiency and sustainability of the programme, the study makes the following recommendations:
The programme design must include not only technology transfer, but also the transfer of the other managerial functions.

It requires a blend of effective skills in all the other functional areas for a firm to be successfully managed. In other words, it takes more than technology upgrading and transfer to catapult a firm or an alliance into successful operations. The Danish partners must spend a lot more time working with the alliances so that learning by "observing and doing" could be achieved.

Moreover, the business plan that is drawn must be properly scrutinised to ensure that the working capital component has been adequately catered for. It appears the partners contribute their equities in kind, leaving out the vital working capital component. As a result, the alliances are as a result starved of cash. To ensure adequate resourcing of the alliances, partners must contribute both in cash and kind into the alliance. Moreover, the soft loans that have been given out to the alliances must be recovered. The notion that aid money is free money must be a thing of the past. As at the time of the interview, none of the firms that received loans from the PSD had paid anything back. If the loan is recovered, it could be used as a revolving fund for further loans to other alliances.

The PSD programme is a boost in the cup of the recipient countries to develop their private sectors. However, commitment and honesty on the part of the participating firms as well as vigilance on the part of the PSD office will help the programme achieve its intended objectives.

Notes

---

[1] This is a programme that aims at bringing firms from selected countries into long term commercial relationship with firms from Denmark. Danida supports this programme with funding through its programme co-ordinators in the respective countries.

[2] Esprit is the European Strategic Programmeme for Research Development in Information Technologies. It was founded in 1984, sponsored by the European Commission and aims at finding European partners to collaborate in information technology.

References

Beamish, P.W. (1993): "The characteristics of joint ventures in the People's Republic of China." *Journal of International Marketing*. 1, 29-48

Beamish; P.W. (1988): *Multinational Joint Ventures in Developing Countries* (London, Routledge).

Beamish, P.W., and Delos, A., (1997): "Joint ventures in LDCs: Partner Selection and Performance" *Management International Review*. 34: Special Issue. 60-74.

Bleeke, J. and Ernst, D. (1993): *Collaborate to Compete* (New York, John Wiley)

Bo, B. Nielsen, (2003): "Managing knowledge in International Strategic Alliances: Theory and practice". Unpublished doctoral dissertation, Copenhagen Business School.

Boateng, A., Glaister K.W., (2002): "Performance of joint ventures: Evidence for West Africa." *International Business Review*, (11) 523-541.

Bruner, R., and Spekman, R., (1998): "The dark side of alliances": Lessons from Volvo-Renault. *European Management Journal* 16(2) 136-150.

Child, J and Yan, Y., (2003): " Predicting performance of international joint ventures: An empirical investigation in China" *Journal of Management Studies*. 40 (2) 284-320)

Child, J. and Faulkner, D (1998): *Strategies of Co-operation: Managing Alliances, Networks and Joint Ventures*. (Oxford)

Child, J., and Markoczy (1993): "Host country managerial behaviour and learning in Chinese and Hungarian joint ventures". *Journal of Management Studies*, 30(4) 611-631.

Cohen, W.M., and D. A. Levinthal, (1990) "Absorptive Capacity, A new perspective on learning and innovation", *Administrative Science Quarterly*. **35**. 128-152.

Das, K.T. (2000): "A resource-based theory of strategic alliances", *Journal of Management*. ***http://www.findarticles.com.***

Doz, Y.L., and Hamel, G. (1998): ***Alliance Advantage: The Art of Creating Value Through Partnering*. Boston, Ma: Harvard Business School Press.**

Doz,Y.L, (1986) "The evolution of co-operation in strategic alliances: Initial conditions, or learning processes" *Strategic Management Journal*, Summer Special Issue, **17**, 55-75

Ducin, M.T. and Hitt, M.A. (1997): "Selecting partners for successful international alliances: Examination of U.S. and Korean firms" *Journal of World Business*. 32 (1) 3-16.

Geringer, J.M. (1990): "Strategic determinants of partner selection criteria in international joint ventures" *Journal of International Business Studies*, 22. 41-46.

Geringer, J.M., and Herbert, L., (1991): "Measuring performance of international joint ventures". *Journal of International Business Studies*.22: 249-263

Glaister, K.w. and Buckley, P.J. (1996): "Strategic motives for international alliance formation". *Journal of management Studies*, 33, 301-332

Gronroos, C. (1994): "From Marketing mix to relationship marketing: towards a paradigm shift in marketing", *Management Decision*, **32** (2) pp.481-510.

Gulati, R., (1995): "Does familiarity breed trust? The implications of repeated for contractual choice in alliances." *Academy of Management Journal*. 38: 85-112.

Hamel, G. (1991): "Competing for competence and inter-partner learning within international strategic alliances", *Strategic management Journal*, Summer Special Issue, **12**, 83-108.

Harrigan, K. (1998): "Joint ventures and competitive strategy", *Strategic Management Journal*, **9** (2) pp. 141-158.

Harrigan, K.R.,(1988): Strategic alliances and partner asymmetries. *Management International Review. 28: 53-72.*

Inkpen A.C. and Curral C.C., (1998): "The nature, antecedents, and consequences of joint venture trust". *Journal of International Management* 4(1) 1-20.

Inkpen, .A.C and Crossan, M.M, (1995): " Believing is seeing: joint ventures and organisational learning" *Journal of Management Studies*, **32** (5) 595-618.

Inkpen, A., C., and Dinur, A., (1998): "Knowledge management processes and international joint ventures." *Organisational Science*. 9 (4) 454-468.

Inkpen, A.C., and Beamish, P.W (1997): "Knowledge, bargaining power and international joint ventures instability." *Academy of Management Review*. 22 (1) 177-202.

Inkpen, A.C., and Dinur, A., (1998): Knowledge management processes and international joint ventures" *Organisational Science*, 9 454-468

Kale, P., Singh, H., Perlmutter, H. (2000): "Learning and protection of proprietary assets in strategic alliances: building relational capital" *Strategic Management Journal*. 21, 217-237

Killing J.P. (1983): *Strategies for Joint-Venture Success* (New York: Praeger)

Kogut, B and Zander, U., (1995): "Knowledge and the speed of the transfer and imitation of organisational capabilities: An empirical test" *Organisation Science*: 6(1) 76-92.

Kogut, B. (1988): "Joint ventures: Theoretical and empirical perspectives", Strategic Management Journal, 9 (4), 319-332.

Kuada, J. (2002) "Collaboration between developed and developing country-based firms: Danish-Ghanaian experience" *Journal of Business and Industrial Marketing*. 17 (86) 538-557

Kuada,.J and Sørensen, O.J. (2000) "Institutional support for international strategic alliances: some Danish-Ghanaian experience" *Journal of management Studies*, 15 (1) pp.114-130

Lane P.J., and Lubatkin M., (1998): "Relative absorptive capacity and interorganisational learning" *Strategic Management Journal.19 (5): 461-478.*

Lane, H. W and Beamish, P. W, (1990) " Cross-cultural co-operative behaviour in joint ventures in LDCs" *Management International Review*, Special Issue. 87-102

Levitt, B, and March J, (1988): "Organisational Learning". *Annual Reviews Social*, 14: 319-340,

Lyles, M.a, (1988): "Learning among joint venture sophisticated firms" *Management International Review*. 28. 85-98

Lyles, M.A.; and Salk J.E., (1996): "Knowledge acquisition from foreign parents in international joint ventures". *Journal of International Business Studies*. 27(5) 877-904.

Mahoney, T. A. and Deckop J. R., (1993): "Y'gotta believe" Lessons from American-Vs. Japanese-run U.S. factories." *Organisational Dynamics*, 21(4) 27-38.

March, J.G. (1991): "Exploration and exploitation in organisational learning". *Organisational science*. 2: 71-87.

Meschi, P. and Roger, A. (1994): "Cultural contexts and social effectiveness in international joint ventures" *Management International Review*, 34, (3) 197-215.

Mowery, C.D., Oxley, E. J., Silverman, B. S, (1996) "Strategic Alliances and Interfirm Knowledge Transfer" Strategic *Management Journal*, 17 (Winter Special Issue)

Nonaka, I., and Takeuchi, H., (1995): *The knowledge-Creating Company: How the Japanese Create the Dynamics of Innovation.* Oxford : Oxford publisher

Simonin, B.L., (1999): "Ambiguity and the process of knowledge transfer in strategic alliances". *Strategic Management Journal,* 20: 595-623.

Tsang, E.W. (1999): "A preliminary typology of learning in international strategic alliances". *Journal of World Business.* 34(3) 211-229.

Zinn,W. and Parasuraman, A. (1997): "Scope and intensity of logistics-based strategic alliances", *Industrial* Marketing Management. 26, 137-147.

Lecraw, D.J., (1983): "Performance of Transnational Corporations in Less Developed Countries." *Journal of International Business Studies* 14(1) 15-33.

Tomlinson, J.W.C., (1970): *The joint Venture Process in International Business: India and Pakistan,* Cambridge, MA: MIT Press.

Grant, R.M., (1996): "Prospering in a Dynamically-Competitive Environment: Organisational Capability As Knowledge Integration" *Organisation Science.* 7: 375-388.

7

BUILDING TECHNOLOGICAL CAPABILITIES IN GHANAIAN SMEs THROUGH PRIVATE SECTOR DEVELOPMENT PROGRAMMES

Peter Kragelund[1]

Introduction

The private sector is at the forefront of today's development agenda. A growing consensus is emerging among donor agencies that the private sector is a fast-growth area and therefore a tool for poverty alleviation (Kragh, Mortensen et al. 2000; Gibbon and Schulpen 2002; Cox and Healey 2003). The increased focus on the private sector as an engine of growth that will lead to economic progress and thereby to poverty reduction is a logical outcome of the reorientation in development thinking dating from the beginning of the 1980s.

This reorientation began with a shift from considering the state as the prime mover of development to a focus on the private sector, which was seen as more efficient and more conducive to economic dynamism. However, after a decade of neo-liberal structural adjustment programmes (SAP) all over sub-Saharan Africa with dubious results, a change occurred in the beginning of the 1990s. Many donors acknowledged that the past emphasis on macroeconomic policy, stabilisation and extensive privatisation of state-owned enterprises failed to create a dynamic private sector. The donors expected the domestic private sector to diversify its exports and bring about structural change in the economy, but this did not happen. Hence, major bi- and multilateral donors put more emphasis on sectoral development to transform the economy. A synthesis of public and private initiative became recognised as the way forward. It is within this new 'consensus' that the private sector development programmes of today should be understood (Harrigan and Younger 2000; Gibbon and Schulpen, 2002; Schulpen and Gibbon, 2002).

In accordance with this trend of the 1990s, the Danish International Development Assistance (Danida) initiated its Private Sector Development Programme (PSDP) in Ghana in 1993. Based on a study on how Danida could contribute to strengthen the productive sector in the programme countries, carried out by the Federation of Danish Industries (DI), Danida decided to initiate a three-year trial programme (1993-1996) which was committed to targeting the private sector as a stimulant to development. On the basis of an internal review, Danida (1995), the Danida Board approved a continuation of the programme over a five-year period.

The programme was extended from the original three countries, viz. Ghana, India and Zimbabwe, to Egypt, Uganda and Vietnam[2]. Later, foreign aid to India was suspended due to tests of atomic weapons, and Bangladesh was included. In 2001, the programme was broadened to include all Danida programme countries. The overall aim of the programme is to promote the formation of long-term business links between Danish and developing country-based companies in order to facilitate a transfer of Danish management and technology skills to the developing country-based companies (Kuada, 2000).

The underlying rationale behind the programme is that inter-firm co-operation can contribute to economic as well as social development in the developing countries that host these companies. Hence, the support is conditional on agreements between companies being mutually binding and having a long-term perspective. Within the PSD-programme, the Danish and the local companies can get financial support for both the preparation and the implementation of the project.

However, hardly any studies of the effects of the past decade's support to the private sector in developing countries exist. Moreover, only a few of these studies have looked beyond the effectiveness of the programme, i.e. has the programme fulfilled its objectives or not? The aim of this paper is to go a step further: it will seek to explore the impact of the programme, both at the enterprise level and at a broader developmental level, i.e. it acknowledges that the PSD-programme has a dual role to fulfil, viz. economic gains for the participating entrepreneurs, and traditional developmental goals on a national level. Moreover, it aims at pinpointing programme internal as well as programme external factors, which impede the fulfilment of its objectives.

The paper starts by presenting central characteristics of the private sector in Ghana (section 2). Thereafter, it briefly introduces the methodological considerations (section 3) before scrutinising the foreign aid evaluation literature in order to draw attention to limitations of traditional aid evaluations and instead, propose a broader approach to the impact of aid in section 4. Section 5 examines the literature on technological capabilities with the purpose of suggesting an illustrative framework to measure changes in technological capabilities. The sixth section deals with the impact of the PSDP in Ghana on the two levels suggested in the preceding sections. It starts out by looking at previous studies before continuing with an examination of effects of the programme at the enterprise level before it proceeds with an analysis of the impact of the PSDP in relation to its developmental objectives, i.e. the formation of technological capabilities in Ghanaian enterprises.

The Private Sector in Ghana

Most of the literature on the private sector in Ghana takes the Economic Recovery Programme (ERP) of 1983 as its point of departure[3]. It covers as diverse fields as the development of the informal sector during the era of structural adjustment programmes (SAP) (Nikoi, 1995; Barwa, 1995), the effects on medium and large-scale enterprises (Acheampong and Tribe, 2001), the response of the entrepreneurs (Amposah, 2000), export of traditional products (Owusu, 2001), mobilisation of action in relation to the new policies (Awuah, 1997), and the impact on the female workforce (Panford, 2001).

This is not in itself a problem as long as the discussion takes us beyond the rather dull question of whether the ERPs worked according to the objectives or not, or whether the right indicators were used to measure the results or not (Lall, 1995). However, there is more to the development of the private sector in Ghana than the policies conducted under the ERPs. This section will briefly discuss some key features of the Ghanaian private sector that influences the way the PSDP impact on the Ghanaian private enterprises. This will include a brief description of the historical development of the private sector and a consideration of significant aspects of the Ghanaian private sector that affect the building of capabilities through the PSDP.

It is not surprising that the Ghanaian ERPs are mentioned in almost every book and article on the private sector development in Ghana. Looking at the crude figures of manufacturing production in Ghana from the late 1970s to the mid 1990s, it soon becomes apparent that something happened in the mid-1980s: Manufacturing output was roughly halved between 1977 and 1985, and more than doubled from 1985 to 1996 (Tribe, 2002: table 15.3a). However, it is not correct to make a direct causal link between the ERPs and the subsequent growth. A number of reasons can be put forth for the economic decline, among them: government mismanagement, shortages of foreign exchange for the purchase of imported inputs, poor infrastructure, and economic decline associated with loss of consumer purchasing power. Of course, the reverse explanations can be used to account for the recovery, but one has to bear in mind that a considerable proportion of the recovery of manufacturing production was due to improvements in capacity utilisation rather than capacity expansion and technological change (ibid). Moreover, much of the growth occurred because of the special attention that was accorded the manufacturing sector, i.e. import of inputs and liberalisation of the exchange rate and imports and the increased intermediate and capital input and improvement in the infrastructure performance (Acheampong and Tribe, 2001)[4].

Moreover, using 1983 as a point of departure might skew the results in-as-much-as the output in 1983 was particularly low due to draught, electricity rationing, shortages of foreign exchange etc. (ibid: 21f). Recovery was therefore comparatively easily achieved, and was not the result of a dynamic private sector. Rather, the result of the ERPs was a booming micro and small-enterprise sector that did not manage to create the necessary economic growth to boost economic development in Ghana.

These enterprises contain the majority of the economically active population in Ghana (Nikoi 1995). This is worth mentioning as one of the central goals for the ERPs was to improve conditions for the domestic private sector by reducing state involvement in the co-ordination of economic activities. Likewise, an (intended) consequence of the programmes has been the lay off of a large part of the workers in the public sector. In other words, the ERPs were meant to put up a framework for a new dynamic private sector that could absorb these laid off workers. However, this did not happen. Rather, these workers were forced into various forms of self-employment. Moreover, an increasing pressure to open the Ghanaian market for foreign products has made the local private entrepreneurs distressed as their technological capabilities are too low to compete with e.g. Chinese consumer goods and many Small and Medium-sized Enterprises (SMEs) are closing down (Cletus Kosiba, Association of Ghana Industries, personal comment).

Many explanations have been put forward in order to explain why the domestic private sector has not responded, including poor institutional environment (Amponsah, 2000). This is not the only factor explaining the poor response, though. The reason should also be sought in a protected market and inadequate incentives for private enterprises, which have resulted in a "missing middle"[5], i.e. a dual structure of companies with parastatal firms imbued with a high degree of vertical integration on the one hand, and a group of small, informal firms on the other (Kragh, Mortensen et al. 2000). As Pedersen (1998) points out, this phenomenon is not limited to the Ghanaian context but can be found elsewhere in sub-Saharan Africa. On a more general level, Pedersen argues that medium-scaled enterprises are almost non-existent because the large enterprises tend to operate in their own closed production and distribution network or institutional setting to which the medium-sized enterprises do not have access, while the small enterprises operate in a local family-based network, which is insufficient for the larger enterprises.

Moreover, the special state-business relationship in Ghana since independence has to be taken into consideration as well. Private entrepreneurs have faced several constraints since independence. Even though a large proportion of the MPs during the first years of CCP leadership (1957-61) were businessmen, they were soon driven out of the party through an attack on private capital accumulation and as such kept out of influence of economic policies. Even though the relationship between the businessmen and the state changed to the better during the Busia regime (1969-72), the indigenisation decrees of 1969 and 1972 only reserved small business sectors to Ghanaian private capital, the rest was given to the state as majority shares in foreign companies. During the PNDC regime headed by Rawlings (1982-1992) the government officially recognised the private sector as an 'engine of growth' (especially after a Consultative Group meeting in Paris in 1984) but due to its fierce attack on *kalabule*[6] activities including intensive interrogation, searches, punishments and arrests of private businessmen, many fled Ghana[7]. In the words of Hutchful (2002: 176):

> "...to business...the PNDC had introduced technically pro-business policies but its rhetoric and political actions...remained frequently antagonistic to the private sector".

Following the inauguration of the fourth republic in 1993 the business-state relationship became less tense. A new business class emerged consisting of, among others, expatriate Ghanaians investing in enterprise and real estate but the Ghanaian economy was still highly vulnerable to shocks and the level of corruption increased and economic growth never really took off.

The NPP government (2001-) has continued the former regimes' focus on the private sector as an engine of growth, and President Kufuor has even dubbed his presidency 'the Golden Age of Business'. A number of innovations have been launched among them the Ministry for Private Sector Development and Special Presidential Initiatives to boost the non-traditional export commodities. However, it is yet to be seen how the centralisation of programmes and the introduction of new initiatives targeted at the private sector will affect the latter (Tangri, 1992; Nugent, 1995; Hutchful, 2002; Kraus, 2002).

In addition, we need to know more about the specific characteristics of this sector in order to understand how the PSDP impacts on the private enterprises in Ghana. Here, the work by Sørensen and Kuada (2001) can guide us. They have studied the background and proximate institutions that make up the special characteristics of the Ghanaian business system[8]. They pinpoint that the family is the primary social unit in the Ghanaian society. Hence, the family influences the individual's activities and even though the fulfilment of family obligations does not always impede the management of business entities the "*...Ghanaian social structure appears to offer a weak basis for effective market-firm interaction*" (ibid: 176).

When it comes to the private sector, they argue that the outcome is a pronounced mistrust among Ghanaian business people for non-kin partners[9]. Therefore, hardly any long-term horizontal linkages between enterprises exist and joint ownership arrangements with fellow Ghanaians are seldom. This, however, is not solely related to mistrust, but relates to the fact that there is no mechanical way in which information about other businessmen's trustworthiness can be shared in Ghana as Fafchamps (1996) reminds us. Thus, the business contracts are mainly transactional rather than relational. Furthermore, to protect themselves from periods of economic decline and to take account of the historically high inflation rates entrepreneurs often engage in several unrelated businesses (Kraus, 2002).

The organisation of enterprises is important in the diffusion knowledge related to the building of capabilities to further enhance growth. Here too, Sørensen and Kuada (2001: 172f) offer us some insight. They characterise the most widespread leadership style in Ghana as authoritarian-benevolence, i.e. comprising close supervision, elaborate instructions on all matters and disapproval of deviations from these instructions on the one hand, and provision of extra opportunities and privileges to the closest and most obedient, on the other hand.

Likewise, the technical and managerial skills among the workforce are important for building capabilities. Unfortunately, these skills in general seem to be too low to even compete internationally in labour-intensive goods.

The companies with higher skills are according to Lall (1995) largely foreign owned; among local enterprises the better ones have entrepreneurs that are well educated.

To sum up, the ERPs did not foster the expected vibrant private sector in Ghana and policies in recent years geared towards creating economic growth have merely kept up with population growth (ISSER, 2003). Moreover, the special characteristics of the Ghanaian business system, especially the background institutions and lack of technological capabilities have resulted in a very fragmented economy that is unable to compete internationally.

Methods

In 2001, eight years after the PSD was initiated, funding for 84 collaborative arrangements between Danish and Ghanaian companies had been approved. These collaborative arrangements cover both the so-called Start-up facilities (lasting ½ year) and the partnerships (lasting up to 3 years). This study is based on a list provided by Danida of disbursed grants in the period 1993-2001. According to this list, Danida has funded 37 partnerships and 47 "start-up" facilities. However, I have chosen to limit the number of partnerships to 29 as 7 enterprises did not have a (private) counterpart either in Denmark or in Ghana, and 1 partnership received two grants. Likewise, the number of "start-up" facilities was reduced from 47 to 40 as 1 had no Danish partner and 6 had continued to full partnerships and is thus included in the partnerships. Thus, all together 69 collaborations qualify to be included in this study. However, six Ghanaian companies have had more than one partner, thus reducing the amount of enterprises to 63. Unfortunately, not all the companies exist anymore. Moreover, some general managers (GM) were not available during my three months stay in Ghana in 2002. Thus, only representatives of 41 Ghanaian enterprises were interviewed (covering 45 different collaborations as depicted in appendix 1). The purpose of these visits was first and foremost to interview managing directors and staff directly related to the PSD-programme regarding the direct effects of the collaborations, e.g. transfer of knowledge, employment generation, linkages to suppliers, customers etc., but also to assess some of the derived impacts of the programme. Likewise, the intention was to get a first hand impression of changes that have taken place during the course of the programme because no systematic gathering of the effects of the PSDP in Ghana has taken place.

Wherever possible, I participated in strategy meetings between the partners and observed the actual transfer and training process between a Danish 'expert' and his or her Ghanaian counterpart. Additionally, I conducted interviews with representatives from the Danish embassy and involved business organisations in Ghana as well as in Denmark. The information gathered from interviews and direct observation has been linked to feasibility studies, application forms, and progress reports generously given to me by most partners.

The Narrow Focus on Success or Failure in Traditional Aid Evaluations

Evaluation of foreign aid programmes and projects have been widespread for the last couple of decades, but until recently, very little focus has been given to aid impact. Up until recently, aid evaluations have tried to answer the question posed by e.g. (Cassen, 1986): *Does aid work?* Thus, the core objective of an evaluation has been to answer the question of whether a project or programme for which a donor has provided funds has achieved its stated objectives[10]. This is especially true when dealing with funds that are spent in other parts of the world, far away from the taxpayers and where risks of failure are higher (Cracknell, 2000: 39). Besides, not adding new knowledge to how aid works, this particular purpose of aid evaluations has raised a number of methodological concerns, e.g. how are results from one evaluation to be generalised to other settings (the problem of context), is it possible to conduct a value-free evaluation (whose interests are you pursuing – agencies' accountability needs or stakeholders information needs?)

During the last decade this has changed. Impact is now *the* buzz-word of aid evaluation. However, even though there seems to be some kind of agreement that impact is more than the outputs or the effects of a programme, impact is more often seen as the last (seldom reached) stage in a linear monitoring and evaluation process that is closely linked to the planning and monitoring process and the aim of the external stakeholders, as depicted in figure 1 (Oakley, Pratt et al., 1998). Hence, in this respect impact (at the very most) refers to a more thorough examination of the consequences of a project/programme implementation on the intended beneficiaries and does not lead to a more comprehensive understanding of the changes that are generated in a particular setting when development projects are implemented.

Figure 1: A linear perception of impact

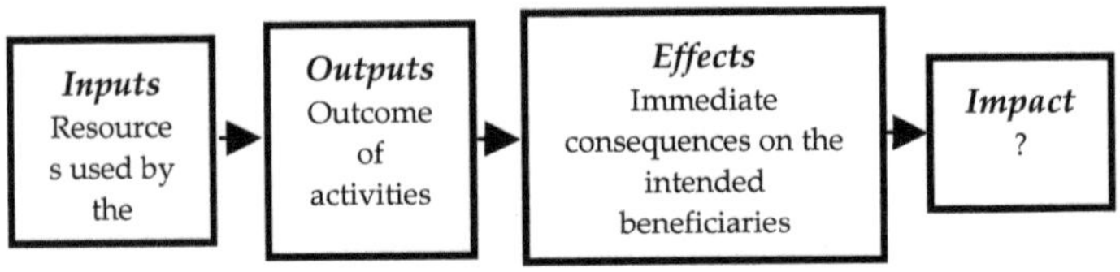

The linear approach presented above does not make it possible to grasp derived impacts and unintended consequences, including wider developmental effects of a project/programme as the focus is concentrated on measuring the outcomes of the inputs in the project.

Even more worrying, however, is the exaggerated significance given to the project in relation to other societal changes. As pointed out by for instance Olivier de Sardan (1988), development (and development projects) is a social phenomenon that involves several actors, both among the developers and among those to be developed. The result is a complex interaction that cannot be grasped using a linear model. Several reasons can explain this narrow focus on intended consequences, e.g. the role of taxpayers, the limited timeframe etc. However, I will argue that this is only part of the explanation.

The main reason should rather be sought in the very structure of foreign aid. Possibilities for learning how aid works exist in theory. Two different forms of evaluations can be distinguished: viz. the *formative* evaluation that is conducted for the benefit of those managing the project and therefore seeks to deepen the understanding of what has happened in order to enhance future performance, and the *summative* (goal-based) evaluation that is conducted for the benefit of external stakeholders (e.g. politicians, tax-payers etc.) in order to register achievements (Kruse, Kyllönen et al., 1997; Commission, 2001).

It seems more fruitful, though, to consider these two forms of evaluations as possible components in an evaluation. Thus, an evaluation can contain both elements (Olivier de Sardan, personal comment). However, seen in retrospective the summative components have been much more powerful than the formative ones. This is partly due to the demand of the external stakeholders and partly due to the close link between the aid management tool, logical framework approach (LFA)[11] and the aid evaluations in most donor agencies (see, e.g. Commission, 2001)[12].

The LFA focuses solely on the achievements of intended effects by intended routes and therefore, it is difficult to identify unintended outcomes and get a richer understanding of how aid works. Moreover, it has been argued that the mere form of the logical framework excludes the analysis of politics in as much as all problems (including political tensions) must be defined as technical in order to be dealt with successfully (Bierschenk, 1988: 153)[13].

Without mentioning the word *impact* a group of social anthropologists have tried to uncover how development aid worked for more than one decade. They focused on the study of the meaning and the processes of development (aid). They understand development projects as political arenas with conflicting interests, e.g. who are the recipients, how are the resources allocated, and what is the objective of the development project. Moreover, they have approached the various logics that determine the way the different actors act. Above all, however, they have shown us that development projects are not implemented in a vacuum. They are implemented in societies characterised by complex political, economic and cultural process. Thus, the impact of the development project is only one out of many processes taking place simultaneously (Bierschenk, 1988; Crehan and von Oppen, 1988; Olivier de Sardan, 1988; Bierschenk and Olivier de Sardan, 1997; Harrison, 2003).

It seems that this line of thought has inspired Folke (2000) who argues that in order to dig deeper into how development aid works, it is necessary to adopt a *broad impact study* that incorporates both the intended and the unintended effects and at the same time includes an analysis of changes during a longer time-span and sees the intervention as one of several factors influencing a particular development (Folke,1998). This approach is directly related to the work of (Roche 1999: 21), who while referring to an NGO impact study, defines impact assessment as *"the systematic analysis of the lasting or significant changes – positive or negative, intended or not – in people's lives brought about by a given action or series of actions"*[14].

This definition has a number of advantages. Firstly, it allows the researcher to incorporate many different factors in the analysis. Hence, not only aid flows and directly targeted subjects are studied, but also the surrounding society. This way, the lack of clear boundaries (spatially, socially and economically) of the project/programme is taken into consideration. Secondly, this definition does not attempt to propose a single method to assess impact. Rather, the researcher can let the particular field of interest guide the selection of methodologies, i.e. the theoretical framework(s) relating to the particular field should direct the choice of method(s). Thirdly, it includes an attempt to go beyond the unexpected effects and instead, measure the unintended and derived 'effects' of a particular aid intervention as part of an aid impact evaluation (Hopkins, 1995; Coles, Evans et al., 1998; Madsen, 1999; Roche, 1999; Adams, Batchelor et al., 2000)[15]. However, as pointed out by e.g. Sørensen (2000) one should bear in mind that the momentary effect of a project eventually may have a large impact on the society. Thus, the examination should not be confined to lasting changes but also include temporary changes.

The above approach is closer to what we have been looking for, namely an approach that examines the processes of development aid in a particular setting. Impact is thus perceived as the result of a complex interplay of intervention and context, hence both the social context in which a programme/project is implemented and the objective of the programme/project will influence the outcome. However, in the case of foreign aid to the private sector it is important to bear in mind that the effects of the project at enterprise-level, i.e. for the immediate intended beneficiaries is different from the broader impact of the programme, even though e.g. generation of employment and foreign exchange could be regarded as benefiting both the enterprise and the society.

The objective of the programme is essentially to alleviate poverty through the creation of long-term business relationships and thereby transfer technological, managerial and organisational skills from the Danish to the Ghanaian partner. However, there is no causal relationship between the two variables. Moreover, the immediate and long-term consequences are not necessarily the same. Thus, in order to examine the impact of the programme, the analysis will be divided into two parts. One part is related to the effects of the programme that are of immediate interest to the participating Ghanaian enterprises.

The effects concerned correlates with the specific objectives of the collaborations stated in the application forms and include employment generation, export earnings, improved product quality, enhanced product range, increased productivity, bigger profit margin, higher salary, and larger turnover. The other part is concerned with the building and diffusion of technological capabilities in the Ghanaian private sector, as this is seen as a way to generate competitiveness and thereby, economic growth.

This part, thus, deals with the interest of the donor agency. However, no ready-made methods exist to measure the changes in technological capabilities in SMEs in Africa through inter-firm collaborations. Therefore, the next section will set out to unravel the concept and propose ways to measure the changes.

Building Capabilities Through Inter-firm Collaborations: A Theoretical Overview

A major part of the PSD-programme consists of a transfer of technology in the broad sense, i.e. transfer of knowledge, managerial skills and organisational skills. Hence, I need a framework to understand how this transfer affects the private Ghanaian enterprise.

A number of schools of thought have dealt with how technology and society are related, but one school of thought, the "diffusing technology" stands out as more relevant as the focus has centred on the acquisition and building of technological capabilities, both at firm level and on a national level. However, most studies have focused on technological capabilities in large companies and only a few have scrutinised these processes in SMEs in developing countries (Romijn, 1999: 11)[16]. Moreover, third party involvement, e.g. the development agency as a mediator for the transfer and training is almost non-existent in the literature[17]. Therefore, this section sets out to build a framework for measuring changes in technological capabilities in the Ghanaian enterprises.

The "diffusing technology" heading refers to the neo-Schumpeterian school of thought, which addresses factors such as technological capabilities, access to resources and incentives for change in its attempt to explore the economic and social conditions for technological change. A main concern in these studies is the diffusion of technology into society and how this diffusion creates economic development. These concerns are highly relevant in the examination of how the PSD-programme impacts on the Ghanaian private sector.

Central in this line of thinking are the evolutionary theories expressed for instance by Nelson and Winter (1982). This approach draws attention to the heterogeneity of firms caused by for instance different learning routines and difference in work efforts between firms, i.e. the efficiency with which firms operate a given technology and the effort with which the firms pursue technological improvements (Romijn, 1999: 14)[18]. Moreover, it does not accept the assumption of readily available technology that can easily and instantaneously be transferred and utilised, which was put forward by the neoclassical economists at the time. Instead, proponents of this line of thought argue that technology is not simply available from the "international technology shelf" in-as-much- as the mere choosing and acquiring of technologies create obstacles and difficulties (Archibugi and Pietrobelli, In Press). Thus, a central theme within the evolutionary theory is the analysis of the acquisition and adaptation of new technology at national, sector as well as at enterprise level.

Even though most evolutionary contributions do not have an explicit microeconomic perspective, their focus on differences in productive capabilities point to the need for a more microeconomic focus in order to understand fully the concepts of knowledge, information and learning, and according to Lall (1992: 166) this school of thought has given inspiration to most subsequent micro-level analysis of technology in developing countries. It is therefore no coincidence that central terms within the diffusion technology approach are directly derived from the evolutionary school of thought, i.e. *competences, capabilities, resources* and *capacities*. These terms refer to different levels of technological skills and abilities needed within a given enterprise.

According to Lall, Navaretti et al. (1994: 5) *technological capabilities* (TC) in an industry are the information and skills (technical, managerial and institutional) that allow productive enterprises to utilise equipment and technology efficiently. The TCs can neither be reduced to the physical equipment, blueprints and patents nor to formal skills. TCs are better described as the way in which a firm combines the physical equipment, blueprints and patents, and the skills in order to function as an organisation (Lall and Latsch, 1999: 42). However, this definition misses out one important aspect, namely that the TCs are not only the skills, knowledge etc. to utilise the technology efficiently but also the capacity to generate and manage change as pointed out by Bell and Pavitt (1993: 159).

The TCs are firm specific in-as-much-as they are a form of institutional knowledge that is made of the combined skills of its members over time. Thus, the process of developing TCs is *evolutionary,* i.e. it builds upon past efforts and choices. The process itself involves buying skills and information from the market as well as providing some in-house. Hence, it is not a passive process as the choice depends on the technology, the market conditions and the specific firm strategy, but rather it is driven by conscious and purposive efforts undertaken by the enterprise. Hence, technological efforts in Ghana should not be thought of as investments at the global frontier of technology, but rather as a wide range of efforts that the enterprise must undertake in order to access, implement, absorb and build upon the knowledge required in production (Lall and Latsch, 1999: 41).

Normally three main types of TCs can be distinguished: investment capabilities, production capabilities and adaptive innovation capabilities. However, the precise labels can vary. Lall, Navaretti et al. (1994: 111ff) and Lall and Latsch (1999: 48ff) for instance differentiates between the following three broad categories that equate the technological tasks facing a manufacturing company. Each of these functions is performed either implicitly or explicitly by all manufacturing companies:

- Investment capability is an umbrella category for the skills and information that the entrepreneur is required to have to be able to identify (realistic) investment projects, to (systematically) search for and buy at the right price appropriate technologies for the enterprise, plus install and absorb the tacit elements of the technology.
- Production capability is first and foremost related to the skills and knowledge required to operate a firm and subsequently related to the improvement of the production process. The production capabilities can be subdivided into three headings[19]: *Product centred* that includes design, re-design and improvements of products, *process centred,* which refers to the general organisation of production and thereby the improvement of the process as such, and *equipment related,* which refers to activities like maintenance, adaptation to new materials etc.
- Linkage capability is defined as the skills needed to establish, maintain and exploit production and technological links with other firms and institutions. These linkages go beyond anonymous purchase of products and services and involve exchange of information, know-how and skills and thereby work as an efficient way to diffuse technology. This category is of utmost importance as not all technology flows generate TCs and as linkage with local suppliers and other groups within the local economy are critical for enhancing TC (Wei, 1995).

A number of authors have attempted to quantify these capabilities by constructing proxies for the TCs. These indirect indicators can be classified in the following three broad categories:

1. ***Input indicators:***

a. *R&D spending* is often used as a proxy for TC as comparable R&D spending data exists and as these figures are easily compared. However, as pointed out by Figueiredo (2002b: 6) one should be wary even in developed countries to assume that innovative activities are only confined to R&D laboratories. Rather, technical change in companies is most often associated with trial and error in the design process. Moreover, in SMEs, technological activities are performed on a part time basis and often not categorised as R&D but design and product engineering (Bell and Pavitt, 1993: 166).

b. *Investment in* (technologically more advanced) *machinery* does not by itself lead to new TCs but according to Romijn (1999: 84f) the literature on the small-scale metal sector in developing countries suggests that introduction of new production equipments leads to mastery of new skills and most often to product development and thereby TCs.

c. *Number of days of training* of employees is at times used as an indicator for TCs. This measure assumes a direct link between training and capability building that does not always exist as the quality and absorption of the training is not taken into account.

d. *Educational enrolment rates* represent the human capital base in a country. However, education by no means equals TCs rather; it provides the base for which learning takes place. Also *enrolment at the tertiary level in technical subjects* and vocational training are often used (Lall, 1999; Lall, 2000)[20].

2. ***Output Indicators:***

a. *Production output*: In-as-much-as this indicator can quantify TCs at all (a number of external factors, such as foreign exchange and raw material shortages can make the company stand idle for longer periods of time), it only captures part of TC development as it does not take quality changes into account (Alänge, 1987: 27).

b. *Patent data* has regularly been used as a substitute for TCs in developed country companies, but as pointed out by Evenson and Westphal (1994: 28) such data on the one hand articulate differences of inventive activity between countries and on the other hand, reflect differences in laws governing Intellectual Property Rights.

c. *Export* can be seen as an indicator for TCs on an international scale and is seen as one of the most useable indicators to measure national TCs in-as-much-as this indicator is easy to calculate while simultaneously measuring international efficiency (Lall, 2000: 31). However, this indicator does not distinguish between different levels of technology used in the production process, nor does it differentiate among domestic and foreign firms.

3. Any combination of input and output indicators:

a. *Total Factor Productivity,* which includes two other combination indicators; *capital productivity* and *labour productivity,* is the most used single indicator for TCs by the proponents of the new growth theories[21]. The indicator itself does not measure TCs, but rather technical (in)efficiency (Lall 2000).

As shown above, there is no agreement as to what constitutes the most optimal indicator for a quantitative assessment of TCs, nor is there any objective indicator that can be used for a systematic assessment across countries or even sectors (Romijn, 1997: 360; Wignaraja, 2001: 11). Moreover, the indicators listed above have been used in a wide variety of studies, covering national inquiries (e.g. Lall (1992) and Lall (2000)), industrial branch level studies (e.g. Putranto, Stewart et al. (2003)) as well as firm-level investigations in developed as well as developing countries (e.g. Okejiri (2000)). In addition, all the input indicators presented above have a common weakness, namely they are valuable only when the inputs they represent are directly linked with the output of the related technological activity, which is seldom the case (Babu, 1999).

As mentioned above, the various approaches to the TCs all propose different categorisations of these capabilities. In general, the various authors conceptualise the particular TC as the ability to undertake a corresponding set of technological activities. Many of these writers had no intention of actually measuring the capabilities in the disaggregated form. Hence, some degree of overlap was not a major concern. However, this becomes a major concern when the aim of a study is to assess *changes* in TCs rather than develop theory. In this case, the construction of indicators with a minimum of overlap is of utmost importance. Moreover, the indicators should correspond to the performance of a given firm in the study.

In order to overcome these hurdles I'll propose the following illustrative framework that on the one hand, distinguishes between the three major forms of TCs and on the other, distinguishes between various levels of TCs. Hence, the columns in table 1 below set out the TCs by form. The rows set the level of difficulty as well as the development over time. Hence, the various cells in the table below point to an activity the company is able to do on its own at a given point in time. Thus, following Figueiredo (2002a) the accumulation of TCs in a company is identified when that particular company has acquired the ability to use a particular piece of technology that the company has previously been unable to use.

Table 1: Technological Capabilities in SMEs in Ghana – An Illustrative Framework

Forms of TC		Investment		Production			Linkage
Levels of TC		*Pre-investment*	*Preparation & implementation*	*Product – centred*	*Process - centred*	*Equipment*	
Basic	Simple -> Complex	Identification of a suitable project			Routine production control	Basic equipment maintenance	Local procurement of goods and services
		Pre-investment studies	Preparation of feasibility study	Replicating specifications set by partner	Basic quality control	Routine replacement of components	Development of suppliers / subcontractors
		Search for suitable technology	Installation of equipment	Minor adaptations[22] to market needs	Minor adaptations incl. material substitutions	Trouble shooting	Establishment of links with technology suppliers, industry associations and universities
		Negotiation of technology transfer	Specification of project incl. product mix, input requirements & scale of production	Adaptation to export market needs	Obtaining certification for routine process quality control		
Intermediate	Simple -> Complex		Equipment procurement, training and recruitment of skilled personnel	Quality improvement & reverse engineering	De-bottlenecking, capacity stretching & cost-saving	Minor adaptations in equipment to adjust to local materials.	Supply of technical advice to buyers
		Execution of feasibility studies incl. search, evaluation and selection of technology	Basic engineering of individual facilities, expanding plant without technical assistance	Expansions of product mix.		Equipment repair	Transfer of know-how to buyers
				Inventive adaptations	Integrated automated operation systems	Modifications of core technology	
Advanced				In-house product innovation and related R&D	In-house process innovation and related R&D	In-house design and manufacturing of equipment and related R&D	Turn key capability

Time + Qualitative increase in 'depth of knowledge'

Sources: This table is inspired by Lall (1992); Lall, Navaretti et al. (1994); Wei (1995); Gonsen (1998) and Figueiredo (2002a).

It was argued that in order to assess how the PSD-programme affects the private sector in Ghana it is crucial to distinguish between the level of the immediate beneficiaries and the broader developmental level. The effects on the immediate beneficiaries will be assessed according to the stated objectives whereas the broader impact of the programme will be considered through an analysis of its role in building TCs, as this is an indispensable part of the upgrading process that eventually (*ceteris paribus*) should pave the way for a more dynamic private sector. Here, it is worth reiterating the importance of the linkage TCs for upgrading beyond the PSD-programme. Thus, TCs in general and linkage TCs in particular, are linked to the long-term effects of the programme. The next section is devoted to the analysis of the direct effects and the building of TCs in the PSD-programme.

The Effects of a Decade of PSD Support to Ghanaian Enterprises

This section will set out to analyse the data on 45 business collaborations between Danish and Ghanaian companies funded by Danida during the period 1993-2001. An overview of the companies, the main objective of the collaboration, the current situation (spring 2002), immediate positive and negative effects, derived impacts and the changes in technological capabilities is provided in appendix 1. This appendix also includes a column that indicates matters outside the collaboration, which have affected it. However, before proceeding to the analysis a brief overview of previous studies of the PSDP in Ghana will be provided.

Previous Studies of the PSDP in Ghana

Based on visits to 17 Ghanaian enterprises in the spring of 2001 an evaluation team looked into the effect of the programme in relation to the following six criteria: employment generation, foreign exchange earnings, technological relevance, environmental improvements, sustainability, and additionality. This was the first time an external evaluation team were to assess the merits of the then eight year old programme[23]. They constructed impact indicators ranging from low, through medium to high impact in the above six criteria and grouped the projects accordingly. In brief, they found that the technology transfer related to the PSDP had in general been positive. However, *"…the improved technologies transferred to the local companies do not in general appear to have resulted in visible increases in profitability*" (Danida, 2001: 28).

In addition, the introduction of new technology had not resulted in employment generation as the new technologies were labour saving. Likewise, the foreign exchange earnings had been meagre as only a few enterprises had been able to export their products. Taken together, the results of the programme were seen as rather small in comparison to the amount of money that had been used. Even though such an evaluation thus presents us with an indicator of the effectiveness of Danida's PSDP, it does not offer us an insight into why a particular project has succeeded or failed.

In the autumn of 2002, the Danish Audit Department studied 16 collaborations between Ghanaian and Danish enterprises as part of a study that aimed at estimating the effects of the PSDP (and the Business-to-Business programme in South Africa). However, it only visited 5 partnerships and 2 "start-up" facilities in Ghana[24]. It found that in almost half of the visited collaborations the stated objectives were not fulfilled. Moreover, it found that the compulsory progress reports often were faulty and did not reveal problems of managerial and co-operative character. It thus, indirectly points to the need for more knowledge about the PSDP in Ghana (Rigsrevisionen, 2003).

In contrast, John Kuada and Olav Jull Sørensen have written a number of articles and papers dealing with partner perception, the impact of alliance-promoting institutions, motives for entering the programme, and the impact of different national business systems on inter-firm relations based on three successive fieldworks in 1997, 1998 and 1999 with 16 PSDP collaborations, see e.g. (Kuada, 2000; Kuada 2002, Kuada and Sørensen, 1999; Sørensen and Kuada 2000). From these articles it is possible to get an insight into the processes at work at the enterprises, especially at the level of the general manager. Moreover, these studies also provide us with some detailed case studies. Among the most interesting findings are the examinations of why the Danish partners decided to enter into collaboration with a Ghanaian partner, how the partners were matched, the initial interaction between the partners, the different perception of the standard of second hand equipment (Kuada, 2002), and the main motives for the Ghanaian entrepreneurs to enter the programme (Kuada and Sørensen, 1999). It is proposed that the main motive for the Ghanaian owner-managers to enter into the PSD-programme is resource leveraging due to:

- The increasing pressure on local firms to improve the quality of their products as a result of the liberalisation of the Ghanaian economy.
- A general awareness among the manufacturing firms that their low-level technologies place them in a competitive disadvantage.
- The extreme costs of local funding forces owner-managers to seek foreign funding.

This is in contrast to the motive of the Danish companies, which should rather be sought for in the opportunity to enter the Ghanaian market with limited risk (90% of the costs are borne by the PSDP). This difference in incentives for taking part in the programme may explain some of the results presented below.

The Ghanaian PSDP

The collaborating Ghanaian companies represented a wide spectrum of the private enterprises in Ghana and cover among others the following sectors: agro-industry, transport, fishery, wood and furniture, pharmaceuticals, and food and beverages. Most of the companies are located in Accra (33) and Tema (11), the capital and main industrial harbour in Ghana, respectively. The latter 18 are located in Kumasi (7), Takoradi/Sekondi (4), Ho

(2), Winneba (2) and a few villages in the southern part of the country (4). The number of employees in the participating Ghanaian companies spans from 1 (a small textile company) to more than 2000 (one of the largest logging companies in Ghana). Moreover, the relative importance of the PSD-programme for the Ghanaian partner differs enormously.

At the one end of a continuum, an ID-card producer set up his business with the specific purpose of getting PSD-assistance. He had no previous experience within this line of business, and now, 3 years after the collaboration was initiated, the company has not managed to develop further. At the other end of the continuum, a producer of polystyrene products obtained a mobile polystyrene injection machine from its Danish partner for cold stores insulation. A couple of technicians were employed to use the equipment. It had absolutely no influence on the main production line and after a couple of years, the machine broke down, and the technicians were transferred to other operations within the company.

As regards the immediate success or failure of the collaboration the cases also differs a lot. An airline company ended before it really took off. A large amount of money was invested (including funds from Ghana Venture Fund and the Industrialisation Fund for Developing Countries) but due to fraud and corruption, the company went bankrupt after less than 2 years of operation. All 12 employees were laid off, but while the Ghanaian partner and the financial controller hide in the UK and Zimbabwe, respectively, the pilot and four stewardesses are now working in the US, flying internationally because of the international certificates they obtained as part of the training. At the other end of the spectrum, a producer of furniture components and parquet strips perceives the collaboration with the Danish partner as a "tremendous success". Within a 2-year period, the Ghanaian company has increased its number of employees from 7 to 33 (mostly unskilled labourers from the surrounding villages). The company has been able to develop its line of products from export of rough components to also include some of the finishing. So far, all the furniture components have been exported to the Danish partner, but due to the fact that Ghanaian wood is not FSC certified, the Danish partner is not able to sell it anymore, and the production has come to a stand-still.In order to understand the impact of the PSDP on the Ghanaian enterprises, this section will proceed with an overview of the immediate effects of the collaborations on the enterprise level, before digging deeper into the underlying causes. The effects concerned correlates with the specific objectives of the collaborations stated in the application forms and include employment generation, export earnings, improved product quality, enhanced product range, increased productivity, bigger profit margin, higher salary, and larger turnover.

As pointed out in section 3 above, 41 different Ghanaian companies were visited during the spring of 2002. These companies comprised 45 different collaborations. Among the 41 companies the number of employees had increased in 18 of them since the start of the collaboration. In 3 of these cases the increase could definitely not be attributed to the PSD and only in 12 of the remaining enterprises the increase could be ascribed to the collaboration with some accuracy. In contrast, 13 companies have dismissed employees since the initiation of the project.

Similarly, it is difficult to attribute this decrease in number of employees to the project itself. However, in at least 7 cases employees that were employed as part of the collaboration has been fired due to failed projects and in 3 cases employees were made redundant as a part of the restructuring of the enterprise that came along with the cooperation. Thus, in crude terms of employment generation it is difficult to state that the PSDP has been a success. However, these figures should not be overinterpreted. Six Ghanaian companies were established with the specific purpose of participating in the PSDP. Five of these are still running and have created a total of 114 new jobs.

The demand for extra staff in the enterprises seems to be of a different character in the partnerships and start-up facilities, respectively. Whereas organisational changes are observable in many of the Ghanaian enterprises that have augmented the number of staff as part of a partnership with a Danish enterprise[25], this is not the case in the start-up facilities. Here the reason should be sought in the immediate demand for new staff that the introduction of new machines creates. Most start-up facilities are confined to technical assistance, i.e. one or two new machines are brought from Denmark or elsewhere to fill out a vacuum in the production or to introduce a new line of production and Ghanaian employees are trained to operate them.

However, the start-up facilities seldom change managerial or administrative routines in the Ghanaian enterprise. The nature of this immediate demand for extra staff is best illustrated by the following example: A supplier of equipment for the Ghanaian health sector approached the embassy with the purpose of finding a partner that dealt with laboratory equipment. Concurrently, a Danish producer of ultrasound scanners was looking for a Ghanaian partner in order to expand its market to West Africa. The partners were matched and a start-up facility was initiated. The objective of this collaboration was to sell the Danish partner's scanners in Ghana. However, ultrasound scanners are not sold once and for all. Firstly, they come with a 1-year warranty and secondly, even though price matters in this fairly competitive market, service also matters. Therefore, the collaboration called for extra staff to market the new products, to subsequently service them, and to teach doctors in the health clinics how to use them. In total 5 employees were employed to take care of these new operations.

Table 2: Selected Direct Effects of the PSDP in the Ghanaian Companies

Selected parameters	Partnerships		Start-up facilities		Total	
	Rise	Decline	Rise	Decline	Rise	Decline
Employment	7	6	11	7	18	13
Exports	2	-	-	-	2	-
Product quality	4	-	5	-	9	-
Product range[26]	4	-	7	-	11	-
Productivity	4	1	7	-	11	1
Profit margin	2	-	-	-	2	-
Salary	1	1	-	-	1	1
Turnover	3	-	5	.	8	-

However, employment is not the only parameter by which the collaborations should be assessed. As is evident from table 2, product quality, product range, productivity, and turnover have increased in a number of enterprises due to the collaboration with the Danish partner. 11 companies have broadened their product range due to the PSDP. Likewise, 11 companies have experienced an increase in productivity. This is partly due to enhanced production methods and partly to organisational changes brought about by the Danish partner. As one would expect because of the different time horizons, organisational changes are more profound in the partnerships than in the start-up facilities, whereas new production methods (and new equipment) account for the productivity changes in the start-up facilities. In addition, turnover has increased in 8 companies since the collaboration was initiated. Only in one of these cases the increased turnover was neither related to increased product range nor increased productivity. Instead, the Ghanaian partner in this ice cream company was able to obtain contracts with a big retail chain because in the eyes of this chain, the partnership with a Dane guaranteed good quality products. Thereby, the products became available in more outlets, which increased sales. On the other hand, the company changed its marketing and distribution channels in order to meet the customers at their daily endeavours instead of having the customers buy the products at specified outlets. Inspired by the distribution system of Fan Milk, this company bought a number of tricycles equipped with mobile freezers and was thus able to make the products available where mostly young customers were regular visitors, e.g. at the university campus.

As is evident from appendix 1, some direct negative result can also be attributed to the collaborations. Among them is the decline in number of employees, the loss of customers, the decrease of salaries, and loans that are not repaid. These negative effects are partly caused by the factors proposed by Kuada and Sørensen (1999) and Kuada (2002), viz. different reasons for entering into collaboration, problems related to the matching of partners, initial interaction between the partners, and different perceptions of the standard of second hand equipment, and partly to incomplete feasibility studies, fraud, and lack of managerial skills. The factors are many, and often intertwined. Therefore, the following two examples are provided in order to illustrate some of the processes at work in the less successful collaborations.

A producer of fruit juices and fruit concentrates met a Danish manager at a TechChange fair in Denmark. The Ghanaian manger wanted a foreign partner in order to get access to capital whereas the Danish company wanted to enter the Ghanaian orange concentrate market. Representatives from the Danish company had for a long time surveyed the Ghanaian market and had come to the conclusion that an excess of oranges existed and the price was relatively low.

It could have started its own factory but found that it was both easier and better for Ghana if an already existing partner was found. Hence, it looked for a Ghanaian partner to be able to exploit the possibilities. Fortunately, the local partner already had a pineapple extractor including all the equipment to make the concentrate from the juice. Hence, all it needed was a citrus extractor that could be connected to the existing system. In addition, both companies were used to deal with foreign companies. The managing director of the Ghanaian company has both educational and working experience from abroad. Moreover, the company collaborates with a Dutch partner on a regular basis.

The Danish partner solely works abroad and has extensive experience from the PSDP, having participated in five other Danida funded PSDPs. Thus, on the face of it, the future prospects were bright. However, the partners did not match. According to the Danish partner the Ghanaian partner was unable to run a business. He would not listen to advice and during the course of the collaboration; the economic situation in the Ghanaian company *"went from bad to worse"*. The Ghanaian partner, on the other hand, claimed that the main representatives from the Danish company only spent 10-20% of their time in the company; the rest was spent on looking for new partners. His feelings were expressed in the following statement: "... [their] *approach to* [our company] *is a neo-colonial approach. They just want to go to Ghana to exploit the market"*.

However, the problems were not confined to interpersonal disputes. Firstly, it turned out that it was difficult to acquire oranges of a satisfactory quality on a regular basis, and secondly world market price decreased. Thus, in this case it appears that many factors were at play at the same time causing the poor outcome of the collaboration, viz. incomplete scrutiny of the availability of raw materials including infrastructural problems, poor matchmaking, and conflicting interest.

A Ghanaian graphic designer was also invited to a TechChange fair in Denmark. He had a relatively sound business designing greeting cards for the Afro-American community in the United States. Moreover, he designed calendars and sales displays for the Ghanaian market. However, the company was facing problems finishing the products it was producing as the companies that it outsourced the pre-printing and printing of the products to often failed to meet both the quality and the deadline the customers demanded. Thus, he was looking for a partner that could help him establish a pre-print and a printing unit in the company.

From the initial meeting with the Danish partner that had just closed a successful partnership with a Zimbabwean partner; the Ghanaian graphic designer was made to believe that these two units could be established quite quickly. Therefore, he was reluctant to initiate new projects because he felt that any new mistakes from printing and finishing companies would ruin his good reputation. He scaled down the business and focused mostly on what the company could do in-house. However, the actual process of getting started was procrastinated and when the new equipment eventually came, a large part was dysfunctional and minor parts were missing altogether.

Furthermore, the Danish partner lost interest in the project and left the management of it to a former employee. In order to earn a living the graphic designer increased his (personal) business of designing greeting cards. This involved a lot of travelling and thus, he did not take interest in the daily management. All the profitable jobs slipped away and the employees either left the company for better offers or were made redundant due to lack of new orders. The graphic designer still believes that at the end of the day, the collaboration will benefit the company, but two years after the collaboration took off, and fours years after the first meeting the essential image-setter was still not working, all qualified staff were gone and the company hardly ever got new contracts. Additionally, many new companies have entered the market forcing down the profit. Similar to the fruit juice case presented above, it is difficult to point to one causing factor in this case. Rather, a number of factors have been at play, among them too high expectations, prolonged procedures, loss of interest in the project, and dysfunctional machines.

Building Technological Capabilities in Ghanaian Enterprises

Building and diffusion of TCs in the Ghanaian private sector is seen as a way to enhance value-added activities in the enterprise and economy, respectively. Moreover, the applications forms and feasibility studies related to the collaborations all indicate that the building of TCs through technical, managerial, administrative and marketing training is a central component of the PSDP. Thus, changes in TCs are a useful indicator for the developmental impact of the programme. As argued in section 5 above, changes in technological capabilities in Ghanaian SMEs are best analysed through a division of TCs into investment, production and linkage capabilities. This section will set out to analyse how the PSDP has affected capability building in the Ghanaian enterprises and which factors that have either encouraged or constrained it.

Table 3: Capability- building in Ghanaian Enterprises

	Investment capabilities	Production capabilities	Linkage capabilities
Partnerships	5	10	4
Start-up facilities	3	8	5

To facilitate clarity, positive changes in TCs as a result of the PSDP are presented in table 3 above. The number of Ghanaian enterprises that have experienced positive changes in any of these forms of capabilities has been added. Consequently, table 3 merely presents the number of enterprises that have encountered changes but not the quality of these changes. As is observable from appendix 1, positive changes in TCs most often come together, viz. production and investment capabilities, production and linkage capabilities, etc. The exception is changes in production capabilities that are present in eight cases without any changes in other forms of capabilities. However, in order to avoid misunderstandings I will make it clear that only a couple of enterprises have reached the level of intermediate TCs (two in investment capabilities and one in production capabilities) the rest are confined to changes in basic level TCs. Given that building of TCs is the main objective in most PSD-collaborations, the results are rather meagre. The question is why this is so.

Some factors seem to encourage the building of TCs, among them training, organisational and administrative changes, openness, membership of business organisations, and increased forward and backward linkages. Technical training of blue collar workers relating to the operation and maintenance of new equipment is directly related to the enhancement of production capabilities. However, production capabilities are not confined to the act of feeding e.g. raw rubber into one end of a machine and subsequently collecting the finished product in the other end, including frequent cleaning and lubrication of it. Basic production capabilities also involve the skills of, for instance, adapting the equipment for local needs and if necessary, modify the raw materials. Thus, enhancement of production capabilities entails organisational changes in as much the blue collar staff have to acquire information about suppliers and customers in order to adapt the process/product to the required specifications.

Likewise, openness is often a precondition for the enhancement of TCs in as much as openness allows employees from one company to benefit from advances achieved in another company, be it product or process-wise. Openness can be facilitated through membership of business organisations where networks can be established and new ideas and opportunities fostered. By the same token both forward and backward linkages can enhance TCs through new ideas and new demands that have to be fulfilled. Failing to accomplish these account for much of the failure to build TCs in the Ghanaian companies. Moreover, the very PSDP seems to counteract the enhancement of linkage capabilities because many Ghanaian owner-managers leave the initiative to either the programme or their Danish partner, or both.

As soon as the matchmaking is finished and the application for funds has been approved, many owner-managers expect the enterprise to develop instantly due to access to the Danish market, new machines and a steady inflow of capital. However, this is seldom the case. Firstly, administrative procedures are lengthy due to the specific routines in Danida. Secondly, time-schedules are seldom kept as a result of financial constraints, difficulties of obtaining the right equipment, problems procuring high quality inputs etc. Thirdly, the partners underestimate the time it takes to get to know each other. Finally, many owner-mangers over interpret the collaboration agreements and assume that even though it is specifically stated that the collaboration is confined to a technical cooperation the Danish partner will eventually invest in the company. Instead of searching for alternative markets, other funding channels etc. the owner-managers slow down operations and wait. The result is often that they lose customers and pull out of agreements with sub-suppliers thereby worsening linkage capabilities.

The rather poor result with regard to generating TCs in Ghanaian SMEs are also caused by the specific features of the Ghanaian business system. The hierarchal organisational structure and the authoritarian-benevolent leadership conducted in most enterprises impede employees, especially at floor level, to get sufficient knowledge to upgrade the TCs. Family members are often employed in top positions in the company, even though they do not have the crucial qualifications and are often included among the employees that are trained.

Many owner-managers engage in other business activities in order to minimise risks and therefore often neglect activities that do not immediately pay off, and often rely on connections in the political establishment to obtain contracts. In addition, there is no culture of sharing information among Ghanaian businessmen and it is impossible to obtain reliable information about company assets and activities except for the very few enterprises that are listed on the Ghanaian Stock Exchange (Grant, 2002).

The same causes also account for the fact that capabilities that are transferred from Danish to Ghanaian companies are only spreading into the rest of the Ghanaian private sector to a minor extent. Diffusion of capabilities occurs through the following modes:

1. Trained employees leave the company to start their own company or get employed elsewhere.
2. Subcontractors are upgraded as part of the improvement of the products and processes in the Ghanaian company.

3. Customers' quality awareness is raised, resulting in the demand for higher quality products from other local enterprises.

However, a combination of the specific features of the Ghanaian business system described above and the limitations of the PSDP seem to impede this diffusion of capabilities. For instance, the very fact that companies in general do not go bankrupt but instead remain inactive implies that (trained) employees and equipment are kept instead of being spread. Of course the economic situation in Ghana reinforces this tendency in-as-much-as it is very often very difficult to get another job, particularly in smaller communities. Thus, it is better to stay with the "big man"[27] than to seek for other employment.

The tendency to stay with the "big man" instead of seeking other employment is illustrated by the following example: A Ghanaian businessman from the capital of the Volta region was familiar with the PSDP from his activities at the Association of Ghana Industries and approached the embassy with the purpose of finding a partner for his furniture company. However, the embassy had difficulties finding him a suitable Danish partner and instead matched him with a dealer of kiln dryers in order to produce impregnated teak poles. The Ghanaian partner had a vacant plot of land in an industrial zone and the collaboration was initiated. However, it never became a success, the partners did not match and furthermore, the Ghanaian partner had no former experience in this line of business.

Now, some eight years after the collaboration was initiated, the activities are still tickling over; most often the machines are standing idle due to lack of orders and malfunctioning equipment but all employees keep with the "big man". No other jobs are available and they still believe that eventually the owner-manager will obtain new contracts through his connections in Accra.

As regards the PSDP in Ghana, it seldom involves a strengthening of the linkages between the involved enterprises and the rest of the Ghanaian private sector. The majority of the Ghanaian companies either act as subcontractors for their Danish partner, i.e. raw material is bought in Ghana whereupon the Ghanaian partner does the basic finishing (in order to keep freight costs down), or as a possibility to gain access to the Ghanaian market, i.e. all inputs for a particular productions is imported from the Danish partner whereupon the assembly is done in Ghana (in order to minimise the import duties and thereby become competitive). In some cases either the local inputs or the local customers have been pushed aside in favour of the Danish partner or the PSDP companies have started to trade with each other.

Thus, the capabilities are kept in certain companies and only in rare cases do they diffuse. Moreover, in a few cases in which external funding from the Industrialisation Fund for Developing Countries (IFU) is involved, the Danish company simply has taken over the shares from the Ghanaian partner. On the one hand, this has made the company profitable and, thus facilitated the continuation of an otherwise bankrupt company but on the other hand, it has limited the diffusion of TCs in the Ghanaian private sector.

Conclusion

The effects of the PSDP in Ghana described above are not the only ones to be found. The impact of most development projects/programmes far transcends the immediate beneficiary group and could thus be sought for in competing enterprises that did not receive funding, or in the families of the employees of a particular company. However, in order to make this analysis more manageable changes in technological capabilities were chosen as the focus of the study. Even though the study was thus limited, it has shown us that a simple success/failure criterion in aid evaluations fails to offer any insights into the development process of the PSDP. Moreover, it proposes that the history of the projects should be taken into consideration when examining the impacts. Additionally, it suggests that the development project cannot be examined in isolation. Rather, the financial situation in Ghana as elsewhere, the role of business organisations, trends in international consumer preferences etc. have to be taken into consideration. Thus, development projects must be analysed within the wider societal and economic context. Finally, it illustrates the centrality of unintended and derived impacts.

It has been shown that a number of interwoven factors determine the outcome of the programme. Among the most important internal factors are training of blue collar workers, managerial and organisational changes, openness, and forward and backward linkages. Likewise, the conflicting interests and expectations among the Ghanaian and Danish participants, respectively, influence the impact of the PSDP. However, just as important are factors outside the realm of the programme, viz. the specific features of the Ghanaian business system, e.g. the hierarchal organisational structure of Ghanaian enterprises and the authoritarian-benevolent leadership, and the socio-economic situation prevailing in Ghana, i.e. lack of inputs, few job opportunities, and lack of working capital.

The linkages between the participating Ghanaian enterprises and the rest of the Ghanaian private sector have been touched upon. The analysis suggests that technological capabilities do not diffuse due to the lack of collaboration between Ghanaian companies, the tendency to keep employees even though no production is taking place, the fact that hardly any companies go bankrupt, and the built-in inclination to work solely for the Danish partner.

Overall, we have seen a variety of cases and illustrations of collaborations each with pros and cons; that there is not one causal explanation for these outcomes; that the building of technological capabilities is not confined to training blue collar workers; and that there is a need for a broad approach to impact studies in order to understand the underlying causes. My depiction of each argument can be improved but I hope that I have given a usable introduction.

Notes

[1] The research for this paper is based on fieldwork conducted for my PhD, which has been funded by the Danish Institute for International Studies (formerly: Centre for Development Studies, Copenhagen), International Development Studies, Roskilde University, and the Council for Development Research, Copenhagen. I am grateful to the researchers at the School of Administration, University of Ghana, Steen Folke and Laurids S. Lauridsen for very helpful comments and support. I also received valuable suggestions from one anonymous reviewer. The usual caveats apply.

[2] Concurrently, the grants were raised to cover 90% of the costs with a maximum limit of Dkk 3 million.

[3] The Structural Adjustment Programmes in Ghana evolved in three phases: ERP I (1983-86), II (1987-93), and III (1993-95). Basically the ERP I included a stabilisation package and a programme to promote economic development, ERP II sought to deepen the ongoing reforms, and ERP III focused on accelerated growth through sustainable development and poverty alleviation. The ERPs included liberalisation of prices, rationalisation and privatisation of state-owned enterprises, de-subsidisation of food and social services, devaluation etc. For excellent insights into the socio-economic and political realities that made the ERPs possible, see Hutchful (2002) and Nugent (1995), respectively.

[4] Hutchful (1995: 179) reminds us that the commercial and manufacturing enterprises reacted differently towards the ERPs precisely due to the different ways the programmes affected the two sectors.

[5] The medium-sized enterprises are regarded as an important pillar in the development of the domestic private sector, see e.g. Dia (1996).

[6] The word *kalabule* entered the Ghanaian vocabulary in the 1970s and referred to *"profiteering, either by manipulation of the state machinery or merely by evasion of official controls"*. Apparently, during the end of the 1970s fortunes were made on the basis of speculation and hardly any profit could be made on productive activity. All entrepreneurial activity was increasingly associated with *kalabule* activities and regarded as underhand and parasitic (Nugent, 1995: 27f).

[7] It is worth remembering that the actions taken by Rawlings in mid-1979 (confiscation of a number of small private manufacturing firms) still remain deeply imprinted in the memories of local entrepreneurs (Tangri, 1992).

[8] The business system is defined as nationally distinctive systems that are *"particular arrangements of hierarchy-market relations which become institutionalized and relatively successful in particular contexts"* (Whitley 1992: 10). It was developed to describe the major differences in the organisation of market economies and explain them in terms of variation in the nature of dominant societal institutions among countries (Whitley 2001).

[9] It seems, however, that non-kin networks are slowly emerging among educated members of the Ghanaian society (Sørensen and Kuada, 2001)

[10] It should be noted, that the definition of evaluation adopted by Danida also include impact and sustainability as stipulated in the following definition recommended by DAC for its member countries: *"An evaluation is an assessment, as systematic and objective as possible, of on-going or completed aid activities, their design, implementation and results. The aim is to determine the relevance and fulfilment of objectives, developmental efficiency, effectiveness, impact and sustainability"* (Danida, 1999a: 2).

[11] The logical framework provides an overview of the project objectives, i.e. goal, purpose, outputs and activities, measurable indicators, possible data sources and major assumptions and risks related to the project. Moreover, it links these aspects in a matrix and connects the various levels in the logical framework with evaluation criteria, e.g. results are related to efficiency, purpose to effectiveness, and objectives to impact (and sustainability) (Gasper, 1997; Coles, Evans et al., 1998; Mosse, 1998; Cracknell, 2000; Gasper, 2000; Commission, 2001).

[12] The ToRs of external evaluations most often specifically demand LFA-like approaches. The following quote is a typical example of the close link: *"The overall objective is to evaluate the programmes' long-term impact…Based on the ToR, the team is required to evaluate the B-t-B Programmeme* [business-to-business programme in South Africa] *in terms of the achievements of its objectives"* (Danida 2000:4).

[13] From a critical point of view, it has been argued that development policy as such is nothing but a rationalising discourse that conceals hidden political intent of development and purposes of bureaucratic power. Development issues are portrayed by donor agencies in a way that makes technical solutions possible as political tensions and power relations simply cannot be dealt with. See James Feguson's description of a World Bank project in Lesotho for a magnificent account of this view (Ferguson, 1990).

[14] A number of impact studies have been made using a similar definition; see e.g. (Sultana and Folke, 1999; Folke, 2001; Adam and Nielsen, 2002).

[15] Danida, for instance, defines impact to include: *"...both positive and negative consequences, whether these are foreseen and expected, or not"* (Danida, 1999a: 56). The important word here is expected in as much as Gasper (2000: 23) reminds us that: *"...unintended is a broader category than unexpected, since all unexpected effects are unintended but so are some expected ones"*.

[16] Romijn (1999: 33) even goes as far as to state that many of the firms covered in these studies are not only among the largest in the country but also the leaders of their particular sector and sometimes even large by international standards. Thus, the image that is generally presented is biased towards the large-scale sector. However, most of these studies relate to an Asian or Latin American context. In an African context the picture is somewhat different in-as- much-as the works of (Alänge, 1987; Lall, Navaretti et al., 1994; Biggs, Shah et al., 1995; Teitel, 2000; Wignaraja, 2001) all include SMEs in their analysis.

[17] Notable exceptions from this general picture are (Alänge, 1987; Olsen, 1995; Motoki and Taichi, 1999; Romijn, 2001).

[18] The starting point of the evolutionary school of thought was a critique of the orthodox microeconomic theory of the time which, on the one hand, assumed the behavioural patterns of the firm was based on rules that reflected the seek for maximisation (usually profit or present value) and on the other, was guided by the concept of equilibrium. Moreover, it emphasised the similarities between firms and argued that in-so-far-as differences existed; they were a product of differences in market environment. Neoclassical economists did not focus on the causes of technological change. Rather, they focused on the labour and capital intensity of technology and the estimation of economic contribution of technology by its move outwards of the production function (Nelson and Winter, 1982; Fransman, 1984: note 9).

[19] Lall, Navaretti et al. (1994) have proposed slightly different subgroups, namely process technology, product technology and industrial engineering, but due to the fact that only the former two have any relevance in a Ghanaian context, I've have chosen to subdivide the production capabilities differently.

[20] In relation to the creation of necessary skills in manufacturing companies in developing countries, the skills needed for creating (basic) production capabilities ultimately are formed within the framework of the enterprises and not in the formal schooling system. However, it is important to note that even the most basic TCs often demand skills acquired in primary school, such as the ability to read and write and the ability to carry out arithmetical calculations. The capabilities that are more advanced are normally partly created in universities and R&D departments, and partly within the company (Enos, 1991).

[21] See Biggs, Shah et al. (1995: 37ff) for an example of how to calculate Total Factor Productivity in three African countries.

[22] The classification of adaptations proposed by Evenson and Westphal (1994: 34) is used here. Hence, minor adaptations change the technique but leave its core

unaffected whereas, inventive adaptations do not make use of the technique, but of the knowledge that underlies it. Thus, inventive adaptations are often associated with formalised R&D capabilities.

[23] It should be noted that two internal reviews of the PSDP have been completed in 1995 and 1999, respectively. Unfortunately, these two reviews offer little but an overview of the amount of money spent and a recommendation of continuation of the programme. Even the annexes with data on the various enterprises that have participated in the programme offer nothing but the name of the partners, the objective(s) of the collaboration, and the grant disbursed. This is, however, not surprising as the team of the 1999 review only visited Ghana for 3 days! (Danida, 1995; Danida, 1999b).

[24] The validity of the Audit Department's result is questionable as the team was accompanied by the PS-coordinators from the embassy. Thus, in order to be able to apply for further funding one would suspect that the Ghanaian entrepreneurs tended to highlight the positive effects and downgrade the negative effects of the collaborations.

[25] Organisational changes of course also account for the decline of the number of employees in some enterprises.

[26] Excluded are activities that were totally outside the scope of the Ghanaian enterprise before the initiation of the collaboration but were introduced with it, and companies that were set up with the specific purpose of getting funding from Danida, e.g. an engineering company which previously also sold educational toys but started an institution for caretakers as part of the PSDP, and a producer of teak poles that only had the plot of land when the collaboration started, respectively.

[27] This term is borrowed from Nugent (1995) to denote both economic and political power, but primarily to denote the relationship between the big men and the small boys in Ghana that implies that employees will keep with the owner if he has some political power because they know that as soon as he will obtain new contracts they will once again be able to work.

References

Acheampong, I. and M. Tribe (2001): "Sources of Industrial Growth: The Impact of Policy on Large and Medium Scale Manufacturing Performance in Ghana". *Economic Policy and Manufacturing Performance in Developing Countries.*

Adam, Y. and H. Nielsen (2002): *The Agricultural Development Project in Tete, Mozambique: An Impact study*. Copenhagen, Danida.

Adams, J., S. Batchelor, et al. (2000): "Developing A Methodology For Measuring the Impact of a Development Network". Unpublished paper.

Alänge, S. (1987): *Acquisition of Capabilities through International Technology Transfer: The Case of Small Scale Industrialisation in Tanzania.* Göteborg, Chalmers University of Technology.

Amponsah, N. (2000): "Ghana's Mixed Structural Adjustment Results: Explaining the Poor Private Sector Response." *Africa Today* **47**(2): 9-32.

Archibugi, D. and C. Pietrobelli (In Press): "The globalisation of technology and its implications for developing countries. Windows of Opportunity or Further Burden?" *Technological Forecasting & Social Change*

Awuah, E. (1997): "Mobilizing for Change: A Case Study of Market Trader Activism in Ghana." *Canadian Journal of African Studies* **31**(3): 401-423.

Babu, M. (1999): The Determinants of Firm-level Technological Performances: A Study on the Indian Capital Goods Sector." Maastrict, United Nations University, Institute for New Technologies: 101.

Barwa, S. D. (1995): *Structural Adjustment Programmes and the Urban Informal Sector in Ghana*. Geneva, International Labour Office.

Bell, M. and K. Pavitt (1993): "Technological Accumulation and Industrial Growth: Contrasts between Developed and Developing Countries." *Industrial and Corporate Change* **2**(2): 157-211.

Bierschenk, T. (1988): "Development Projects as Arenas of Negotiation for Strategic Groups. A Case Study." *Sociologia Ruralis* **28**(2-3): 146-160.

Bierschenk, T. and J. P. Olivier de Sardan (1997): "ECRIS: Rapid Collective Inquiry for the Identification of Conflicts and Strategic Groups." *Human Organisation* **56**(2): 238-244.

Biggs, T., M. Shah, et al. (1995): *Technological Capabilities and Learning in African Enterprises*. Washington D. C., The World Bank.

Cassen, R. (1986): *Does Aid Work? Report to an intergovernmental task force*. Oxford, Clarendon Press.

Commission, E. (2001): *Evaluation in the European Commission. A Guide to the Evaluation Procedures and Structures currently operational in the Commission's External Co-operation Programmes*. Brussels, Commission of the European Communities, EuropeAid Co-operation Office, Evaluation Unit H/6: 20.

Cox, A. and J. Healey (2003): "The Poverty Reduction Strategies of the Development Cooperation Agencies in the 1990s: Their Record and What They Need to Do" in A. Booth and P. Mosley(eds). *The New Poverty Strategies. What Have They Achieved? What Have We Learned?* Houndmills, Palgrave Macmillan: 21-43.

Cracknell, B. E. (2000): *Evaluating Development Aid. Issues, Problems and Solutions*. New Dehli, Sage Publications ltd.

Crehan, K. and A. von Oppen (1988): "Understandings of 'Development': an Arena of Struggle." *Sociologia Ruralis* **28**(2-3): 113-145.

Danida (1995): *Review af privat sektor konceptet og dets gennemførelse*. København, Udenrigsministeriet.

Danida (1999a): *Evaluation Guidelines*. Copenhagen, Ministry of Foreign Affairs: 125.

Danida (1999b): *Review Report: Danida's Private Sector Development Programme*. Copenhagen, Royal Danish Ministry of Foreign Affairs.

Danida (2001): *Evaluation. Private Sector Development programme*. Copenhagen, Ministry of Foreign Affairs. Evaluation Secretariat.

Dia, M. (1996): *Africa's Management in the 1990s and Beyond. Reconciling Indigenous and Transplanted Institutions*. Washingthon, IBRD. The World Bank.

Enos, J. L. (1991): *The Creation of Technological Capability in Developing Countries*. London, Pinter Publishers.

Evenson, R. E. and L. E. Westphal (1994): *Technological Change and Technological Strategy*. Maastricht,
Institute for New Technogies, UNU: 83.

Fafchamps, M. (1996): "The Enforcement of Commercial Contracts in Ghana." *World Development* **24**(3): 427-448.

Ferguson, J. (1990): *The Anti-Politics Machine. "Development," Depolitization, and Bureaucratic Power in Lesotho*. Minneapolis, University of Minnesota Press.

Figueiredo, P. N. (2002a): "Does Technological Learning Pay off? Inter-Firm Differences in Technological Capability-Accumulation Paths and Operational Performance Improvement." *Research Policy* **31**(1): 73-94.

Figueiredo, P. N. (2002b): "Technological Capability-accumulation and the Underlying Learning Process: Analytical Frameworks and Differences between latecomer Steel Firms" Paper presented at the DRUID Summer Conference on *"Industrial Dynamics of the New and Old Economy - Who is Embracing Whom?"* Copenhagen/Elsinore: 54.

Folke, S. (1998): "Evaluering af udviklingsbistandens virkninger." *Den ny verden* **31**(1): 75-90.

Folke, S. (2000): "Hvad ved vi om NGO-bistandens virkninger?" *Den ny verden* **33**(3): 5-20.

Folke, S., Ed. (2001): *In The Wake of A Fflagship : Ex-post Impact Study of the Noakhali Rural Development Project in Bangladesh.* Copenhagen, Danida evaluation report 2001/5.

Fransman, M. (1984): "Technological Capability in the Third World: An Overview and Introduction to some of the Issues raised in this Book" in M. Fransman and K. King: *Technological Capability in the Third World..* London, MacMillan Press, 3-30.

Gasper, D. (1997): *'Logical Frameworks': A Critical Assessment: Managerial Theory, Pluralistic Practice.* The Hague, Institute of Social Studies: 36.

Gasper, D. (2000): "Evaluating the Logical Framework Approach Towards Learning-Oriented Development Evaluation." *Public Administration and Development* **20**(1): 17-28.

Gibbon, P. and L. Schulpen (2002): *Comparative Appraisal of Multilateral and Bilateral Approaches to Financing Private Sector Development in Developing Countries.* Helsinki, World Institute for Development Economics Research: 47.

Gonsen, R. (1998): *Technological Capabilities in Developing Countries: Industrial Biotechnology in Mexico* Houndmills, MacMillan Press.

Grant, R. (2002): "Foreign Companies and Glocalizations: Evidence from Accra, Ghana" in R. Grant and J. R. Short: *Globalisation and the Margins.* Houndmills, Palgrave MacMillan: 130-149.

Harrigan, J. and S. Younger (2000): "Aid, Debt & Growth" in E. Aryeetey, J. Harrigan and M. Nissanke: *Economic Reforms in Ghana. The Miracle and the Mirage.* Oxford, James Currey: 185-208.

Harrison, E. (2003): *The monolithic development machine? A Moral Critique of Development" in* P. Q. van Ufford and A. K. Giri: *In Search of Global Responsibilities*. London, Routledge: 101-117.

Hopkins, R. (1995): *Impact Assessment: Overview and Methods of Application*. Oxford, Oxfam GB & Novib: 70.

Hutchful, E. (2002): *Ghana's Adjustment Experience. The Paradox of Reform*. Geneva, UNRISD.

ISSER (2003): *The State of the Ghanaian Economy in 2002*. Accra, The Institute of Statistical, Social and Economic Research, University of Ghana, Legon.

Kragh, M. V., J. B. Mortensen, et al. (2000): Foreign aid and private sector development. *Foreign Aid and Development: Lessons Learnt and Directions for the Future*. F. Tarp and P. Hjertholm. London, Routledge: 312-331.

Kraus, J. (2002): "Capital, power and business associations in the African political economy: a tale of two countries, Ghana and Nigeria." *Journal of Modern African Studies* **40**(3): 395-436.

Kruse, S.-E., T. Kyllönen, et al. (1997): *Searching for Impact and Methods: NGO Evaluation Synthesis Study*. Helsinki, Ministry of Foreign Affaiars of Finland.

Kuada, J. (2000): "Partner Performance Perception in Danish-Ghanaian Strategic Alliances. A Gap Analysis" in O. J. Sørensen and E. Arnould: *Marketing and Development Challenges in The 21st Century. Proceedings of The 7th International Conference on Marketing and Development*. Accra, International Society for Marketing and Development: 91-108.

Kuada, J. (2002): "Collaboration between developed and developing country-based firms: Danish-Ghanaian experience." *Journal of Business & Industrial Marketing* **17**(6): 538-557.

Kuada, J. and O. J. Sørensen (1999): "Upstream and Downstream Processes of Internationalisation: Some Ghanaian Evidence." *Journal of Euromarketing* **7**(4): 7-41.

Lall, S. (1992): "Technological Capabilities and Industrialisation." *World Development* **20**(2): 165-186.

Lall, S. (1995): "Structural Adjustment and African Industry." *World Development* **23**(12): 2019-2031.

Lall, S. (1999): "Introduction and Setting" in S. Lall: *The Technological Response to Import Liberalisation in SubSaharan Africa*. Hampshire & London, MacMillan Press Ltd.: 1-25.

Lall, S. (2000): "Technological Change and Industrialisation In the Asian Newly Industrialising Economies: Achievements and Challenges" in L. Kim and R. R. Nelson: *Technology, Learning, & Innovation. Experiences of Newly Industrialising Economies*. Cambridge, Cambridge University Press: 13-68.

Lall, S. and W. W. Latsch (1999): "Import Liberalisation and Industrial Performance: Theory and Evidence" in S. Lall. Hampshire: *The Technological Response to Import Liberalisation in SubSaharan Africa*. London, MacMillan Press Ltd.: 26-56.

Lall, S., G. B. Navaretti, et al. (1994): *Technology and Enterprise Development. Ghana under Structural Adjustment*. London, MacMillan Press Ltd.

Madsen, H. L. (1999): *Impact Assessment - undertaken by Danish NGOs*. Copenhagen, Centre for Development Research.

Mosse, D. (1998): "Process-oriented Approaches to Development Practice and Social Research" in D. Mosse, J. Farrington and A. Rew: *Development as Process: Concepts and methods for working with Complexity*. London, Routledge: 3-30.

Motoki, T. and S. Taichi (1999): "Can 'the Miracle' be Replicated?: Official Development Assistance and Technological Transfer from Japan to East Asia and Southern Africa." *Journal of Developing Societies* **15**(1): 61-94.

Nelson, R. R. and S. G. Winter (1982): *An Evolutionary Theory of Economic Change*. Cambridge, The Belknap Press of Harvard University Press.

Nikoi, G. (1995): "Change Agents in the Development of Financial Services for Small-Scale Enterprises in Ghana" in P. English and G. Hénault: *Agents of Change. Studies on the Policy Environment for Small Enterprise in Africa*. London, Intermediate Technology Publications Ltd: 144-160.

Nugent, P. (1995): *Big Men, Small Boys and Politics in Ghana. Power, Ideology and the Burden of History, 1982-1994*. Accra, Asempa Publishers.

Oakley, P., B. Pratt, et al. (1998): *Outcomes and Impact: Evaluating Change in Social Development*. Oxford, INTRAC.

Okejiri, E. (2000): "Foreign technology and development of indigenous technological capabilities in the Nigerian manufacturing industry." *Technology In Society* **22**(2): 189-199.

Olivier de Sardan, J.-P. (1988): "Peasant Logics and Development Project Logics." *Sociologia Ruralis* **18**(2/3): 216-226.

Olsen, O. E. (1995): *Small Steps Towards Great Changes. Enterprise Development in Aid Supported Technology Transfer Projects*. Trondheim, Institutt for organisasjons- og arbejdslivsfag. Universitetet i Trondheim. Norges Tekniske Høgskole.

Owusu, J. H. (2001): "Determinants of export-oriented industrial output in Ghana: the case of formal wood processing in an era of economic recovery." *The Journal of Modern African Studies* **39**(1): 51-80.

Panford, K. (2001): "Structural Adjustment Programmes, Human Resources and Organisational Challenges Facing Labour and Policy Makers in Ghana" in K. Konadu-Agyemang: *IMF and World Bank Sponsored Structural Adjustment Programmes in Africa: Ghana's experience, 1983-1999*. Burlington, Ashgate: 219-239.

Pedersen, P. O. (1998): "The Development of Small- and Medium Sized Enterprises in Developing Countries – The Case of Zimbabwe." *CDR Working Paper* **98**(5).

Putranto, K., D. Stewart, et al. (2003): "International technology transfer and distribution of technology capabilities: The Case of Railway Development in Indonesia." *Technology In Society* **25**(1): 43-53.

Rigsrevisionen (2003): *Beretning om privatsektor programmer i udviklingslande*. København, Statsrevisoratet.

Roche, C. (1999): *Impact Assessment for Development agencies: Learning to Value Change*. Oxford, Oxfam GB.

Romijn, H. (1997): "Acquisition of Technological Capability in Development: A Quantitative Case Study of Pakistan's Capital Goods Sector." *World Development* **25**(3): 359-377.

Romijn, H. (1999): *Acquisition of Technological Capability in Small Firms in Developing Countries*. Houndmills, MacMillan Press.

Romijn, H. (2001): "Technology Support for Small-scale Industry in Developing Countries: A Review of Concepts and Project Practices." *Oxford Development Studies* **29**(1): 57-76.

Schulpen, L. and P. Gibbon (2002): "Private Sector Development: Policies, Practices and Problems." *World Development* **30**(1): 1-15.

Sørensen, O. J. and J. Kuada (2000): "Institutional Support for International Strategic Alliances: Some Danish-Ghanaian Evidence." *The Journal of Management Studies* **15**(1): 114-130.

Sørensen, O. J. and J. Kuada (2001): "Institutional Context of Ghanaian Firms and Cross-national Inter-firm Relations" in G. Jakobsen and J. E. Torp: *Understanding Business Systems in Developing Countries*. Thousand Oaks, Sage Publications (place of publication and publisher: 163-201.

Sørensen, P. (2000): "Fødevaresikkerhed og udviklingsprojekter i Nord Wollo." *Den Ny verden* **33**(3): 43-58.

Sultana, P. and S. Folke (1999): *Bangladesh In-Depth Study. Project Impact at the Local Level - A Study of LIFT - Patuakhali*. Copenhagen, Danida.

Tangri, R. (1992): "The Politics of Government-Business Relations in Ghana." *The Journal of Modern African Studies* **30**(1): 97-111.

Teitel, S. (2000): *Technology and Skills in Zimbabwe's Manufacturing. From Autarky to Competition*. **Houndmills, MacMillan Press .**

Tribe, M. (2002): "An overview of manufacturing development in sub-Saharan Africa" in D. Belshaw and I. Livingstone: *Renewing Development in Sub-Saharan Africa: Policy, Performance and Prospects*. London, Routledge: 263-284.

Wei, L. (1995): "International Technology Transfer and Development of Technological Capabilities: A Theoretical Framework." *Technology In Society* **17**(1): 103-120.

Wignaraja, G. (2001): *Firm Size, Technological Capabilities and Market-Oriented Policies in Mauritius*. Maastrict,

The United Nations University, Institute for New Technologies: 41.

APPENDIX 1

PARTNERSHIPS								
№	**Sector**	**Main objective**	**Current situation**	**Positive effects**	**Negative effects**	**Derived & unintended effects**	**TC changes**	**AOB**
P1	Waste collection	Mechanisation of liquid waste collection	Just started due to initial problems. Ghanaian partner out.	Employment•	No profit Loans not repaid	Company is now almost entirely on European hands	+Investment cap. +Production cap. +Linkage cap.	AMA sets the prices for waste
P2	Consultancy	Capacity building especially as regards road construction	The coll. has ended but the partners still collaborate on a project-basis	Employment• Product quality• Productivity• Product range• Turnover• Profit margin•	÷	Able to bid for international contracts	+Investment cap. +Production cap. +Linkage cap.	
P3	Education	Establish Inst. for caretakers. Sales of edu. toys	Coll. has ended. No contact	Caretakers can get education	No profit Employment•		NA	New activity. Same Gh. as № S4.
P4	Pharmaceuticals	Create modern pharmaceutical factory	On the verge of bankruptcy.	Product range•	Loans not repaid	Spent capital reserves on Indian machines. No working capital	Machines never came to work. Staff changed	Competition is very hard on this market.
P5	Environment energy	Assembly and sales of solar collectors	No activity is taking place in the company	Employment•	No profit		+Production cap. Assembly of imported inputs	Devaluations made products too expensive. New activity. Same Gh. as № S7.
P6	Textiles	Production of textiles for export	Coll. has ended due to dispute btw partners	Product quality•	Employment• Customers•	Increased imports	+ Production cap.	

P7	Furniture	Production of doors and window frames	Coll. has ended due to accusations of fraud. No activity	÷	Loans not repaid		÷	GM continuously seeks new foreign partners. Same Gh. as № P8 & P10.
P8	Furniture	Production of doors, window frames and office furniture	Running with a loss No activity Sporadic contact	Safety conditions improved			÷	Same Gh. as № P7 & P10.
P9	Sustainable forest operation	Reforestation and improved forest management	Partners are still collaborate	Employment•		Positive economic development in the area	NA	Employment generation cannot be attributed to PSDP.
P10	Teak poles	Production of impregnated teak poles	Coll. has ended. No contact. No activity	Employment•	Running with a loss	Negative environmental effects	÷	Teak not certified Same Gh. as № P7&P8 (diff. comp). New activity.
P11	Refrigeration plant	Export of fish	Money has been spend to make already installed machines work	÷	Employment•		+Production cap.	Both partners ran into financial problems. Dk. partner has other partners.
P12	Airline company	Establish a domestic airline company	Project has been cancelled due to fraud	÷	Money lost	Int. licenses have enabled pilots & stewardesses to work in US	NA	Fraud and cultural barriers. New activity.
P13	Metal industry	Assembly of wheelbarrows	Coll. has ended. No contact. Hardly any activity	Safety conditions improved	Employment•		+Production cap.	Gh. owes Dk partner money. New activity. Same Gh. as № P14. (diff. comp).

P14	Furniture	Production of parquets strips and furniture parts for export	Until recently a success, but due to changing market preferences in Europe production has stopped	Employment● Exports● Product quality● Productivity● Salary●	÷	The employees are mostly unskilled labour from the surrounding area	+Investment cap. +Production cap.	Same Gh. as № P13. (diff. comp). Faces problems due to uncertified wood
P15	Plastic containers	To widen product range and improve quality	Making a profit and expanding operations in Ghana and abroad	Environmental● Product range● Turnover●	Employment● Trained personnel laid off.	Ghanaian partner has sold all shares to the Danish partner	+Investment cap. +Production cap. +Linkage cap.	Virtually bankrupt when the Danish partner took over.
P16	Graphic design	In-house print and pre-print	The coll. has encountered numerous problems but is still running.	Product quality● Product range●	Employment● Productivity● Salary● Loans not repaid	All qualified personnel left due to financial problems. Not able to employ good people.		Some essential machines didn't work upon arrival. No spare parts. Dk. partner lost interest
P17	Publishing	Broaden range of products and in-house pre-press	Project ongoing and successful	Employment● Exports● Product quality● Productivity● Turnover● Profit margin●	÷	Books printed outside Ghana	+Investment cap. +Production cap. +Linkage cap.	Has benefited from a development project to buy books from dev. Countries
P18	Engineering	Upgrade technical skills	Project never finished as the Dk. Partner withdrew because it won another contract	Productivity●	÷	Some former employees now work as sub-contractors for the company	+Production cap.	Partners still collaborate on a project basis

8

CULTURE, LEARNING, AND THE INTERNATIONALISATION OF GHANAIAN FIRMS

John Kuada and Gitte Thomsen

Introduction

The international business literature reflects two dominant streams of research. One group of scholars have focused attention on understanding the processes that relate to firms' entry into foreign markets, their choice of entry modes (i.e. export, contractual and local production), and the strategies adopted to improve their marketing performance (Bilkey and Tesar 1977, Johanson and Vahlne 1977, Cavusgil 1980, Cavusgil and Nevin 1981, Leonidou and Katsikeas 1996). This line of research is labelled as downstream internationalisation (Kuada and Sørensen 1999). In contrast, the second stream of research concerns itself with a hybrid of cross-border linkages between firms, aimed at strengthening production processes and leveraging resources through joint tasks, input deliveries, as well as upgrading technological and managerial capacities of collaborate firms. This approach is denoted as upstream internationalisation in the literature (Welch and Luostarinen 1993, Kuada and Sørensen 1999).

Upstream internationalisation relates both to local firms' relationship with foreign partners and to the location of foreign firms in a local economy. It conveys the expectation that foreign firms would enter into vertical (backward and forward) linkages with local firms, providing a ready outlet for their products and at the same time introducing new performance standards that will raise the overall competitiveness of the firms. Scholars working within each of the two streams of research generally register their awareness of the importance of knowledge management to the processes of internationalisation and the role of culture in the learning process.

In spite of this awareness, researchers have not adequately explored the impact of culture on cross-border inter-firm learning and knowledge management in developing country firms that establish either upstream or downstream linkages with developed country firms. Several factors justify such a research focus. Firstly, internationalisation is believed to provide developing countries with the best avenue for growth (Fafchamps et al 2001). As such many developing countries now pursue some form of internationalisation-driven growth strategy. Second, the limited resources of developing country firms have compelled many of them to adopt off-shore resource leveraging strategies. Thirdly, and due to the first two reasons above, many policy-makers and managers in the developing countries are in search of guidelines on how to effectively manage linkages with foreign firms and to stimulate the location of foreign companies in the developing parts of the world.

The objective of this paper is therefore to contribute to filling the knowledge gap and to provide a basis for policy and strategy formulation in the developing countries. In specific terms, the paper seeks to address the following two research issues:

(1) To study how developing country-based firms manage their relationships with their key partners from the developed parts of the world, and
(2) To explore the impact of macro and organisational cultures on the learning process of developing country-based firms.

Building on the existing literature on learning and culture, the paper offers a more comprehensive framework for understanding how knowledge management takes place in the internationalisation process of firms. It argues that upstream inter-firm linkages provide an important avenue for leveraging scarce resources globally, since it links these firms to foreign firms that have financial resources, improved technology and management skills. The inputs so obtained constitute several years of accumulated knowledge. The developing-country firms are therefore spared the resources and time that would otherwise be needed to develop these skills in-house and raise the quality of their products and management up to international levels. The downstream internationalisation allows firms to grow faster as they respond to international competitive pressures and improve their efficiency in the process. Proper management of cultural differences and knowledge underpins both processes.

The next section of the paper is devoted to a review of the theories of internationalisation, discussing the distinction between upstream and downstream internationalisation. This is followed by two sections in which we discuss the dominant views on culture and learning and draw attention to challenges that firms are likely to face in cross-border inter-firm knowledge transfer processes. The three sections together provide a backdrop against which some Ghanaian evidence is discussed. The final section discusses the strategy, policy and research implications that can be derived from the Ghanaian evidence.

Downstream and Upstream Internationalisation Processes of Firms

Downstream Internationalisation

A large proportion of the most cited publications on the internationalisation process of firms tend to view internationalisation as a downstream activity. The dominant models of internationalisation are predicated on the general assumption that firms proceed with their foreign market entry decisions in a gradual, sequential manner.

The most popular model, commonly referred to as the Stages Model, consists of a number of identifiable and distinct stages with higher level stages indicating higher degrees of internationalisation, and with each stage forming the precondition for the subsequent stage (Bilkey and Tesar 1977, Cavusgil 1980). Varieties of the Stages Model differ only in terms of the number of stages and the actual parameters triggering the change.

The stages model presents market knowledge acquisition as one of the critical factors in the internationalisation process of firms. The understanding from the model is that there are two main types of knowledge that firms need during the early stages of their internationalisation: (1) knowledge about market opportunities and (2) knowledge about how various market-related activities (e.g. distribution and payment) should be performed. The acquisition of such knowledge is believed to proceed in a gradual and incremental manner following and influencing the overall tempo of internationalisation (Johanson and Vahlne 1977).

Critics have argued that the models focus primarily on a single activity of firms (i.e. exporting) rather than viewing that activity as part of a company's overall portfolio of activities. In doing so, they fail to capture overall investment and organisational development requirements of firms during their internationalisation process.

The approach has also been criticised for being too mechanistic. As argued by (Leonidou and Katsikeas 1996 P. 527). "a linear and predictable pattern of single, orderly or progressive export development may not always occur due to intra- and inter-firm variability in resource endowments, market opportunities and managerial capabilities". Some firms may enter a new market via a direct export route but may serve the same market subsequently through an indirect export route, depending on their assessment of the relative pay-offs of the two entry strategies (Turnbull 1987).

Upstream Inter-firm Relations

As mentioned earlier, upstream internationalisa-tion refers to a hybrid set of collaborative arrangements that link local and foreign firms.

It basically involves internationalising the input side of the value chain. A simple approach to upstream internationalisation is the import of inputs. The more embracing approaches require strategic ownership arrangements of a long-term character. This involves not only the purchase of raw materials and equipment but also the acquisition of new skills and financial resources. Collaboration tends to be formed among companies whose resources are perceived by their managers to be complementary. This happens either through vertical (upstream and/or downstream) joint activities or through horizontal linkages between competitive firms.

The international business literature abounds with evidence of varieties of collaborative arrangements between firms. These include joint ventures, license agreements and other forms of contractual arrangements (Boryd and Jamison 1989). The collaboration is presumed to proceed in two broad ways: either by planning or through an incrementally emerging process. Although the two approaches are not mutually exclusive, they reflect dominant management orientations of the partner firms. The planning approach endorses a sequential and progressive process of collaboration. Objectives, resource contributions of partners, and performance measures are all decided upon in advance and included in an overall business plan. The planned approach is however hardly feasible in most operational environments due, partly, to uncertainties produced by environmental dynamics (Doz 1996), shifts in strategic priorities of partners (Koza and Lewin 1998) and differences in the cultures of the collaborate firms.

Iyer (2002) divides the collaborative process into four phases. First, prospective partners must explain the economic justification of collaboration with other firms. Once top management is convinced of this need the partner search begins, first by going to firms that they already have some relationship with. If these firms are not suitable, the partner-seeking firm will rely on the recommendations of third parties who can vouch for the prospective candidates' performance and trustworthiness.

The literature advises firms to select partners with similar values, beliefs, and practices in order to minimise tensions during the process of collaboration (Weitz and Jap 1995).

The second phase is one of "exploration", where partners lay the groundwork for a lasting relationship in the form of norm adoption for mutual conduct and "setting the ground rules for future exchanges" (Dwyer et al. 1987 p: 17). However, the relationship at this stage is assessed as being very fragile, still with minimal investment and interdependence, leaving a very easy outlet for quick dissolution. At this stage serious partners start building a common culture to speed up the social bonding process critical for achieving mutual goals. In addition to this, partners' learning needs expand and various learning processes are called into operation, including the transfer of institutionalised practices and procedures from the two partners. As Iyer (2002) observes, there emerges (towards the end of the phase) a systematic effort by the partners to vicariously learn deeply embedded knowledge such as skills, processes and routines.

Phase three is described as the expansion phase, where partners acknowledge their interdependence and mutual vulnerability as a result of investment and technology sharing as well as adaptation of processes and products/services to satisfy each other's requirements. As partners tap into cumulative experience of each other they gain the opportunity to improve productivity in their respective firms (Levitt and March 1988). At the fourth and most advanced stage in the interfirm collaboration, structural bonds as well as norms and values are established to such an extent that the relationship is further institutionalised, making it very difficult to terminate.

In sum, both upstream and downstream processes of internationalisation may involve inter-firm collaboration as partners become integrated into the international value creation process. The initial stages of the collaborative relationships are characterised by a high degree of uncertainties and tensions as partners size each other up and establish rules of behaviour that would guide the collaboration. The degree of uncertainty is possibly correlated with the degree of dissimilarity in the operational backgrounds of the collaborate firms. As the relationship matures, the uncertainties give way to mutual trust and commitment.

Culture and Cross-border Inter-firm Relations

How does culture impact the learning processes in cross-border inter-firm relationships? An answer to this question must start with the concept of embeddedness, which has been popularised in more recent years by the work of Granovetter (1985). In simple terms, this concept holds that every economic action is embedded in a social structure. Related to the central thesis of this paper, it can be argued that the shared space of inter-firm relationships entails the presence of embeddedness (Granovetter 1985, Gulati 1999, Gulati and Gargiulo 1999).

Building on this understanding, Whitley (1994) has argued that there exists a diversity of successful business strategies and economic development "recipes". Whitley's studies have shown that what proves to be successful business strategies in most Asian nations are those that are consistent with their cultures. Other studies have indicated that cultures do not always facilitate economic activities. They can also constrain economic processes by inhibiting the creation of successful management practices (Moore 1997).

The importance of culture in business management has been empirically demonstrated in Hofstede's (1980, 1991) study of IBM workers in 50 countries. This study revealed highly significant differences in the behaviour and attitudes of the respondents across countries - differences that did not change over time. Hofstede's major contribution to the analysis and understanding of cultural differences lies in the submission that managers and employees vary on four primary cultural dimensions. These dimensions were labelled "power distance" (large vs. small), "uncertainty avoidance" (strong vs. weak), "individualism" vs. "collectivism", and "masculinity" vs. "femininity". In 1988 a fifth dimension, "confucian dynamism", was added to the previous four. This dimension contrasts a long-term orientation to work and life with short-term orientation.

Two of these dimensions, power distance and uncertainty avoidance deserve particular attention for our analysis since they relate closely to leadership styles and their impact on organisational learning.

> *Power distance* indicates the extent to which junior managers accept that those above them in the managerial hierarchy have powers over them. In the larger power distance cultures, superiors, and subordinates consider each other un-equals.
>
> *Uncertainty avoidance* describes the lack of tolerance for ambiguity and the need for formal rules, or the adoption of other measures that provide stability in life. A society characterised by high uncertainty avoidance is likely to establish formal rules to guide behaviour and members of these societies are more willing to adhere to these rules.

Learning and Culture

To gain an insight into how these cultural dimensions impact organisational learning in general and knowledge transfer process in particular, we need to examine views presented by socio-cognitive scholars of organisational learning. To them, knowledge is a 'situated action'. This implies that knowledge and the meaning of words are not independent from context. They lie partly in the context of use, and they shift from one context to another. This implies that learning and interpretations, although they entail cognitive process, cannot be isolated from the context within which they take place. In other words, individuals' ability to perceive, interpret and evaluate phenomena depends on the sustained and intensive interactions that they have with other people in a given community or context.

These interactions help create shared mental models and enable people to make sense of their environments. The situational setting provides a constellation of meanings that both informs and constrains socially acceptable behaviours, including socially constructed identities and forms of participation—that is, it both informs and constrains social practices.

One stream of research that has adopted this perspective is represented by scholars emphasising learning within "communities of practice" (Brown and Duguid 1991, 1996 and 2001). In general terms, these scholars argue against the implicit distinction between learning and working found in mainstream organisational learning literature. They see working and learning as rather compatible – both being part of the normal flow of organisational life. Building on both Orr (1987) and Lave and Wenger's (1991) research, Brown and Duguid (1991) argue that to understand working and learning, it is necessary to focus on the formation and change of the communities in which work takes place. The argument that knowledge and learning are contextually embedded led these scholars to coin the term "communities-of-practice" to describe the locus of knowledge stock and learning processes. Community in this regard may refer to members of an organisation or a group that interact on a continuous basis in the execution of an assigned task.

Thus the "communities of practice" view of learning places emphasis on the interactions (both social and professional) that take place among a given group of workers, the stories and anecdotes that they narrate to the group members concerning their earlier work experiences and how such accounts influence their interpretations of current and subsequent task-related events. Their individual accounts of why and how they confront specific task-related problems converge into collective sense making of similar task situations. As Brown and Duguid (1991:8) put it "stories act as repositories of accumulated wisdom. In particular, community narratives protect [people's] ability to work from the ravages of modern idealizations of work and related downskilling practices".

To summarise, learning takes place within a context. It is therefore a socially embedded process involving dialogue, reflections and behavioural changes. This implies that each culture has its implicit rules of learning and dissemination of knowledge. When knowledge flows across cultures the disparities between cultures within which partners are located do impact (positively or negatively) the learning process.

A Review of Some Ghanaian Studies

The viewpoints discussed above provide a useful frame of reference for understanding the challenges of learning and knowledge transfer to Ghanaian firms. This section of the chapter draws on the results of empirical studies conducted by one of the present authors in Ghana at various times from 1992 to 2002. (See Kuada and Sørensen 1999; 2000 and Kuada 2002). The section seeks to explore the extent to which the Ghanaian (macro business) cultures impact knowledge generation and diffusion within Ghanaian companies. This is done at both organisational and inter-organisational levels.

The organisational level discussions focus attention on how culturally prescribed leadership and management styles influence individuals' learning behaviour. The inter-organisational discussions examine the relationships between local companies as well as between local and foreign companies. In this manner, the discussions attempt to uncover the complexities in knowledge transfer between companies with disparate cultural backgrounds.

Leadership Styles and Organisational Learning

The earlier discussions suggest that organisational culture is a factor that exerts its influence in a significant way in the process of organisational learning. Where organisational culture supports learning, managers would adopt leadership styles that allow the generated knowledge to be shared by all the members of the organisation outside the limits of space, time and hierarchy (Huber 1991).

Our studies in Ghana indicate that aspects of the Ghanaian culture tend to inhibit the flow of knowledge within Ghanaian organisations. Using Hostede's cultural dimensions as a frame of reference, the evidence shows that superior–subordinate relations in Ghana are characterised by high power distance. Kuada (1994) coins the term *authoritarian-benevolence* to describe the dominant leadership style in Ghana. He argues that Ghanaian leaders see their role as providing clear-cut instructions and solving specific problems. Subordinates correspondingly define their role as not taking responsibility, but simply following, responding and carrying out instructions from their superiors. As such many of them fail to reflect on work-related problems that they face, let alone consider the possible solutions to them. They may suffer silently or grumble quietly at the inactions of their superiors, but refrain from acting on their own volition for fear of inviting their superiors' rage at mistakes that they might have made.

Subordinates' reluctance to question superiors' actions is further reinforced by their awareness that superiors patronise their subordinates selectively, providing extra opportunities and privileges to those closest and most subservient to their interests. The Ghanaian employee therefore knows that it is necessary to cultivate the "right" people, particularly his immediate superior, in order to have a successful career. Since seniority in traditional social structures commands unflinching loyalty, a subordinate tends to believe that his superior is likely to value personal loyalty and goodwill over and above competence.

This observation is consistent with studies conducted by Ghanaian sociologists into social relations in Ghana. Assimeng (1981:76), for example, observes that, "conformity and blatant eschewing of individual speculations" as well as "unquestioning acquiescence and accommodationism" are dominant characteristics of the behaviour of young Ghanaians. This, he argues, is due to the collectivist social structure that strongly encourages the maintenance of status quo and avoidance of any serious disruption of the specific social order. In other words, certain cultural orientations can transmit to its members, *a priori,* the sense of powerlessness, although individuals might not actually have experienced such powerlessness in their work-related situations.

Thus the evidence from Ghana confirms the prevailing view in the literature that learning is not politically neutral. That is, organisational members cannot always challenge existing root assumptions in their organisations without penalty. To the extent that the power of key organisational members (e.g. top management) shape the process of organisational learning and determine the survival of new ideas, what receives attention and therefore influences the learning process may be determined by organisational politics. Thus, the power configurations within organisations, leadership styles, bureaucratic structures and the roles organisational members are expected to play have determined influence on the learning process.

The implications of such culturally induced superior-subordinate relationships are quite evident. Organisational learning literature informs that learning occurs in organisations when individuals, acting as learning agents for the organisation, detect and correct errors in the organisation's behaviour patterns which in turn become embedded in the culture of the organisation (Argyris and Schön, 1996). Thus organisations that learn are those that facilitate the learning of all individuals within them and therefore can respond to internal and external changes (Pedler et al 1991). To the extent that the leadership styles in Ghanaian organisations do not facilitate individual learning it is difficult to imagine how the organisations can be rightfully described as learning. Knowledge tends to reside in the minds of top management. This particularly holds true for small owner-managed firms in which power distance between the owner and other organisational members must be expected to be high. (See Puplampu's empirical study in this volume for corroborating evidence).

Knowledge Acquisition in Ghanaian Exporting Firms

Turning to the internationalisation process itself, the Ghanaian evidence only partially confirms the theoretical understandings that underlie the stages model. Ghana embarked on export-led growth strategy fairly recently, i.e. in the late 1980s and most exporting firms in the country are of recent origin, established purposefully to sell to export markets. Thus, they have not had the privilege of being nurtured by the domestic market. Furthermore, many of them are relatively small, mostly owner-managed firms, exporting single products to few European markets. In effect, the internationalisation of most Ghanaian firms does not begin from the geographically close-by markets, as the stages model predicts.

There are however some exceptions to this pattern of internationalisation. Few of the manufacturing companies target the nearby West African markets, particularly where the domestic supply of such products are limited in the target markets, thus providing opportunities for the Ghanaian exporters.

In the light of the above evidence, acquisition of even the most basic international business knowledge is of great importance to most of them. Our empirical investigations indicate that the lack of reliable market knowledge is a key constraint to the operations of Ghanaian exporters. Export performance therefore depends partly on the ability to acquire reliable information in potential export markets and for the companies to learn fast. The studies also showed that even the successful Ghanaian exporters relied on rudimentary sources of information such as friends and family members living abroad or foreigners living in Ghana (Kuada and Sørensen 2000). Information coming from these sources is described as being erratic, inadequate and sometimes of dubious validity since some of the sources are not in regular contact with key actors in the markets that they report on. Few companies have been fortunate to build stable relationships with foreign distributors and learn quickly from these relationships. Two of these companies are Combined Farmers Limited (CFL) and Kiku

Limited, whose relationships with a Swiss and a Dutch distributor respectively have played an important role in their market knowledge acquisition processes.

Upstream Linkages and Knowledge Transfer

The upstream approach to internationalisation has been adopted by an increasing number of Ghanaian firms, sometimes with the support of bilateral aid organisations (Kuada 2002). This strategy has been adopted in response to the realisation that their technological capacity, production and management know-how fall short of the requirements for successful performance on the global market. These cross-national business relations invariably entail interaction between two business systems, i.e. the Ghanaian business system and the business systems of the various European countries in which their partners are located. The interacting business systems may provide opportunities in some respects and create constraints for the relationship in other respects.

Contrary to the understanding in the literature that inter-firm collaborations involve a fairly long-term relationship rather than episodic transactions, the Ghanaian evidence suggests that relationships between developed and developing country-based firms are most likely to be contractual and of relatively short duration. Knowledge transfer also takes place within the defined contractual period. Thus firms with low learning capacities are not likely to take full advantage of the knowledge transferred. Furthermore, the contractual and terminal characteristics of these relationships mean that they do not develop the commonality of purpose, mutual learning processes, or the multiple levels of personal and emotional relationships that Iyer (2002) has suggested in her model. The low levels of trust and the weak structural bonds between the partners mean that the relationships usually lack dynamism and innovative drive.

Our studies also show that the collaboration process between Ghanaian and foreign firms tend most often to be initiated by a chain of fortuitous events that occur through informal interactions of organisational actors. This is the case when the collaborating firms are relatively small and owner-managed. Thus the planning approach, which is suggested in the literature, appears to apply only to those cases where the collaboration is initiated and nurtured by a third party such as a donor organisation or the government.

The challenges of knowledge transfer from foreign firms to Ghanaian firms is illustrated by the Dixcove Solar Project case presented below.

Dixcove Solar Project- An Illustrative Case[1]

Dixcove Engineering (a Ghanaian company) has been engaged in assembling solar water heating systems for the Ghanaian market since 1993. In 1996, Dixcove took the strategic decision to expand its product line to include solar electrical systems. The new product line was targeted at hospitals (serving their emergency lighting needs), households, as well as infrastructural facilities such as street lighting and traffic lights. The implementation of this strategic decision entailed purchases of new equipment by Dixcove Engineering as well as upgrading the technical capacity within the company to be able to design, assemble, install and service the solar electrical systems. Danish International Development Assistance (Danida) agreed to support the project.

Jylland A/S (A Danish firm) was commissioned to collaborate with Dixcove Engineering to find the most suitable technology for the purpose and to help Dixcove acquire the requisite competencies for the implementation of the project. The choice of Jylland A/S for this task was based on the compatibility in the two companies' lines of business, the relatively superior technological capacities and capabilities of Jylland A/S, and its previous business experiences in Ghana and Zimbabwe.

The technical assistance agreement specifically required Jylland A/S to upgrade Dixcove Engineering's technical capacity to "supply photovoltaic system solutions to energy requirements in Ghana." A successful transfer of skills and knowledge would enable Dixcove to assess the energy requirements of its prospective customers, determine the sizes and combinations of individual components of the electrical system (panels, inverters, batteries, cables, etc.) that would fulfil the needs and provide appropriate post-installation services to the customers.

Jylland and Dixcove designed an elaborate plan for the technology transfer.

Key activities in the plan included:

- Training of Dixcove's staff, in both Ghana and Denmark.
- The design and production of marketing materials.
- Procurement and installation of demonstration units.

Out of a staff of 27 at Dixcove Engineering, the training was limited to the General Manager, the Workshop Manager and a newly appointed engineer. The expectation was that the knowledge and skills acquired by these people would be effectively disseminated throughout the organisation. Post-training evaluation showed that the learning effects were limited.

The trainees were unable to analyse the implications of differences in weather patterns and atmospheric conditions for the performance of the solar electrical systems they had designed after the training, apparently due to the nature of training methods used. Subsequent analysis of the training process indicated that the trainers lacked adequate understanding of the context within which the technology was to be used. As such they could not successfully transfer core skills required to effectively utilise the imported technology. This led to sub-optimal performance of the systems under weather conditions that were very different from those under which the systems were designed and tested in Denmark. Furthermore, the knowledge acquired by the few trainees did not flow effectively to other workers almost two years after the training was conducted, apparently due to limited organisational capacity to facilitate the knowledge flow. Understandably, some of the Ghanaian customers were grossly dissatisfied with Dixcove Engineering since their lights did not work at all or worked intermittently.

Implications

The discussions above clearly show that transferring knowledge between organisations located in disparate cultures is always problematic. Addressing the problems calls for new strategic and policy orientations in Ghana.

First, efforts must be made to strengthen the learning and knowledge absorptive capacity of individual firms. This requires conscious efforts by top management to change from authoritarian leadership style to transformative leadership, i.e. a leadership that empowers subordinates to ask critical and constructive questions that motivate them to learn. This process entails integrating the experiences that individuals acquire into their existing mental models or concepts. Without changes in the existing leadership styles, these learning efforts cannot be effectively developed.

Second, Ghanaian companies must endeavour to operate in several European markets rather than depending on relationships with a single distributor in a single market. They must also endeavour to make greater use of the network of relationships that industry associations at home and abroad offer them. The breadth and heterogeneity of inter-firm ties determine a firm's capacity to learn and accumulate knowledge. The theoretical justification of this suggestion derives from the network approach to internationalisation, which suggests that firms placed centrally in a network receive more, better, and early knowledge than their competitors. Furthermore, networks may produce unexpected random information to firms. As Burt (1992) argues, weak ties (rather than strong ties) provide firms with the greatest variety of new knowledge. From this perspective it can be argued that Ghanaian firms that operate within a network of weak ties are likely to obtain unexpected valuable information that could position them advantageously in relation to their competitors.

But the effect of new information on the prevailing mental models in an organisation will depend on the degree of homogeneity of the organisation's culture (Gullestrup 2003), and the superior-subordinate relationships. The reasoning here is that heterogeneous cultures are more flexible in accepting new ideas. Some members in the culture may see the wisdom in the new idea and may take initiatives to implement it. Homogeneous cultures are more likely to resist changes until top leadership endorses the adoption of new ideas.

Third, the Ghanaian government must adopt policies that will strengthen the legal and judicial system and improve institutional contract enforcement arrangements in the country. Following the internationalisation literature, it can be argued that the management of uncertainty in international business is influenced significantly by the reliability of the prevailing systems of sanction in the focal countries, and the degree of trust within the business system and between partners (Moore 1999). The strength and reliability of the institutional system of sanctions impact partners' willingness to extend trust. That is, people operating in countries with strong and reliable legal institutions stand a greater chance to be trusted. Where foreign investors are confident that judicial systems are well functioning and capable of expeditiously redressing grievances of contracting parties, they will be more willing to enter into long-term contractual arrangements and commit more resources to the collaborations.

Fourth, efforts must be made at macro, industry and firm levels to build a trustworthy business culture in Ghana. Building a high trust business culture means that partners will reduce their cost of monitoring the relationships and devote more resources to activities that will enhance business to the mutual benefit of the parties. It is not uncommon for collaborate parties to initially exhibit high levels of sensitivity to each other's behaviours, i.e., viewing each other with suspicion until such a time that mutual trust has emerged.

Deepening trust involves a learning process. Factors such as honest dealing (Das and Teng 1998), veracity, openness, acceptance, support and dialogue (Fukuyama 1995) have been found in earlier studies as creating conditions for trust building among collaborate business partners.

Conclusions

The aim of this paper has been to explore the impact of culture on learning during the internationalisation process of Ghanaian firms. The discussions above suggest that Ghanaian firms are generally relatively young. Most of them were established in the early 1990s in response to the export-led growth strategies initiated by the Government. They are also relatively small, mostly owner-managed firms, exporting single products to few European markets. They therefore have limited international business knowledge and lack resources to acquire new knowledge fast enough to operate effectively in export markets. Inter-firm collaboration is the most promising avenue for rapid learning for most of these firms.

The discussions further reveal the challenges that the Ghanaian culture creates for effective knowledge absorption. It has been argued that certain cultural orientations have important psychological impact on managers' and subordinates' perception of their role in organisations. This culturally motivated collective disposition tends to influence leadership styles in Ghana. It has been further argued that the impact of individual learning on overall learning and activities in Ghanaian firms would occur through modifications of relationships between top management and other organisational members. Relationships may be modified through changes in organisational structure and its resulting rearrangement of roles, authority, and communication channels. It also requires changes in top management orientation to power, control and domination of subordinates, i.e. a change from authoritative to transformative leadership. This will motivate individuals to question existing practices in the organisation and strive to acquire new ways of doing things.

Notes

---

[1] This case is based on a study conducted by Felix Quansar as part of his Master's degree thesis at Aalborg University.

References

Argyris, C; Schön, Donald A (1996): *Organisational Learning II.* (Reading, Massachussetts: Addison-Wesley Publishing Company).

Assimeng, Max (1981): *Social Structure of Ghana* (Accra: Ghana Publishing Corporation)

Bilkey, W. J. & G. Tesar (1977): "The Export Behaviour of Smaller-sized Wisconsin Manufacturing Firms". *Journal of international business studies,* (Vol. 3, Spring pp. 93-98).

Boryd Bryan and David B. Jemison (1989): "Hybrid arrangements as strategic alliances: Theoretical issues in organisational combinations", *Academy of Management Journal* (Vol.14, No.2. 234-249).

Brown, John Seely; Duguid, Paul (2001): *Organisation Science,* (12) 2, 198-213

Brown, John Seely; Duguid, Paul (1996): "Organisational Learning and Communities-of-Practice" in M.D. Cohen and L.S. Sproull (Eds.) *Organisational Learning,* (Thousand Oaks, CA: Sage). 124-162.

Brown, John Seely; Duguid, Paul (1991): "Organisational learning and communities-of-practice: Toward a unified view of working, learning and innovation". http://www2.parc.com/ops/members/brown/papers/orglearning.html. 31-10-2003.

Burt, Ronald S. (1992): *Structural Holes* (Cambridge, MA: Harvard University Press)

Cavusgil, S.T. (1980): "On the internationalisation process of firms". *European Research,* Vol. 8. No 6., 273-81.

Cavusgil, S.T. and Nevin, J.N. (1981): "Internal determinants of export marketing behaviour: An empirical investigation" *Journal of Marketing Research* vol. 18 no 1 114-19.

Cavusgil, S. Tamer (1984): "Organisational characteristics associated with export activity" *Journal of management studies* 21, 1 pp. 3 - 22.

Das, T.K. and Teng, Bing-Sheng (1998): "Between Trust and Control: Developing Confidence in Partner Cooperation in Alliances" *Academy of Management Review* Vol. 23, No.3, pp.491-512

Doz, Y.L. (1996): "The Evolution of Cooperation in Strategic Alliances: Initial Conditions or Learning Processes? *Strategic Management Journal,* Vol.17 pp:55-83

Dwyer, Robert F., Paul H. Schurr, and Sejo Oh. (1987): "Developing Buyer-Seller Relationships." *Journal of Marketing* Vol. 51 No. 2 pp: 11-27.

Fafchamps, Marcel, Teal, Francis, and Toye, John (2001): *Towards a Growth Strategy for Africa* (University of Oxford Centre for the Study of African Economies Working Paper REP/2001-06)

Fukuyama, F. (1995): *Trust. The Societal Virtues and the Creation of Prosperity*. (New York, Free Press)

Granovetter, M. S. (1985): "Economic Action and Social Structure: The Problem of Embeddedness", *American Journal of Sociology,* 91, 3, pp. 481-510.

Gulati, R. (1999): "Network Location and Learning: The Influence of Network Resources and Firm Capabilities on Alliance Formation", *Strategic ManagementJournal,* 20, pp. 397-420.

Gulati, R. and M. Gargiulo (1999): "Where Do Network Forms Come From?",*American Journal of Sociology,* March, pp. 177-231.

Gullestrup, Hans (2003): *Kulturanalyse – en vej til tværkulturel forståelse.* Danmark: Akademisk Forlag.

Hofstede, G (1980): *Culture Consequences.* (California: Ed. SAGE).

Hofstede, Geert (1991): *Cultures and Organisations: Software of the Mind.* (London: McGraw-Hill Book Company)

Huber, G.P. (1991): "Organisational Learning: The Contributing Processes and the Literature" in M.D. Cohen and L.S. Sproull (Eds.) *Organisational Learning,* (Thousand Oaks, CA: Sage). 124-162.

Iyer, Karthik (2002): "Learning in Strategic Alliances: An Evolutionary Perspective." *Academy of Marketing Science Review.* http://www.amsreview.org/articles/iyer10-2002.pdf . 02-12-03.

Johanson, J. & J. Vahlne (1977): "The internationalisation Process of the firm - A Model of Knowledge Development and Increasing Foreign Market Commitments". *Journal of International Business Studies.* 8 (1) 23-32

Koza, M.P. and Lewin, A.Y., (1998): "The Co-evolution of Strategic Alliances" *Organisation Science,* Vol. 5 No. 1 pp: 255-264

Kuada, John (1994): *Managerial Behaviour in Ghana and Kenya – A Cultural Perspective* (Aalborg, Denmark: Aalborg University Press)

Kuada, John and Sørensen, Olav Jull (1999): "Upstream and Downstream Processes of Internationalisation: Some Ghanaian Evidence" *Journal of Euromarketing* Vol 7 No. 4 pp:7-41

Kuada, John and Olav Jull Sørensen (2000): Internationalisation of Companies from Developing Countries (Binghamton, N.Y: The Haworth Press, Inc.,)

Kuada, John (2002): "Collaboration between developed and developing country-based firms: Danish-Ghanaian experience" *The Journal of Business & Industrial Marketing* Vol. 17 No. 6 pp. 538-557

Lave, J.; Wenger, E. (1991): *Situated learning. Legitimate peripheral participation.* Cambridge, UK: Cambridge University Press.

Levitt, B.; March, J.G., (1988): "Organisational Learning" Annual Review of Sociology, 14: 318-340

Leonidou, Leonidas C. and Katsikeas Constantine S. (1996): "The Export Development Process: An Integrative Review of Empirical Models" *Journal of International Business Studies,* Third Quarter 517 – 551

Moore, Mick (1997): "Societies, Polities and Capitalists in Developing Countries: A Literature Survey" *The Journal of Development Studies* Vol. 33 No. 3 pp. 287-363

Moore, Mick (1999): "Truth, Trust and Market Transactions: What Do We Know?" *The Journal of Development Studies* Vol. 36 No. 1 pp. 74-88

Orr, J. (1987): Narratives at work: Story telling as cooperative diagnostic activity. *Field Service Manager:* 47-60.

Pedler, Mike; Boydell, Tom; Byrgoyne, John (1991): *The Learning Company: A Strategy for Sustainable Development.* (London: McGraw-Hill).

Quansar, Felix Panyin (2001): *Adaptive Technological Capabilities: Transfer of Solar Electric Technology to Ghana* (Unpublished MSc. Thesis, Denmark: Aalborg University)

Turnbull, P.W.(1987): "A challenge to the stages theory of the internationalisation process" in Rosson, P.J. and S.D. Reid (Eds). *Managing export entry and expansion* (New York,: Praeger). pp. 21-40

Weitz, Barton A. and Sandy D. Jap. (1995): "Relationship Marketing and Distribution Channels." *Journal of the Academy of Marketing Science* Vol. 23 No.4 pp: 305-320.

Welch, Lawrence S. and Luostarinen, Reijo (1993): "Inward-outward connections in internationalisation", *Journal of International Marketing,* Vol. 1, no. 1, 44-56.

Whitley R., ed. (1994): *European Business Systems. Firms and Markets in their National Contexts.* (London, Sage Publications).

9

THE IMPACT OF FINANCIAL LIBERALISATION AND CAPITAL FLOWS ON ECONOMIC OUTPUT IN SUB-SAHARAN AFRICA[1]

Anthony Q. Q. Aboagye

Introduction

Many sub-Saharan African countries in search of ways to improve the performance of their economies have been liberalizing the financial sectors of their economies. This has taken the form of abolishing of minimum and maximum deposit and lending rates, abolishing of mandatory requirement to lend to selected sectors of their economies such as agriculture, revamping of banking supervision, relaxing state control of foreign exchange markets, establishment of stock exchanges, etc. Liberalisation is expected to enhance the process of financial intermediation by allocating financial resources, both domestic and foreign, from surplus areas to deficit areas more efficiently. This in turn is expected to lead to higher rate of growth of economic output than otherwise.

In recent times, support for financial Liberalisation may be traced back to the works of McKinnon (1973) and Shaw (1973). This school of thought considers imposition of interest rate ceilings, high reserve ratios and government role in directing where credit should be granted as sources of financial repression resulting in low savings, credit rationing and low and poor quality of investments.

Several authors have explored the subject. These include King and Levine (1993a, 1993b), Arestis and Demetriades (1997),

Demetriades and Hussein (1996), Fry (1997) and others. These generally found strong support for positive relationship between economic output and the level of financial development. On the other hand, economists such as Singh (1997), Minsky (1986), Grabel (1995) and Federer (1993) have cautioned that financial Liberalisation (including stock market development in developing countries) makes financial systems in these countries fragile and may not lead to long-term economic growth.

To date, 15 sub-Saharan African countries have functioning stock exchanges.[2] Typically, these are countries that have implemented programmess that are meant to reform the structures of their economies significantly. Some of these have been in existence for well under 10 years. But before establishing stock exchanges, many had liberalized their banking systems. This study investigates the impact of banking systems and stock exchanges on economic output.

With Liberalisation history of about 10 years, most individual sub-Saharan African countries will not have enough data points with which one can perform individual country analysis as most data are reported as annual aggregates. Bearing this in mind, this study is designed as a short-run analysis. Short-run impact responses of this type have been used extensively in econometric investigations. They are useful in informing short-run policy reviews and evaluations for example. Thus the conceptual approach envisaged here is different from cross-country regressions of the type popularized by Barro (1991) and others.

Anecdotal evidence about sub-Saharan African countries suggests that living standards in economically liberalized economies are no better than within non-liberalized economies. This paper will attempt to determine econometrically whether there is an association between economic output and the level of formal financial activity (banks and stock markets). As well, it will also seek to establish whether the impacts of stock markets and banks on economic output in 'de-repressed' economies are different.

Another issue of concern in respect to SSA's economic growth is the role of physical capital. The poor economic performance is sometimes blamed on inadequate or inappropriate capital (equipment, technology, etc.) in addition to wrong policies. To obtain further insight into the impact of physical capital, it is proposed here to go a step further and disaggregate physical capital as a factor input into its domestic and foreign components.

This study is organised as follows. In the next section we discuss previous empirical findings and the conceptual framework driving this study. This is followed by methodology of the study and data issues. Then we present and discuss empirical findings. We then conclude with a summary and policy implications of the study.

Economic Theory

We first review related literature and then discuss the conceptual framework within which we posit the model we wish to explore. The topical literature with a direct bearing on the subject matter of this paper is growth theory. The typical starting point for most growth regressions is a production function stated in levels of output and explanatory variables. Subsequently equations of interest are derived. This paper will try to estimate parameters of a production function rather than a growth equation. The two will have a lot in common. Unlike growth equations, interpretation of variable estimates made here will be within the context of production functions. We review the related literature next.

Review of Literature

As noted above, the McKinnon-Shaw school promotes financial Liberalisation as a means of ensuring investment and hence economic growth in developing countries. That is, financial Liberalisation ensures faster financial deepening which in turn promotes economic development. In explaining the lack of conclusive evidence in support of their stated position, the McKinnon-Shaw school has focused the argument on conditions that must be in place at the outset before financial reforms can be expected to work. These include adequate banking supervision, low and stable inflation and sustainable government deficit. In his contribution, Cho (1986) showed analytically that for efficient resource allocation to occur, credit markets must be supplemented by well-functioning equity markets.

In their study, King and Levine (1993a) find that financial development and economic growth are 'robustly correlated'. While agreeing with this finding, Arestis and Demetriades (1997) question King and Levine's assertion of causality running from finance to economic growth. Using time series data for the United States and Germany, Arestis and Demetriades provide evidence suggesting that the causality between financial development and real economic output varies across countries. In an earlier paper, Arestis and Demetriades (1996) suggest that causality link between finance and growth is determined by the nature and operation of financial institutions and policies. Demetriades and Hussein (1996) also suggest that causality between financial development and economic growth varies across countries.

Singh (1997) has however pointed out drawbacks in respect of Cho's (1986) formulation. For example, Cho overlooks the fact that even in well-functioning markets agency problems plague large corporations controlled by management, and asymmetric information problems exist between management and investors. Exploring the issue earlier, Singh (1995, 1997) focused on the role of stock markets in addition to financial depression in developing countries. When he examined the evidence from major developing countries, he concluded that in these countries (a) stock market pricing processes are a poor guide to efficient resource allocation, (b) interactions between stock markets and currency markets may lead to increased macroeconomic instability in the face of negative economic shocks, and (c) stock market development may undermine the group-banking system that has been of some merit in some developing countries.

Stiglitz (1994) has also criticized financial Liberalisation on the grounds that financial markets are prone to failures.

Yet others such as Levine and Zervos (1996) and Atje and Jovanovic (1993) suggest that stock market development has positive impact on economic growth by providing services different from those provided by banks, or by making investments more liquid.

The studies cited above have not used data from African countries. It is proposed here to investigate currently the existence or otherwise of a positive relationship between economic output and the financial sector in sub-Saharan Africa. Given recent emphasis on economic Liberalisation and restructuring (i.e. beyond financial Liberalisation), it will be instructive to use ideas from endogenous growth theory in formulating a relationship between economic output and financial Liberalisation.

Conceptual Framework

We hypothesize a model of economic output that is rooted in both neo-classical and endogenous growth theories. Neo-classical growth theory emphasizes the role of exogenous factors, given the rate of growth of technology and factor accumulation in the production process. Endogenous growth theory on the other hand, emphasizes the orientation of economic policy, institutions, and intangible inputs such as knowledge acquisition, in addition. These later models are thus able to explain non-decreasing returns to reproducible factor inputs.

We posit here a Cobb-Douglas type production function with economic output as the dependent variable, and the stock of labour, physical capital, and human capital as factor inputs, and allow output to be affected by efficiency factors. In this case we broaden the concept of efficiency factors to include macroeconomic policy environment, the level of financial deepening, state or level of infrastructure, etc.

We proxy the macroeconomic environment by an inflation variable. An unstable rate of inflation may be viewed as capturing the impacts of unsound government policies such as persistent budget deficits, political upheavals, ethnic strife, etc. which may undermine economic efficiency and growth.

Financial deepening and intermediation may come about through banking activities or stock market activities. We include in our specification measures of stock market development and the extent or depth of banking activity. In the literature, the variables that have been used to represent stock market development include the *ratio of stock market capitalization to gross domestic product (GDP), number of companies listed on the stock exchange, ratio of the value of shares traded to GDP or market capitalization, volatility of market returns,* etc. Bank based measures include the *ratio of deposits, credit or money supply to GDP*, etc.

Next, we reason that the stock of physical capital is built up overtime by the different capital flows that take place in the economy. We may therefore disaggregate the stock of physical capital into its domestic and foreign components. For countries of sub-Saharan Africa (SSA), the stock of physical capital may be built up from domestic savings, SAV, or net foreign flows. Foreign financial flows to SSA take two forms: official development assistance (ODA) and private foreign commercial capital (PFX).

ODA generally refers to resources that are provided on concessional terms. That is, terms less stringent than obtains in capital markets. In recent years, the importance of development assistance in providing funds to SSA has increased, especially for countries liberalizing their economies. At the same time, domestic savings and private foreign flows have fallen. Unfortunately, while the proportion of total ODA to SSA has remained high, total ODA to developing countries has been declining in real terms since 1990, (World Bank, 1997). Another important aspect of ODA is described by the same source as "... the composition of ODA has shifted, with a significant portion being used to fund emergency relief and peacekeeping activities and less going toward long-term development needs."

PFX are defined to include foreign direct investment, commercial loans from foreign banks and other sources, as well as portfolio equity investments in financial and equity markets. The amount of PFX coming to SSA has fallen substantially from the peak of an annual average of 8.9% of all total private capital flows to developing countries during 1977 to 1982, to an annual average of 1.6% between 1990 and 1995, (Bhattacharya, Montiel and Sharma, 1997). SAV refers to the difference between gross domestic product and consumption.

It is hypothesized here that these different sources of investment capital have different objectives and impact economic output differently. For example, while ODA is provided on humanitarian and ethical grounds, among others, and is development oriented, PFX flows are made on risk and return basis and are trade oriented. The rationale for disaggregating domestic savings (SAV) from foreign financial flows is essentially to emphasize the ideas of the "two-gap planning model" (Chenery and Strout, 1966), and the Harrod-Domar model, (Domar, 1946, and Harrod, 1948). These suggest that, foreign financial flows to a developing country play two roles, (i) providing investment funds, and (ii) making possible investments in areas that require foreign capital, that would otherwise not have been possible with domestic savings only. Indeed, Aboagye and Gunjal (2000) provide evidence of the differential impact of the three forms of capital on SSA agriculture.

Methodology

In this section we discuss the model to be estimated and the data that are required.

Model Specification

This study proposes to pool data, over time, of sub-Saharan African countries that are undergoing substantial financial Liberalisation. Lau and Yotopoulos (1989) formalised the concept of a common production function for a collection of countries and estimated one by regression analysis on panel data. It is proposed to use regression analysis along similar lines to address the issues of concern in this paper. With such formulation, the underlying assumption is that these countries have access to the same production technology. Different countries may however operate on different parts of this production function due to the nature of each country's endowment of natural resources, relative prices of inputs, macroeconomic environment, etc.

The advantages of using panel data are many and are discussed in Baltagi (1995) and Hsiao (1986) among others. They include increased number of observations, increased ranges of variation of the variables in the model thereby allowing for more precise estimates, and reduced multicollinearity among explanatory variables among others.

However, when one pools data across many countries, one must recognise the potential of differences in definition, measurements and even qualities of inputs across countries. There is also the question of differences in economic environment across countries. In addition, one should be careful not to carry the assumption of a common production technology too far. This latter issue may be addressed by statistical tests however.

These disadvantages of pooling data across countries apply to some extent to the countries included in our study. However, we are of the opinion that the advantages outweigh the disadvantages. For example, countries in the panel though different have many things in common. Geographically, they are all low income countries located in sub-Saharan Africa, they all have functioning stock exchanges, have liberalized their banking systems mostly since the 1990s, and have implemented programmess that are meant to reform the structures of their economies significantly since the 1980s.

The relationship can be expressed in the form of:

$$GDP_{it} = \alpha EXCH_{it} + \beta BANK_{it} + \gamma CAPITAL_{it} + \delta X_{it} + \xi_{it} \quad (3.1)$$

where, GDP_{it} is gross domestic output for country ***i*** at time ***t***, (*i* and *t* hold similarly for other variables);
EXCH is a measure of stock market development;
BANK is a measure of the extent of banking activity;
CAPITAL is the stock of physical capital. This may then be disaggregated into the stocks of SAV, ODA, and PFX;
X is a vector of control variables such as the stocks of labour force, human capital, inflation, and other factors which are hypothesized to affect economic output;
ξ is an error term to be discussed below;
α, β, γ, and δ are coefficients to be estimated.

Formulation (3.1) is used often in the literature. (See for example King and Levine (1993a) and Arestis and Demetriades (1997)). Unlike those regressions however, we shall estimate (3.1) in levels. Specification (3.1) enables one to estimate the two parameters of interest α, and β, as well as accommodating the view from endogenous growth theory that there exists a linkage between labour, physical and human capital, public policies and long-run economic growth.

With panel data specification, the error term, ξ_{it}, may be decomposed in general, into an unobservable country-specific effect, a_i, an unobservable time-specific effect, λ_t, and a random term, e_{it}. That is,

$$\xi_{it} = a_i + \lambda_t + e_{it}$$

Country and time effects account for differences between countries and time that affect inputs and outputs. Country dummy variables capture differences in government policies such as infrastructure, external markets for exports, cultural/institutional differences, differences in technical efficiency in production across countries, etc. They also capture inter-country differences in definitions, measurements and qualities of outputs and inputs. Time dummy variables compare effects such as changes in total factor productivity to a base period. Heteroskedasticity and autocorrelation are handled below in section 4.2.1.

The country and time specific components of the error term may be fixed or random. In this context, a fixed effects model is posited on grounds that the countries of the panel are not randomly selected, rather, these are the SSA countries that meet the criteria of financial Liberalisation and for which complete data for this study are available. Inference made in this study may therefore be considered to apply to this group of countries. We posit a one way fixed effects model on the grounds that, comparison to a base year is not the issue of interest in this exercise. Besides, time dummies will use up precious degrees of freedom.

Each country of the panel was represented by a dummy variable.

Data

We require data for the period 1990 to 2000. Secondary data for this data were obtained mainly from *2002 World Bank African Development Database CD-ROM (ADI)*. Some of these data were further processed into forms suitable for this study as explained below.

Impact of banks: We considered several measures of financial deepening: (i) BNK, the amount domestic credit granted by banks (from ADI) divided by GDP. This measures the overall size of the formal financial system. Improving values of this will suggest development of the financial system. DEP, the ratio of broad money to gross domestic product (M2+/GDP). As this measure includes both liquid and quasi liquid liabilities, it measures the total size of financial intermediation, both for the short-term and the medium term. Evidence of how these banking measures impact output will be useful findings for this exercise. M2+ was obtained from the International Monetary Fund (2002).

Stock Market Development: We considered three measures, (i) EXC, annual values of local stock market indices; (ii) MCP, the ratio of stock Market Capitalization/GDP; (iii) TOV, the ratio of total value of traded securities/GDP. All were obtained from International Financial Corporation (2001). A rising stock market index must be due generally to improving economic performance, and vice-versa. Regression finding will indicate whether the performance of stock markets explain economic output and to what extent. In the literature, MCP is interpreted to have positive correlation with ability to mobilise capital and diversify risk. An improving MCP is thus indication of improving financial system development. The literature also interprets high TOV as indication of low transaction costs and vice versa. Falling transaction costs are indication of improving financial intermediation, and this can be expected to enhance output.

GDP, Gross Domestic Product in 1995 United States dollars are given in ADI. This is the dependent variable of interest.

LAB, the stock of labour force in each economy is a factor input to the production process under both neoclassical and new growth economics. This was obtained from Food and Agricultural Organisation, (2001) and earlier issues.

CAP, The stock of physical capital is also a factor input to the production process under both neoclassical and new growth economics. Here it is computed as the sum of the following three stocks: (i) *ODA, physical stock of development assistance*: this was captured as the stock of concessional loans outstanding at the start of each year as given in ADI; (ii) *SAV, the stock of domestic savings*: this was constructed by the perpetual inventory method, using annual savings data from ADI. Stocks were constructed as $K_t = \delta K_{t-1} + I_t$, where K_t is the stock at time t, and I_t is the time t flow. The initial stock of SAV was then computed as $K_0 = I_0/(\delta+g)$, where g is the estimated average growth rate of real SAV, I_0 is the flow at time 0, and δ is the depreciation rate of capital. In this construction δ was set to $10%; (iii) *PFX, the stock of private commercial foreign flows*: the stock of foreign direct investment (FDI) was constructed in a manner similar to KSAV and added to the stock of official non-concessional debt and the stock of private non-concessional debt. All are taken from ADI.

HCP, the stock of human capital stock, is also a factor input to the production process. It has gained prominence under new growth theories. Here the stock of human capital is the average number of years of schooling of the total population over age 15. These are obtained from Barro and Lee (2000). The Barro and Lee data set contains quinquennial stock data for some SSA countries. We interpolated for the intervening years. For the one or so countries for which Barro and Lee did not provide data, we used data from Nehru, Swanson and Dubey (1995) and extrapolated

IFL, the rate of inflation, was computed from consumer price indices obtained from ADI. As discussed earlier an unstable rate of inflation may be viewed as capturing the impacts of unsound government policies such as persistent budget deficits which may undermine economic efficiency and growth.

Estimation results

This section presents and discusses the result of estimating equation (3.1). Before then however, we computed the simple correlation coefficients between pairs of pooled variables in the model. For the specification involving banking variables (measuring financial deepening), there was enough data for 13 countries with which to estimate the model. However, for that involving stock market development, there were enough data for only 8 countries. In both cases, the panel spanned the period 1990 to 2000.

Simple Correlation Coefficients

Table 1 presents the matrix of simple pair wise correlation coefficients between variables. The correlation coefficient between GDP and each of the following explanatory variables are statistically significant: LAB, HCA, EXC, ODA, SAV, PFX, IFL, and CAP, (negative in the case of HCP). We also note that among the explanatory variables, pair wise correlation coefficients among all factor inputs are significant (negative for all cases involving HCP). Even when physical capital is disaggregated only that between ODA and SAV is not significant. We note further that, BNK, a measure of the extent of banking is significantly positively correlated with GDP, whereas DEP, the measure of financial deepening, is not. DEP and BNK are significantly positively correlated. Only one measure of stock market development, EXC, is positively significantly correlated with GDP. All three measures of stock market development, EXC, TOV and MCP are however significantly positively correlated to each other. In addition, EXC and BNK, and MCP and DEP are significantly (positively) correlated.

However, given that simple correlations may not tell a good story in the presence of other variables, we now turn to regression analysis for further insight into the relationship between GDP and the explanatory variables.

Table 1: Abbreviations

GDP	Gross Domestic Product
LAB	Stock of labour force
HCP	Stock of human capital
CAP	Stock of physical capital
SAV	Stock of domestic savings
ODA	Stock of development assistance
PFX	Stock of foreign private commercial capital
EXC	Stock market index
BGT	Budget deficit
IFL	Inflation rate
BNK	Domestic credit extended by banks
DEP	Ratio of broad money to GDP
TOV	Total value of traded shares/GDP
MCP	Total market capitalization/GDP

Table 2: Simple Correlation Coefficients.

	GDP	LAB	HCP	CAP	SAV	ODA	PFX
GDP	1						
LAB	0.87	1					
HCP	-0.60	-0.69	1				
CAP	0.82	0.65	-0.70	1			
SAV	0.760.47	-0.51	0.95	1			
ODA	0.36	0.68	-0.62	0.21	-0.04	1	
PFX	0.85	0.77	-0.75	0.84	0.71	0.46	1
EXC	0.51	0.41	0.08	0.20	0.28	0.14	0.28
BGT	0.04	-0.02	0.06	0.14	0.17	-0.23	- 0.01
IFL	0.33	0.41	-0.09	0.12	0.04	0.21	0.23
BNK	0.66	0.49	-0.16	0.66	0.70	-0.11	0.55
DEP	-0.20	-0.30	0.34	-0.02	0.08	-0.32	0.03
TOV	-0.10	-0.23	0.54	-0.34	-0.22	-0.16	- 0.18
MCP	-0.21	-0.27	0.56	-0.36	-0.29	-0.09	- 0.18

Note:Correlation coefficients with absolute values greater than 0.27 are significant at the 0.01 level

Table 2 continued: Simple Correlation Coefficients

	GDP	LAB	HCP	CAP	SAV	ODA	PFX
GDP							
LAB							
HCP							
CAP							
SAV							
ODA							
PFX							
EXC	1						
BGT	-0.02	1					
IFL	0.27	0.30	1				
BNK	0.42	0.30	0.28	1			
DEP	-0.01	0.13	-0.20	0.42	1		
TOV	0.56	-0.16	-0.02	-0.09	0.18	1	
MCP	0.35	-0.12	0.14	-0.06	0.43	0.70	1

Note:Correlation coefficients with absolute values greater than 0.27 are significant at the 0.01 level.

Regression Coefficients

Regression coefficients were estimated on a personal computer running *Winrats-32 version 5.0.*

Regression Adequacy

Initially, the least squares estimator was employed to estimate all country dummies and other explanatory variables in one step. For variables whose definitions involve GDP in the denominator, one year lags were used as instrumental variables for current values.

However, statistical tests suggested that ordinary least squares residuals were both heteroskedastic and autocorrelated in the first order. As advised by others such as Dagenais (1994) and Mankiw (1995) for example, we hesitate to transform the model to remove serial correlation because of concern that such transformation may introduce more bias in coefficient estimates than otherwise. Our concern stems from the very real chance that measurement errors are present in the data. Economists who work with SSA data generally believe that the data quality should be improved further.[3]

To obtain a consistent estimate of the variance-covariance matrix in the presence of heteroskedasticity and autocorrelation of residuals, we specified the "ROBUSTERRORS" and "LAGS" options in *Winrats*. The ROBUSTERRORS option is important in situations where some forms of the generalized least squares may be "inconsistent because the regressors (or instruments) are correlated with past residuals" (Doan, 1992).

Standard diagnostic tests were performed to assure validity of estimation results however. They include the following. Autocorrelation function tests, which suggested that the variables in the model were stationary in levels.[4] Variance inflation factors (VIF) were also computed. For the variables in regression equations (1) and (2) in table 3 all VIF were between 1.11 and 2.78. The average VIF was 1.79. For regression equations (3) and (4), the VIF were between 1.25 and 9.11. The average value was 4.51. Taking advice from Neter, Wasserman and Kutner (1990), we consider our computed VIF values not to be too big and conclude that multicollinearity is not too much of a problem. We shall also be careful not to make inferences beyond the region of observations. Neter et al indicated that maximum VIF values in excess of 10 and mean VIF values considerably larger than 1 suggest that multicollinearity is influencing least squares estimates. They however add that multicollinearity does not stop one from obtaining good fits, nor does it affect inferences about mean responses or predictions provided inferences are made in the region of observations.

Tests for outlying cases with respect to the regressors (leverage values of observations) and dependent variables (studentized deleted residuals) were performed. No significant leverage values or studentized deleted residuals were determined. Finally, computation of the Cook's distance statistics did not suggest that any observation had significant influence on parameter estimates.

Parameter Estimates

Table 3 presents estimates of the parameters of the production function involving banking variables. Four such regression equations were estimated. All country dummy variables were significant at the 1% level. They are not reported here. Significance of country dummies suggests possible significant country differences in government policies, technical efficiency in production, differences in definitions, measurements and qualities of outputs and inputs.

In regression (1) the typical neo-classical model is augmented by human capital, the amount of credit extended by the banking system and the rate of inflation. All factor inputs except capital stock are positive and significant at the 0.01 level. Capital stock is positive and significant at 0.05 level. This is what one would expect. The magnitude of the coefficients suggests that of these, human capital has the highest impact and capital stock the least. The banking variable is significant at the 0.05 level. But with a magnitude of only -0.007, its impact is very small. Changes in the rate of inflation have negative and significant impact on output.

In regression (2) we use, DEP, the ratio of M2+/GDP, as the banking variable. The impact of factor inputs are unchanged. This time however, the impact of the banking variable is not significant. The impact of inflation is also unchanged.

Table 3: Production Function with Banking

	Regression Equation[1]			
Variable[2]	(1)	(2)	(3)	(4)
LBR	0.373**	0.377**	0.367**	0.367**
	(3.043)	(3.018)	(3.457)	(3.464)
HCP	0.496**	0.436**	0.889**	0.888**
	(4.122)	(3.751)	(5.358)	(5.422)
CAP	0.171*	0.181*		
	(2.286)	(2.376)		
ODA			-0.081	-0.082
			(-1.427)	(-1.511)
PFX			0.004	0.004
			(0.033)	(0.141)
SAV			0.138**	0.138**
			(4.250)	(4.082)
BNK	-0.007*			0.001
	(-2.140)			(0.329)
DEP		-45.733	5.553	
		(-0.414)	(0.148)	
IFL	-0.111**	-0.123**	0.001	0.001
	(-2.732)	(-3.036)	(0.033)	(0.014)
D. F.	102	102	92	92
R^2	0.997	0.997	0.997	0.997

Legend:
[1]t-statistics in parenthesis below coefficient estimate;
* and ** indicate statistical significance at the 0.05 and 0.01 level respectively.
[2]Variables are defined in Table 1. D. F. is degrees of freedom.

When capital stock is disaggregated into the stocks of development assistance, private foreign commercial capital and domestic savings in regressions (3) and (4), the impacts of labour and human capital remain significant. The magnitude of the impact of human capital is almost doubled. The stock of domestic savings is the only component of physical capital to have significant impact on output. Both measures of banking are not significant. Neither is the rate of inflation. These findings for inflation contradict the findings in regressions (1) and (2). The explanation for the different econometric findings may be due to the fact that the model with capital stock variable disaggregated and the one without have different economic meaning. Of the two however, one is inclined to accept the model in which capital is not disaggregated. The reason being that financial Liberalisation also includes Liberalisation of foreign exchange markets such that assets held in one currency can be easily transferred into another. That is, the arguments for the "two-gap planning model" are less tenable now than when the model was first propounded in the early 1960s.

Table 4 presents estimates of the production function with stock market development variables. The findings here differ from regressions involving banking variables. The labour variable is not significant in any of the regressions (5), (6), (7), and (8). Human capital stock is significant and positive in all regressions. Total physical capital stock is significant and positive in (5), (6), and (7). No measure of stock market development is significant. The impact of inflation is once again negative and significant in (5), (6), and (7).

In the disaggregated model (8) the stock of development assistance is not significant, while the stock of private commercial capital is positive and significant only at the 0.05 marginal significance level. The stock of domestic savings is positive and significant at the 0.01 level. Neither changes in the rate of inflation, nor changes in the stock market performance index are significant.[5]

Finally, when both a banking variable and a stock market development variable are included in one specification, neither financial development variable is significant.[6] Labour once again is not significant, while human capital, total capital stock, the stock of domestic savings and inflation are significant and have the same sign and practically the same magnitude as before. (Inflation is not significant when total capital is disaggregated).

Table 4: Production Function with Stock Market

	Regression Equation[1]			
Variable[2]	(5)	(6)	(7)	(8)
LBR	0.006	-0.068	-0.062	0.013
	(0.051)	(-0.660)	(0.560)	(0.082)
HCP	0.401**	0.488**	0459**	0.971**
	(4.460)	(3.288)	(4.803)	(6.221)
CAP	0.417**	0.417**	0.438**	
	(6.417)	(5.673)	(6.565)	
ODA				-0.081
				(-1.754)
PFX				0.046*
				(2.441)
SAV				0.275**
				(3.096)
EXC	-0.001			
	(-1.298)			
TOV		-0.165		
		(-0.713)		
MCP			-0.040	0.001
			(-0.882)	(0.014)
IFL.	-0.123**	-0.125**	-0.129**	0.025
	-4.860)	(-3.868)	(-4.301)	(0.585)
D.F.	67	67	67	56
R^2	0.995	0.995	0.995	0.995

Legend:
[1]t-statistics in parenthesis below coefficient estimate; * and ** indicate statistical significance at the 0.05 and 0.01 level respectively.
[2]Variables are defined in Table 1. D. F. is degrees of freedom.

Summary of Regression Findings

We have already argued that we do not think that with financial Liberalisation, a strong case can be made for disaggregating the stock of physical capital. Other than the use of banking variables in models (1) and (2), and use of a stock market variables in (5), (6) and (7), all other variables are common to these five specifications. With the additional provision that (5), (6) and (7) use data for only eight countries while (1) and (2) use data for four additional countries (for a total of 12). We think the conflicting sets of estimating results for labour and other variables in models (1) and (2) on one hand, and (5), (6), and (7) on the other, are indications of errors in the measurements of the variables used in the estimation.[7]

Of the sets of results however, we put more faith in regressions (1) and (2) as these have more degrees of freedom and results are more in tune with economic theory.

Summary and Recommendations

We summarize the object and findings of this paper here and make policy recommendations

Summary

This study has investigated the impact of financial Liberalisation on economic output in a number of sub-Saharan African countries. A production function is posited in the context of endogenous growth model and estimated by regression analysis using panel data. Variables representing the extent of banking activities and stock market development were included in the model. In addition, the study investigated the hypothesis that the stock of physical capital may be disaggregated into the stocks of domestic savings, development assistance and private foreign commercial capital.

We found that estimation results were sensitive to the inclusion of banking variables, stock market development variables and disaggregation of physical capital stock and concluded that some variables at least have been measured with error.

Most coefficient estimates from models that included banking variables were in accord with economic theory and we accept those. That is, the factor inputs have positive and significant impact on economic output. The macroeconomic policy environment however had a negative impact. Indeed, the rate of increase in the consumer price index has been high and unstable in most of these countries. The coefficient of the banking variables are not significant or have minimal impact, suggesting that banking activities as the proxy for financial deepening are not having significant impact on economic output. Results from disaggregation of physical capital stock suggests that it is only domestic savings that have significant positive impact on output.

Estimation of models involving stock market development variables suggests that the stock of labour force does not have significant impact on economic output. We reject these results on grounds that they are inconsistent with economic theory. The stock market variables (index of stock market development, turnover ration and market capitalization ratio) probably suffer from errors in variables.

Recommendations

Economic theory posits significant positive relationship between financial depth and economic growth. Our study has shown that for this group of African countries the relationship is not significant. And this is the group of countries that is in the forefront of liberalizing the financial sectors of their economies. The implication is that African countries have to do more to ensure that the financial sectors of their economies do impact economic output positively and significantly. We suggest that the way to do this is to encourage more financial deepening by creating environments in which economic agents realize positive real returns on their savings and equity investments. The macroeconomic environment that increases the chances of this happening should therefore be the target of policy formulators. For example, low and stable inflation.

It is recommended that strong emphasis be placed on data collection and management issues as part of structural adjustment programmes.

Notes

[1] The author is grateful to the Danida Centre for International Business, School of Administration, University of Ghana for supporting this study.
[2] These countries are Bostwana, Cote d'Ivoire, Ghana, Kenya, Malawi, Mauritius, Mozambique, Namibia, Nigeria, South Africa, Swaziland, Tanzania, Uganda, Zambia and Zimbabwe.
[3] This study addresses this concern by using data from credible sources, mostly from the World Bank and The Food and Agricultural Organisation.
[4] Remember that each member of the panel has a maximum of 10 observations.
[5] Results for other measures of stock market development are similar.
[6] This regression is not reported.
[7] We have already alluded to measurement errors in African data.

References

Aboagye, A. Q., Gunjal, K., (2000): "An Analysis of Short-run Response of Export and Domestic Agriculture in Sub-Sahara Africa," *Agricultural Economics* 23, 41 - 53.

Arestis, P., and Demetriades, P., (1996):, "Finance and Growth: Institutional Considerations and causality'," Paper Presented at the Royal Economic Society Annual Conference, Swansea University.

Arestis P., and Demetriades, P., (1997): "Financial Development and Economic Growth: Assessing the Evidence," *Economic Journal,* 107, (May), 783 - 799.

Atje, R., and Jovanovic, B., (1993): "Stock Markets and Development," *European Economic Review,* 37, 632 - 640.

Baltagi, B. H., (1995): *Econometric Analysis of Panel Data,* John Wiley \& Sons.

Barro, R. J., (1991): "Economic Growth in a Cross Section of Countries," *Quarterly Journal of Economics* 56 (2), 407 - 443.

Barro, R. and J. W. Lee, (2002): *Economic Growth Datasets at Harvard University.*

Bhattacharya A., P. J. .Montiel, and S. Sharma, (1997):, "Private Capital Flows to Sub-Saharan Africa: An Overview of Trends and Determinants," *Finance and Development,* 3 - 6.

Binswanger, H., Yang, M., Bowers, A., Mundlak, Y., (1987): "On the Determinants of Cross-Country Aggregate Agricultural Supply," *Journal of Econometrics* 37, 111 - 131.

Chenery, H. B., and A. M. Strout, (1966): "Foreign Assistance and Economic Development," *The American Economic Review*, vol. LVI, No. 4, Part I.

Cho, Y. J., (1986): "Inefficiencies from financial Liberalisation in the absence of well-functioning Equity markets," *Journal of Money, Credit and Banking*, vol. 11, no. 2. (May), 191 - 200.

Dagenais, M., (1994): "Parameter Estimation in Regression Model with Errors in the Variables and Autocorrelated Disturbances," *Journal of Econometrics*, 64, 145 - 163.

Demetriades, P. and Hussein, K., (1996): "Financial Development and Economic Growth: Cointegration and Causality Tests for 16 Countries," *Journal of Development Economics*, 51, (December), 387 - 411.

Demirguc-Kunt, A., and Levine, R., (1996): "Stock Market Development and Financial Intermediaries: Stylized facts," *The World Economic Review*, vol 10, no. 2, 291 – 321.

Domar, E. V, (1946): "Capital Expansion, Rate of Growth and Employment," *Econometrica*, 14, 137 - 147.

Edwards, S., (1998): "Openness, Productivity and Growth: What do We Really Know?," *Economic Journal*, 108 (March) 383 - 398.

Federer, P., (1993): "The Impact of Uncertainty on Aggregate Investment Spending," *Journal of Money, Credit and Banking*, 10, 30 - 45.

Fry, M. J., (1997): "In Defence of Financial Liberalisation," *Economic Journal*, 107, (May), 754 - 770.

Grabel, I., (1995) "Speculation-led Economic Development: a post-Keynesian Interpretation of Financial Liberalisation Programmes," *International Review of Applied Economics*, 9, 127 - 149.

Harrod, R., (1948): *Towards a Dynamic Economics*, London, Macmillan.

Hsiao, C., (1986): *Analysis of Panel Data*, Cambridge University Press.

International Monetary Fund (2002): *International Financial Statistics*.

Jaeger, W., (1992): "Effects of Economic Policy on African Agriculture," World Bank Discussion Paper, African Technical Department, Series No. 147.

Keynes, J. M., (1936): *The General Theory of Employment, Interest and Money*, New York: Harcourt Brace.

King, R. G. and Levine, R., (1993a): "Finance and Growth: Schumpeter Might be Right," *Quarterly Journal of Economics*, 108, 717 - 737.

King, R. G. and Levine, R., (1993b): "Finance, Entrepreneurship and Growth," *Journal of Monetary Economics*, 32, 1 - 30.

Lau, L. J., and P. A. Yotopoulos, (1989): "The Meta-Production Function Approach to Technological Change in World Agriculture," *Journal of Development Economics* 31, 241 - 269.

Levine, R., (1996): "Stock Markets: a Spur to Economic Growth," *Finance and Development,* 33, 7 - 10.

Levine, R., and Zervos, S., (1996): "Stock Market Development and Long-run Growth," *World Bank Economic Review,* 10, 323 - 339.

Mankiw, G. N, (1995): *The Growth of Nations,* Brookings Papers on Economic Activity1, 275 - 326.

McKinnon , R. I., 1973, Minsky, H. P., (1986), Swanson, and A. Dubey, 1995, "A New Database on Human Capital Stock: Sources, Methodology, and Results," *Journal of Development Economics,* 379 - 401.

Minsky, H. P., (1986): *Stabilising an Unstable Economy,* Yale University Press, New Haven, CT.

Neter, W., Wasserman, W., and Kutner, M. H. (1996): *Applied Linear Statistical Models,* 2nd edition, Irwin, Boston.

Shaw, E. S., (1973): "Financial Deepening in Economic Development," The Hebrew University of Jerusalem, Working Paper No. 223.

Singh, A., (1995): "Savings, Investment and the Corporation in the East Asian Miracle," UNCTAD Discussion Paper on East Asian Development: Lessons for a New Global Environment}. Study no. 9, Geneva.

Singh, A., (1997): "Stock Markets, Financial Liberalisation and Economic Development," *Economic Journal,* 107, (May), 771 - 782.

Stiglitz, J. E., (1994):, "The Role of the State in Financial Markets," In M. Bruno and B. Pleskovic (ed), *Proceedings of the World Bank Annual Conference on Development Economics,* 1993, 19 -52. Washington: World Bank.

World Bank, (1997): *Global Development Finance,* Washington, D. C.

World Bank (2002): *World Bank African Database 2002,* CD-ROM.

APPENDIX: Central Moments of Explanatory Variables

	CENTRAL MOMENTS*			
	M1	M2	M3	M4
MCAP	0	0.019	-0.001	0.001
KODA	0	5.895	-33.070	254.719
KPFX	0	6.723	-30.129	247.972
KSAV	0	1.295	0.130	4.347
HCAP	0	0.089	0.000	0.014
BANK3	0	10.559	95.244	1387.807
DEEP	0	0.000	0.000	0.000
INFL	0	0.075	0.066	0.103
TNOV	0	0.000	0.000	0.000
LABR	0	2.033	-1.961	9.516
CSTOCK	0	8.407	-64.063	635.539

M1, M2, M3, and M4 = 1st, 2nd, 3rd and 4th central moments respectively.

Notes on the contributors

Aboagye, Kwame is a lecturer in finance at the University of Ghana. He holds a BSc. degree from the University of Ghana, MA from York University, (Canada), MBA from the University of Toronto, and a PhD from McGill University, Montreal, Canada.
His research interests are on Corporate Financial Management, Derivative Securities, and Development Economics. Dr. Aboagye is also an active consultant to the business community.

Kastner, Adelaide is a lecturer at the School of Administration, University of Ghana. She holds a BSc and MBA degrees from University of Ghana and a PhD in International Business from Aalborg University, Denmark. She has served on a number of boards and committees at the University. Her areas of research and publications have been in Marketing, International Business and Strategy.

Kragelund, Peter holds MSc. (Economic Geography) from the University of Copenhagen. He was the Head of Administration at Centre of African Studies, University of Copenhagen (1999-2001). He is currently a Doctoral student at International Development Studies, Roskilde University and Department for Development Research, Danish Institute for International Studies, Copenhagen. His research interests are in the assessment of aid impact, private sector development, and technology change in developing countries. He has worked in Latin America as well as West Africa.

Kuada, John is Associate Professor in International Management at Aalborg University. He received his BSc and MBA degrees from the University of Ghana and PhD from Copenhagen School of Business. He has taught marketing and management subjects in several African and European universities and has been consultant to government organisations and private companies on management related issues. His research interests are on International Marketing, Intercultural Management, and Cross-national Inter-firm Relations.

Narteh, Bedman is a Marketing lecturer at the School of Administration, University of Ghana. He received his BSc. and MBA degrees from the University of Ghana. He is currently a doctoral student at Aalborg University, Denmark, where he is researching on International Strategic Alliances and Organisational Learning.

Ofei, Ansah lectures in Strategic and Change Management at the School of Administration, University of Ghana. He holds Master's degree in Co-operative Economics from Marburg/Lahn, Germany, and MSc. in Systems Development from Trinity College, University of Dublin, Ireland. He also holds a PhD in Management from England. His research interests are in the areas of Organisational Development and Performance Assessment, Strategic Management and Human Resource Management.

Puplampu, Bill is an academic and a practicing Chartered Psychologist (British Psychological Society). He holds a BA degree in Psychology from the University of Ghana; MSc. & PhD in Occupational & Organisational Psychology from the University of East London. He has considerable research, teaching and consulting experience in the application of organisational psychology to Human Resource Management and Organisational Behaviour. He has lectured at the Universities of Westminster, London Metropolitan and East London (UK). He is currently a Senior Lecturer at the School of Administration, University of Ghana. His professional focus is on the development and application of organisational psychology concepts to national development, corporate and individual dimensions of work life.

Thomsen, Gitte is a lecturer at Aalborg Business School. She holds a Master's degree in Business Communication from Copenhagen School of Business. Her research interests are in Information Management Systems and inter-cultural communication.

Index

www.ingramcontent.com/pod-product-compliance
Ingram Content Group UK Ltd.
Pitfield, Milton Keynes, MK11 3LW, UK
UKHW041851031026
15587UKWH00005B/1159/J

9 780954 503789